1974

book may be kept

FOURTEEN DAYS

Life

A BOOK ON ABSOLUTE REALITY

Life

By ALFRED AIKEN

HILLIER PRESS
P. O. Box 3152
Evansville, Ind. 47701

Printed in The United States of America
HILLIER PRESS, P. O. Box 3152, Evansville, Ind. 47701

BOOKS ON

ABSOLUTE REALITY

BY

Alfred Aiken

The Unchallenged Self

That Which Is

Deity (The Only Self)

Now

Supply

Lectures (Series I)

Power

Bachelor God

Forums (Series I)

CONTENTS

Introduction

If you, Dear Reader, earnestly want to discover what Life truly is, ponder this book carefully. Do not read it as a novel, but contemplate each sentence carefully, for this book is your own autobiography.

Hillier Press

Life

Life

What is LIFE? This is a question that has confronted the world since the so-called beginning of time. The answers are as plentiful as there are people on the earth. Each one has his particular sense as to what LIFE is, but this does not make his definition correct.

What is LIFE?

In Truth we discover that LIFE is not the mere "impulse" that appears to animate items, bodies, things. LIFE is not the impulse, the energy, the stimulus, the motivating urge behind each and every movement, motion.

What is LIFE? LIFE IS SPIRIT, GOD, OMNIPRESENCE ITSELF IN ACTION. IT IS BEING, ISNESS, ACTUALITY, CONSCIOUS AWARENESS, MIND FUNCTIONING TO THE FULL, TOTAL COMPLETENESS ALIVE TO ITS OWN FULLNESS, SATISFACTION.

Within LIFE there can be no pause, no delay, no wait, no otherness, no alienness; there can be no doubt, fear, anxiety, question as to degree, amount, quality, characteristics, qualifications; there can be no opposite, no challenge, no sense of frustration, disappointment, unfulfillment. Within LIFE there is TOTALITY, COMPLETENESS, ENTIRE-NESS, GOODNESS IN ITS PURE ABSOLUTENESS, CON-SCIOUS BEING, UTTER ALIVENESS, JOYOUS EXU-

BERANCE, UNCURTAILED ENTHUSIASM, PERFECT PRESENCE, UNCONDITIONAL AWARENESS THAT ALL IS, AND THAT IT IS ALL . . . THERE CAN BE NAUGHT BESIDE, for Perfection cannot be improved upon!

Life cannot be separated from ACTION, FUNCTION. LIFE *is* ACTION Itself — not to be mistaken for movement, motion, commotion, reaction, effect, but rather BEING ITSELF TOTALLY OPERATIVE, WHOLLY PRESENT, FULLY BEING ALL THAT ISNESS IS. That is, Entirety being completely entire everywhere throughout Immensity, Totality, Wholeness, Allness — throughout Infinity. There simply is naught but ISNESS *being;* Existence Itself *existing;* Omnipresence totally present everywhere. There can be naught more, naught less than THIS ENTIRETY entirely being Itself. This solidarity of TOTALITY, this UTTERNESS of ABSOLUTENESS, this COMPLETENESS of the only SUBSTANCE or "stuff" existent, leaves no opposition, for It leaves nothing but THAT WHICH IS.

Nowhere can an absence of EXISTENCE be found, identified, suffered, known, or even spoken of, in Reality! Why? Because there can be no challenge to ALONENESS, THE ONLY, THE ALL, THE PERFECT WHOLE ONE THAT LIFE IS. There is no second mind, no lesser mind, no state, condition, no suggestion of less or more than TRUTH BEING NOW TRUE IN ITS ENTIRETY. Fact precludes error, mistakes, assumptions, and all and sundry that pretense might pretend, if there were a pretender for Truth's throne! But is there such? The answer is an unequivocal and emphatic NO!

WHOLENESS means that LIFE, EXISTENCE IS ONE AND THE SAME AS CONSCIOUSNESS, AWARENESS. SUBSTANCE is naught . other than CONSCIOUSNESS WHOLLY ALIVE TO ITS FULL POTENTIAL, ITS ABSO-

LUTE ENTIRETY, COMPLETENESS, UNDIMENSIONAL ABSOLUTENESS. It means that there can be, and is, ONLY ENTIRE GOODNESS PRESENT, AND THAT THIS GOOD-NESS IS ABSOLUTELY COGNIZANT OF BEING OMNIS-CIENT PERFECTION NOW, EVERYWHERE . . . that is, TOTAL, SINGLE, PURE LOVE wherein no slightest contest or question of reversal, opposition, or otherness can be.

LIFE is not a mental exercise. LIFE is not a mental battle one must wage against evil, opposition, that which is alien, contrary, opposed, vicious, condemnatory, bent on destruc-tion, wanting power, prestige, authority, or some such cognition. Not at all. LIFE simply is THAT WHICH IS NOW THE ONLY PRESENCE, THE ONLY AWARENESS, THE ONLY CONSCIOUSNESS, THE ALONE BEING THAT IS IDENTITY PRESENT. There is no non-Identity, non-Being anywhere, regardless of what education would say to the contrary.

If LIFE were not, there would be naught, hence not even education could pretend to teach or say aught, give examples and seemingly make them appear factual. LIFE IS GENU-INE, IS EXISTENCE ITSELF as pointed out. To LIFE there is no education, no learning, no advancing, growing, under-standing, demonstrating, be it good or bad. LIFE being SUBSTANCE, THE SOLE "STUFF" AMNESS IS BEING (the Absolute Identity-I) cannot be ill, diseased, missing in some way. It cannot be matter, physical, organic, structural or molecular.

LIFE being SUBSTANCE ITSELF, THE ONLY IDEN-TITY PRESENT, CONSCIOUSNESS ITSELF COGNIZANT AS AWARENESS, is single, entire, wholly pure, unadulter-ated, without the possibility of being contaminated by otherness, for such is impossible! How could ALLNESS be touched by Its absence? Absurd!

LIFE IS GOD, OMNIPOTENCY, ABSOLUTE AUTHOR-
ITY because there is naught to oppose It, refute It, admit It,
or deny It! THERE IS GOODNESS ONLY, which is another
way of saying, THERE IS FULLNESS ONLY, TOTALITY,
SELF-SATISFACTION ONLY, ENTIRETY ONLY. There
exists naught else, hence naught to question Fact, to doubt
It, to disagree or agree with It, to know or not know It, to
"use" or fail to take advantage of It! THERE IS GOODNESS
ONLY, REALITY ONLY, THE TOTAL FACT PRESENT IN
ITS ENTIRETY, ONLY. There can be no "besides."

What then do we "do" when it comes to the picture that
salutes our senses in our daily round? Do we attempt to put
these pictures straight? Do we attempt to heal, alter, help,
correct, condemn, punish or reward?

In every case, the answer is negative. We do naught with
aught.

Does this mean that we ignore conditions, ignore the
suffering of the world about us? Does it mean that we
selfishly go about our own affairs and allow the world to
drown in its sorrow, grief, suffering and heartache?

Again the answer is negative. We do not deal with or
through the world. Our work, so-called, is to begin wholly
with WHAT LIFE, WHAT EXISTENCE, WHAT SUB-
STANCE, WHAT OMNIPRESENCE, WHAT POWER ACTU-
ALLY IS – HERE, NOW, EVERYWHERE! This ONENESS,
THIS FACT, THIS TRUTH leaves naught beside anywhere,
or any "reason" for otherness anywhere. Staying with NOW
BEING THE FACT, appears as the dissolution of the seeming
trouble. Why? Because we no longer are caught up on the
thorns of assumption, other-mindedness, absurdity, insanity.
THE ONLY MIND PRESENT BEING INTELLIGENCE
ITSELF WHOLLY ALIVE TO ITS SINGLENESS, ITS
PURITY, LEAVES NO INSANITY OR ITS AFTERMATH,

ANYWHERE! This appears as "healing."

Above all, in pondering LIFE, the reader must define SINGLENESS, WHOLENESS, ONENESS, or Existence has no meaning in the true sense. LIFE is not a mere mass of movement, a universal re-action, a commotion produced by some impulse, a vibration resulting from a stimulus. Neither is LIFE the effect of a cause, the result of a divine command, the outcome of mere animal routine. It is not a perpetually recurring incident within the maze of generalities, the offspring of idleness, the outcome of reason, the expected side issue of desire, a promise of continuity of the species, a matter of adjustment within a limited ecology.

LIFE IS INTELLIGENCE ITSELF, CONSCIOUS SIN-GLENESS ITSELF wherein no possible sub-mentality exists at all. Herein no undermining can occur, no reversal can take place, no impulse exists to contradict, dispose of, befoul, limit, or obstruct Actuality. LIFE knows naught of other-ness, so never has to deal in or with such. TOTALITY alone is the definition of LIFE, for WHOLENESS leaves no incompleteness, naught in addition, nothing missing — leaves no sub-Life, no sub-Consciousness, no sub-Awareness, no sub-Presence.

ALL OF LIFE IS PRESENT IN ITS ABSOLUTE CON-SCIOUS CERTAINTY, FOR IT IS THE SINGLE BEING, SINGLE PRESENCE, POWER, AWARENESS, SUB-STANCE, TOTALITY, IDENTITY, ALIVENESS, ALL-IN-CLUSIVE CONCEIVER-PERCEIVER OF EVERY THOUGHT (THING) COGNIZABLE BY AND WITHIN MIND!

There simply is no additional mind anywhere, or operat-ing as anyone. There is no additional "stuff" of which such could be composed, nowhere or nowhen that such can even appear to operate, or any "mentality" to know or react to

such. SINGLENESS IS POWER ITSELF, AUTHORITY IT-
SELF, FOR IT TOTALLY KNOWS ITS ENTIRETY HERE
NOW.

This SINGLENESS, LIFE, EXISTENCE, BEING, INDIVID-
UAL WHOLE IDENTITY, is the UTTERNESS OF PER-
FECTION, FOR IT IS ABSOLUTE GOODNESS CON-
SCIOUSLY BEING ALIVE TO THE FULL OF POWER,
JOY, BLISS, HAPPINESS, SELF-SATISFACTION, for
naught of ITS TOTALITY can be absent, missing, impaired,
or even challenged. IT IS ENTIRETY THROUGHOUT, and
this alone is your (MY) IDENTITY. But, remember, IT IS
ALWAYS THE SOLE ONE BEING THE UTTER ONE IT IS
IN ITS CONSCIOUS COMPLETENESS. This leaves no
"other" that suggests aught, presumes aught, assumes aught,
hence none beside that can claim, believe, dream, or enact
error, evil, a contradiction to and of ALLNESS, SINGLE-
NESS, LIFE. It leaves naught beside, hence what can take on
the guise of death, limitation, fear, disease, time, history,
prophecy, humanity, astrology . . . take on the conditions
and conditioning of "time" or theology, the would-be
foundation for Satan, "void," evil, error, or oblivion?

Never fight evil, never contradict error, never battle Satan,
never strive to overcome death, never attempt to cast out
lack, never try to heal humanity, or set history right. Never
try to manipulate time, prevent prophecy, wipe out pictures
or change them in any way. All such is a tacit argument that
there is a sub-mind, sub-substance, sub-identity, subjugation
or slavery to otherness, and anyone trying to then "handle"
such is doomed to failure. However, beginning, stating,
starting with WHAT LIFE, EXISTENCE, SUBSTANCE,
TOTALITY, WHOLENESS *IS*, ONE DISCOVERS THAT IT
IS THE VERY ONE PRESENT, THE ONE DECLARING,
KNOWING, BEING AWARE, ALIVE TO IDENTITY.
THERE IS NO OTHER AT ALL.

So many seem to assume that they are the TV instrument and that the pictures projected on the screen of the instrument are stemming from it. This is not so. Nothing that goes on as a body, or the pictures that seem to be subjective therein and thereas, stems from that body, nor from a mind within that body! LEAVE THE INSTRUMENT ENTIRELY ALONE and "dig" at the WHOLENESS OF PRESENT ALL-POWERFUL GOODNESS, the SINGLE SUBSTANCE, NOWNESS PRESENT IN FULL. Keep thought away from TV instruments, from bodies, from states and conditions. STAY WITH REALITY ONLY, if you would behold your SELF AS YOU ACTUALLY NOW ETERNALLY BE! There is no personality existent at all.

Can any portion of LIFE be lost? Can any portion of OMNIPRESENCE be set aside? Can any portion of WHOLE-NESS be separated, deleted, removed, cast off, cast aside, rendered null or void? Can any portion of ALLNESS, ONENESS, ENTIRETY, COMPLETENESS be rendered less than IT IS? If so, by what, where, when, and through what authority?

What Substance EXISTS ASIDE FROM EXISTENCE? Where is N O W save present Itself? Can any of THE PRESENT be shifted backward, or forward, so that THAT WHICH IS is NOT? If so, how? What logic could possibly claim or believe any such nonsense? What would be operating in lieu of Mind, if such conclusions appeared valid? And where would such stem from, there being neither cause nor effect, no duality, no otherness, naught but the TOTAL WHOLENESS THAT ENTIRETY IS FOREVER NOW?

Where REALITY is, where FACT is, where ACTUALITY is, can there be even the suggestion, much less the would-be evidence of otherness? To what would it appear? Certainly not to Mind, Actuality! Is Consciousness ever asleep? Does It ever fail to stay aware of all that It is? If not, then how does the seeming mess come about, or even appear to be present, or require any sort of attention?

While it is true that none of this nonsense is going on in Mind, the picture "appears" to be present, and is usually the reason why a call for help goes out.

We could blame it all on theology, but where does the theological patter originate? There is neither cause nor effect in Mind . . . there is only Reality Itself being. True. But theology seems to have become a pattern, a system of behavior, a belief that has no challenge even from those who are suffering the most from the silly nonsense. People seem to accept it without question, go along with it, put up with the troubles that come to them as a consequence, and finally die of that which has no foundation in Fact at all.

Seldom does the troubled one begin with Reality. Rather he begins with his trouble, tries to discover why he has it, where it came from, what the underlying cause is, what the outcome will be, how long it will take, and what he might normally expect in the meantime. This process is most foolhardy, but try telling that to the suffering one! He will not listen, and if he does, it will be with skepticism, or a feeling that you are giving him the brushoff, are treating him with extreme coolness, or something of the sort.

Time is the life-blood of theology, of evil. Evil is totally the product of religion, of theology. Duality does not exist outside of the nonsense that One is not ONE, but rather is but one of two or more . . . that the WHOLENESS THAT LIFE IS, is separable into portions, parts . . . can be present in degree, and includes within Its nature the ability to share with Its opposite, Its absence, full honors, powers, action, function, and awareness or aliveness, these contrary states, these impossible states!

If it were not for time, theology would be unable to satisfy logic, hence sell its system to its dupes. It takes time for each step to be worked out, and for the nonsense to make good its claim of non-Existence. Should lack appear as a state, outside of time, it would be rejected, for that which gives lack a pseudo life, is TIME. Yes, TIME is the bloodstream for all forms of lack, for only via TIME can NOW be overlooked, bypassed, ignored, denied.

The when is so important if one would sell a bill of lack, limitation, humanity. The great void appeared and then TRUTH STOPPED BEING THE ONLY WHEREIN THERE IS NO OTHERNESS RIGHT NOW. NOW STOPPED COMPLETELY – THE PRESENT STOPPED, ALL STOPPED, AND LACK CAME INTO BEING AS THE SOLE CAUSE, THE ONLY PURPOSE . . . the reason for being. Ask any child who is starting in school as to why they are here, what the purpose of being is, and they will tell you it is to procreate, fill up a hole, overcome a lack of some sort.

Why creation? Was it not totally to compensate for the void, fill it, or wipe it out? Was not this "purpose" supposed to be totally to the good, in fact, GOOD ITSELF? And remember, the seed was within itself – that is, the recurring "cause" for lack was self-perpetuating – would go on forever. Naught would ever question or doubt it. It was assured of its place in history, in futurity. But what thus became of GOODNESS, God, Life? The only "use" for God from here on in was that He purportedly knew all about this mess, gave it its authority, and it would be evil itself to even question or doubt this!

Evil supplants Goodness, Life. It leaves only oblivion, non-Life purportedly existent within time. But is this possible? Why not? Because without Life there is naught.

As before, we come back again to the question: What *is* LIFE? LIFE is not a "feeling," is not a "quest," is not a means of overcoming a void, filling a need, propagating Itself, having a purpose, striving for a goal, an accomplishment, an end of some sort, or supplying Itself with proof of some sort so It will be *sure* that It actually has SUBSTANCE, ACTUALITY, REALITY, PRESENCE, BEING!

LIFE is not a system, a combination of glands, organs, nerves, structures, states and conditions of items all working toward a given point, or to assure themselves of survival.

LIFE is not material, not physical, not based on the atom, nor is It a mystical experience, a nebulous entity that swirls about in or as an ectoplasm, and through refinement of time, experience, pressures, is shaped into a desired entity or identity equipped with a past, and assured of a future!

LIFE is not the outcome of gases mixed in an infinite bowl of space, tumbled about, broken down and built up again in a new series of combinations and compounds, finally coming forth as sentient matter, mystical assumption, presumptive consciousness — more or less as a happenstance, a chance evolution or mutation of some sort, entering within a temporary garment called body, yet with a prearranged plan of ejection, meanwhile wholly subject to subjection!

LIFE is not a chemical, is not an electrical impulse, is not a vibration, is not the product of cause, reason, purpose, intent, or accident. LIFE is not the end result of aught, nor does It ever end in aught, or as aught. LIFE is not shrouded in darkness, confusion, chaos. LIFE is not in shadow, in trouble, in danger, nor is It ever in aught . . . never in matter, never in a shape, never in a form, never in any sort of envelope, container, shell, or dimensional prison. LIFE is never in any thing, dependent on any thing, influenced by any thing, the evidence of anything. And no thing (body, item, idea, thought) can influence LIFE IN ANY MANNER WHATEVER!

Why?

Because LIFE IS CONSCIOUSNESS, as we have repeatedly pointed out. True, many will expect an entirely "new" statement concerning LIFE, or else they will fall back on their so-called intellect and declare that the contents in this book are but a rehash of what has already been stated. They will never stop to consider that possibly they are still attempting to "translate" the statements here into the old pattern with which they are so familiar!

LIFE is AWARENESS ITSELF BEING ALIVE TO ITS OWN OMNIPRESENCE. In other words, LIFE is UTTER COGNITION, CERTAINTY, ABSOLUTE *being.* Herein is no "looking to things" as conveying AWARENESS, nor in any manner whatever being instrumental in assuring Mind that It is present, or existent.

Things, that is, the picture that salutes the so-called senses, are not the issue. They have no importance at all. They neither contribute, nor do they interfere or challenge Intelligence in Its TOTAL AWARENESS AS OMNIPRESENCE *being.* But he who "starts" with the picture, with the senses, will be unable to make "sense" of what is recorded here. Equally they will be unable to make sense of the picture of what "appears" to be going on in their seeming world. They will be unable to cope with it, help it, stop it, or do aught except to go along with it, as "flesh" is always prone to do.

There is no sub-Consciousness, sub-Awareness, or sub-Stance! There is ONLY LIFE ITSELF PRESENT. And where is this PRESENT? Here, for want of a better way of stating it. But what do WE mean when we use this term?

HERE, or THE PRESENT, means, in Truth, that THERE IS ONLY THAT WHICH IS. Obviously, that-which-is-*NOT* cannot BE PRESENT, BE HERE, BE NOW! "TO BE" — can It be said to NOT BE? THAT WHICH IS — can it be said that IT IS NOT? If so, by whom, by what, and why for?

There is such effort spent on the part of intellect to discover the nature, the workings of, the purposes behind LIFE, yet always OUTSIDE OF LIFE! Never, but *never* does the would-be human intellect, the "inquiring mind," begin with ACTUALITY, REALITY, TRUTH, FACT, BEING AS IT IS! Always the inquiry, the searching, the quest is based on GENESIS — a would-be "beginning," a "reason," or "purpose" behind LIFE! This implies that LIFE IS NOT LIFE OF ITSELF, but rather is the effect, the outcome of, the offshoot of, the result of a divine plan, scheme, plot, intention, or else it is a matter of chance, the evolutionary product of nature, heat, light, decay, electrical impulse; that it all came about because of some need, a void, a hole to be filled, and so on, as we have frequently stated.

None of the above is true. The church, education, science, as we would term it — each branch of human endeavor has its pet set of answers, its set of theories, which may fail to give total satisfaction, but at least keeps the hearer busy mulling over, and possibly keeps him from demanding better answers to the embarrassment of the powers that "sit in high places."

"Wherein am I to be accounted of?" is of special concern to him who seeks the nature of LIFE. Generally he is not interested in LIFE ITSELF, save as It has a bearing on his personal longevity, his body, his personal affairs, his world about him, his era. This is the major stumbling block. If the searcher would not begin with the personal pronoun, "I," but rather with LIFE ITSELF — would let go the possessive identification, "I," and state wholly what NOWNESS, IS-NESS, *BEING* IS, he would be forced to omit all body consideration, all material, structural, organic, glandular, chemical, gaseous, evolutionary, or biological foundations. He would have to drop the possessive case altogether from his calculations. He would have to bypass religion, history, cause, effect, reason, impulse, plan, purpose, He would have to set aside his education, his physical importance, his reactions, movements, dimensions, requirements, and genesis. He would have to overlook the pictures that the senses testify to as being real, important, the impulse behind his daily round, or that of the world in which he seems to browse.

Yes, he who begins, starts with, STATES AND THEN DEFINES HIS STATEMENTS HONESTLY, FULLY, IN-TELLIGENTLY (and if not Intelligently, they are not defined at all!) — he who STATES WHAT NOWNESS IS, WHAT ISNESS IS, WHAT THE PRESENT IS, has to hurdle all that education has taught concerning history — all that the church has taught concerning GENESIS and PROPHECY — all that science has taught and believes concerning "time," hence "space," distance, dimension, hence measurement via the senses, hence all electrical impulses, vibrations, subjectivity, hence objectivity!

He who STATES WHAT NOW IS, must begin with ISNESS ITSELF, BEING ITSELF, NOWNESS ITSELF, THAT WHICH IS PRESENCE ITSELF. Note, we do not say: That which is present, but rather, THAT WHICH IS PRESENCE ITSELF! There is a difference.

The intellect, so-called — that is, organized sense-impressions or reactions to impressions, whether they appear as objective, subjective, whether as items, things, or the absence thereof, and the position of the one concerned within the "intellectual, hence personal picture," always predicates its conclusions upon the reaction thereto. The intellect does not generally doubt that what it "sees" or "senses" is nonexistent, but rather is concerned as to the whys, the wherefores, the hows and so on. And often with great urgency because of the implied, if not the actual, threat to the personal well-being.

The entire effort of the intellect is to account intellectually for the circumstance, state, or situation that threatens, or that fails to threaten! It makes no difference if the situation be called "good" or "bad" — what, or how will it effect, or affect? It is this mystical intellectuality that operates as a person, judging, sentencing, and fulfilling all the rules it has set up in accord with its ignorance, its nonexistent authority, its imaginary background and purpose.

There is no intellectualism. There is no personal intellect. There is no humanity. There is none of this judging going on in THE PRESENT, NOW, ISNESS! Why? Because all the ferment, as well as the firmament, depends utterly on the eradication of NOW, ISNESS, AMNESS, THE PRESENT, BEING! Yes, THERE CAN BE NO INTELLECTUALISM, PERSONALITY, PERSONS, DUALITY, CREATION, HUMANITY, EVIL, SATAN, CHAOS, DEATH-BIRTH, END-GENESIS, WITHOUT FIRST BYPASSING FACT, ACTUALITY, REALITY!

Again, you may demand, and loudly: WHY?

The answer is simple, if one is willing to STATE WHAT ISNESS *IS*, WHAT NOWNESS *IS*, WHAT THE PRESENT *IS*.

He who begins, states, then defines ISNESS, AMNESS, NOWNESS, must discover that IT IS ENTIRELY FRESH, NEW, SIMPLE, TOTAL, COMPLETE, ENTIRE, SINGLE, hence IT MUST BE LOVE in Its true sense. And why LOVE? Because It must be WITHOUT GUILE, WITHOUT IMPURITY, WITHOUT ADULTERY, WITHOUT ADDITION OR

SUBTRACTION, WITHOUT SIN, WITHOUT DUALITY, WITHOUT OTHERNESS, hence WITHOUT A GOAL, WITHOUT A PURPOSE, WITHOUT AN INTENTION, WITHOUT A SCHEME, WITHOUT ANY ULTERIOR OR EVEN GENUINE MOTIVE!

Why are these "intentions" classed as impurity, as sin, as evil? Because in every case they each and altogether imply, or depend upon TIME, thus ignoring NOWNESS, ISNESS, AMNESS, THE PRESENT.

Look them over, if you will! Do they not state, or imply, that TIME is required for *NOW* TO BE COMPLETELY *NOW*, FOR *IS* TO BE TOTALLY *IS*, FOR *AMNESS* TO BE TOTALLY *AM*, FOR THE *PRESENT* TO BE ABSOLUTELY *PRESENT*? Do they not, one and all, say that COMPLETENESS WILL COME ABOUT IN THE FUTURE, AND THAT WHATEVER DOES TRANSPIRE "THEN," will depend on the plans made in the past?

Totally aught that is based on purpose, scheme, plan, reason, intent, cause, is predicated on the subjective notion of incompleteness, vacuum, void, want, need, requirement, evolution, growth, development, attainment, additions via the manner in which subtractions of lack have been managed!

He who states what NOW IS, must behold that ISNESS IS LIFE BEING, EXISTENCE OPERATING, FUNCTIONING, ACTING. ALIVENESS AND INTELLIGENCE IS ONE AND THE SELF-SAME ONE IN OPERATION. This has nothing to do with what has been fed into the computer called the human brain, or aught to do with the nervous system (the senses) via which the information was purportedly acquired and registered within the computer.

NOW IS PRESENT, and has never been present BEFORE! There is no "before" for NOW, any more than there has been

an "is" before THIS AMNESS THAT *IS!* It is impossible to
imagine EXISTENCE as "having been," for if such were the
case, then this PRESENT TENSE is NOT, and there is no
identity at all.

As pointed out in one of our earlier writings, NOW IS
NOT A STOPPING-OFF PLACE BETWEEN YESTERDAY
AND TOMORROW. NOW IS THAT WHICH IS . . . ISNESS
BEING NOW . . . AMNESS ALIVE TO ACTUALITY WHICH
IS EVERYWHERE PRESENT, WITHOUT CHALLENGE . . .
WITHOUT "ANOTHER" TO RISE UP AND ASK IT WHAT
IT IS DOING, AND WHY!

The so-called senses are utterly unable to give any "help"
in "discovering" NOW. They deal exclusively with, as already
pointed out, the subjective which, in turn, becomes objective,
or vice versa. TOTAL GOODNESS, UTTER SELF-SATIS-
FACTION PRESENT AS INFINITE UNDIMENSIONAL
INTELLIGENCE IN OPERATION, IS THE SOLE AMNESS
THAT IS YOU (MY) IDENTITY, BECAUSE IT IS THIS
ABSOLUTE ALIVENESS IN ITS FULL POWER, COM-
PLETE WISDOM, ABSOLUTE ACTION, UNCHALLENGED
PRESENCE THAT IS BEING. IT HAS TO BE SINGLE,
INFINITE, BECAUSE IT IS TOTAL.

Ask your Self if NOW can be absent anywhere? Can there
be any surpassing Authority, Power, Action, Function, Being,
Identity above and beyond NOW? Can there be a "was" that
can supplant IS? Will there ever be a "will-be" that can set
aside IS? Does a conjured subjective implication or notion
supplant ACTUALITY, THAT WHICH REALITY IS?

How long do you have to wait for NOW to be? Where is It
missing, and what "caused" such a mishap? What do you
"use" as a mind in making your statement and conclusion?
How, or what was it that challenged NOW? Where was it?

Who or what says so? What will be the outcome? How long will it take before NOW returns to being NOW? With what did NOW tangle, and how badly damaged is NOW? Where and what were you being while all this was "happening" to NOW? What has NOW, ISNESS, AMNESS, BEING, to do with your Identity, your Self? Are you sure, do you KNOW this, and if so, with what, how, where, when?

Does NOW in any way depend upon the items of which you appear to be aware? Do "things" in any way contribute to NOW, in order that AMNESS *BE* NOW? Are "things" essential to NOW? Has NOW a set of parents, a biological background, or did It come forth from the passage of time? Was Its genesis dependent upon sex, gender, an animal urge, or the requirement to perpetuate Its species?

It is obvious to the honest "seeker" that Truth in no way is challenged, effected, or affected by the general nonsense of intellectualism. The approach to what LIFE IS, is as varied as are the would-be seekers, and their approach is as varied as the number of minutes that make up their would-be record of time.

While they pretend to be serious in their "investigation" of LIFE, they take every imaginary precaution to avoid an honest approach, an unbiased viewpoint, a truthful or accurate conclusion. And, without exception, "down the ages," they have never, but simply NEVER started, or even "made contact" with LIFE ITSELF. Always they have played around the edges of their preconceived notion of what they assume LIFE TO BE. In the language of the Bible, they have busied themselves being "about the business" of what LIFE WOULD HAVE TO BE IF IT WERE WHAT THEY ASSUME IT IS! Thus, they have always avoided dismissal of

the void, for it is always within this area only that inquiry
can be safe . . . that is, avoided!

CHAPTER II

Is God Dead?

The entire world seems to have gone mad of late. Even noted prelates have questioned the nature of God. They feel that all things demand modernization, even God Himself! As there have been such "advances" in technical affairs, as our industries have leaped forward to new zeniths in returns, as our technology has enabled us to hurl mighty rockets about the moon and on to the more distant planets in this solar system, then we have — yes, we MUST HAVE — outgrown our swaddling clothes, and are ready for even an advanced and revolutionary notion, an improved, as it were, view of God. The old one is dead, so now, LONG LIVE THE NEW GOD!

Is God dead?

Would you say that LIFE is dead? If so, then where are you? Are you still existent, yet capable of judging LIFE ITSELF? Do you still cling to the notion that LIFE is merely that which enables "things" to function, move about, do the jobs they are assigned to do, until time takes over and forces LIFE "out" of the vessel, the "temple" or canister in which It purportedly has been caged?

Do you look for LIFE, for GOD, in a body? Do you suppose that your body is the envelope covering LIFE, SPIRIT, SOUL, GOD? Do you still assume that body is your IDENTITY, BEING? Do you accept the notion that your

31

parents brought LIFE, SPIRIT, IDENTITY, BEING, into a subjective world, either by divine command, permission, intention, or because they had nothing better to do at the particular moment when "conception" purportedly occurred?

If you accept that God is "dead," then is not the soul within that body you call "I" equally dead? Is it not considered that the spark of life within the body is a portion of the Supreme Soul — and that at the right moment, when your "number comes up," or whatever it is that "sets the date of departure," your soul, your life, will end, going back from whence it came?

As we repeatedly point out, all consideration of what LIFE, what GOD, what SELF, what IDENTITY REALLY IS, begins with body, with item, with thing — with education, with that which was fed into the computer and accepted as Fact. In all cases the computer is geared to input, hence to output "information" predicated wholly on a subjective would-be mind and its equally nonsensical conclusions or experiences. These, purportedly, deal also in and with the objective — always have an object in mind, always a purpose, cause, hence effect, which brings about a new and always changing set of further subjective notions prompting objective ones.

He who would find out if God is dead, let him turn from his computer, his body, and what it has been tooled to report due to its intake. Let him no longer deal in and with the information "timed" to the uttermost, both past and future, but let him, rather, begin, as pointed out in the first chapter of this volume — yes, let him begin, state, declare WHAT NOW IS, WHAT AMNESS IS, WHAT BEING IS, WHAT THE PRESENT IS, in all Its NEWNESS, FRESHNESS, ORIGINAL STATE OF NON-TIMENESS, NON-CHALLENGE, NON-OTHERNESS!

Is NOW dead? Has NOW gone somewhere? Has It been driven off? If so, by what, when, where, why, how?

Is EXISTENCE dead? Is AMNESS dead? Not unless you are back at the old nonsense of dealing with senses, with the computer, with time, with history!

Is REALITY dead, gone off somewhere, run out on Itself? If so, what is left . . . not only what is left to worry about or strive for, but what is left to do the worrying or the striving? That which is GENUINE, REAL, ACTUAL, EXISTENT AS BEING IN OPERATION — COGNITION FUNCTIONING, hence, conscious of FACTUALITY, is not dead, cut off, missing, absent. If It were, there would not even be oblivion, for there would be naught at all, hence naught to even identify the vacuity.

Those who would raise the question as to the death of LIFE, of BEING, of IDENTITY, ACTUALITY, ALIVE-NESS, are merely seeking for new evidence that the struggle is worthwhile, that there is purpose in being, that there will be a reward of some sort that will be commensurate with the effort put forth. They are striving to find new definitions that are in keeping with what they consider evolution, progression, modern evolvement. They wish to be in mode . . . be abreast of the times, for they assume that this world is not standing still, but is expanding out and farther out, and soon will be making its reputation among the stars.

Of course, this is typical of the young . . . and this world is young, in more ways than one. It is decidedly immature, when stacked up against what assumption would say is "time-gone-by." They who are young in this sense fail to see what is important, dwelling entirely on trivia, their desires, on things, gadgets, baubles, trinkets. Things are of so much more importance than BEING, REALITY, UNDIMENSION-AL NOWNESS, ISNESS, ENTIRETY AT HAND. Identity is considered to merely be indicative of a certain frame, covering, physical suit being worn at the moment by the offspring of a biological act, purportedly imprisoned within the proper garments which will enable it to survive a short span of time!

No, things are of no importance, as our work so repeatedly emphasizes. The would-be mentality caught within the net of a physio-chemical impression, is not Mind, not Intelligence, not Amness-I in any sense of the word. This personal equation, this specific computer which is built according to certain specifications, is not genuine, not One, not Individual, not Undimensional, not I!

Things, within the scope of the would-be computer, are purported to have an aura of sanctity, use, identity, history, and an ultimate. That ultimate always without exception, is the dump heap. Why? Because in accord with its "law-of-construction" it is of "dust" and "unto dust it must return." Was it not brought forth for the sole purpose of running the cycle, and going the way of all flesh? Was it not heir to all that flesh is heir to? Was it not brought forth in time, by time, and made to go through its chores according to time? Was there, or is there ever a single moment when "time" is not supervising every move, every reaction, every impulse of that which it conceives, produces, includes, and ultimately excludes?

But has any of this aught to do with ACTUALITY, NOW, REALITY, TRUTH, BEING, IDENTITY, ISNESS? Nothing at all. It never even touches REALITY at any point, nor is it known by ACTUALITY, so why be concerned with it, over it, because of it? To do or be so, is to deny your very PRESENT IDENTITY — is to DENY YOUR SELF, and seem to shut your SELF AWAY FROM ALL THE GOOD THAT YOU FOREVER NOW BE!

No, GOODNESS is not dead. REALITY is not dead. TRUTH, POWER, LOVE, SINGLENESS, WISDOM is not dead. Regardless of how crazy the world seems to be, how chaotic the affairs of politics appear, how disruptive society claims to be, and the reasons behind it all — these are of no importance at all to REALITY, for they DO NOT EXIST WITHIN ACTUALITY, TRUTH, FACT, THE PRESENT. THEY ARE NOT GOING ON, HENCE CANNOT BE STOPPED, NOR DO THEY NEED TO HAVE COUNTER MEASURES USED IN ORDER TO BRING THEM UNDER CONTROL. THEY ARE NOT SPEEDING US TO THE COMPLETION OF A CYCLE, BRINGING US TO THE VERGE OF DISRUPTION, THREATENING EXTINCTION, all in accord with a curse of prophecy, the wage of sin, the payment from Satan, the loss of soul, nor the death of God!

To discover that God, LIFE, EXISTENCE, OMNI-PRESENCE, is not like the concoction brewed up by the theological master-minds that they might keep their followers in bondage, fear, and superstition, does not mean that REALITY HAS BEEN TAMPERED WITH. The only discovery being made is that the god of theology NEVER LIVED IN ACTUALITY, IN TRUTH, IN FACT!

The seekers who have chiseled away some of the fake facade which theology has so carefully guarded, lo, these past many centuries, find naught there but the "rock" spoken of in the Record — a cold, hard unyielding non-sentient accumulation of solidified dust! It was always void of LIFE, WARMTH, LOVE, WISDOM, SINGLENESS, AUTHORITY. No change has occurred at all, except that its deadness is now apparent to those honest enough to judge correctly that which they are looking at. But, remember, THAT PARTICULAR BRAND OF GOD, LIFE, WAS WHOLLY A THEOLOG-ICAL ONE — never did it breathe forth the POWER OF

SINGLE PURITY, UNADULTERATED ALIVENESS, INDI-
VIDUAL, UNDIMENSIONAL ALL-INCLUSIVENESS
ETERNALLY HERE NOW, UNCHANGING, UNCHAL-
LENGED INFINITY, THE SOLE AMNESS THAT IS I.

Such ACTUALITY precludes any theological nonsense.
REALITY precludes a rock as a foundation upon which to
stand, or upon which to establish aught, not even Itself!
TRUTH precludes another to preach for It, to It, or because
of It. TRUTH has no world to save, for Its only universe is Its
thoughts which It is but now conceiving-perceiving. TRUTH
has no history, no fall, no void, no discovery of otherness, an
opposite or absence of Itself, a state of nothingness that
needs filling, or aught else incomplete.

Yes, the god of theology is dead, and always has been.
Why? Because it never had LIFE, ACTUALITY, OMNI-
PRESENT POWER, PURE UNADULTERATED SINGLE-
NESS, ENTIRENESS, LOVE, ABSOLUTE SELFHOOD.

Yes, whatever purportedly stems from a theological god,
is dead. The entirety of the six days of creation as recorded
in Genesis is dead. None of it ever has taken place. And
whatever other type of creation, formation, or transforma-
tion that has purportedly taken place in Genesis, is false
throughout.

There has never been the production or creation of
duality — biology, a scheme whereby the physical world
could be populated and inhabited. No "night and day" has
come into Being. No lesser light or greater light has been
formed. No history whatever exists. No prophecy or curse
has happened. All of it, including the god that supposedly
gave it life, brought it about, instigated and instituted it, is
dead, totally, irrevocably, absolutely dead, in spite of what
the Supreme Court, the ruling heads of government, the
prelates who depend upon a continuity of the old nonsense,
may say to the contrary.

Yes, it is natural that those who earn a living of sorts from preaching the pap of mysticism, will scream for blood, or demand that he who challenges the nonsense, be tossed to the lions of human opinion, but in no case does this change the Fact that ONLY LOVE IS REAL, ONLY NOW IS PRESENT, ONLY ISNESS AM, ONLY FACT IS OPERATIVE, ONLY INTELLIGENCE IS WISDOM, ONLY SINGLENESS IS LOVE!

The god of this world, the lust for personal power and authority, is dead. The sway that the various forms of government have over their victims, the dictates of this and that ism, the beliefs in body, in organs, in money, in things, in people, in prayers, in understanding, in morals, in all manner of diets, whether mental or physical, spiritual or intellectual — these, one and all, are dead. They may appear to be slow in settling down, they may appear to leave their spirits or ghosts free to walk about and haunt those who would still have "things as they were — the good old days," but that "time" is gone, never to return.

It is on the part of so many who cling with a tenacious effort to what has been disproved, that the struggle seems so severe and long drawn out. So many, regardless of how obvious TRUTH IS, refuse to go along with It. They prefer to carve out a place in "time" where they can go and meditate, think about, fret over, and stir up a storm concerning what yesterday did, or failed to do for them, and worry over what tomorrow may bring forth.

How many of our readers are willing to admit that YESTERDAY IS DEAD? THAT TOMORROW IS DEAD? THAT TIME IS DEAD? THAT CAUSE IS DEAD? THAT CREATION, MATTER, PHYSICALITY, HATE, DUALITY, LACK, MANHOOD IS DEAD? Not many, no doubt, in spite of the FACT THAT OMNIPRESENCE ALONE IS REAL, PRESENT, THE ONLY, and herein "time" cannot be.

How many of our readers are willing to drop all sense of "time?" How many are willing to start WHOLLY, HONESTLY, ENTIRELY WITH NOW ALONE? If so, what becomes of all sorts of notions concerning humanity, race, color, creed, history, Satan, evil, disease, fear, darkness, punishment, blame, sin, reward, cause, effect, purpose, plan, goal, ambition, resentment and the like?

How many of our readers are willing to turn their ENTIRE ATTENTION TO AWARENESS, LOVE, PRESENT IN ALL ITS SINGLENESS AND COMPLETENESS, and waste no more effort over things, body, conditions, effects, states, results, money, organs, age, desires, trips, relatives, flags, parents, offsprings, business, and such? If you are HONEST in saying you do so wish, WHAT IS TO PREVENT YOU FROM DOING SO?

How many of us are so eager for wealth, for health, or whatever the particular item happens to be, that we cannot keep our thought from it? Whenever we think concerning TRUTH, we wonder how we can "apply" Truth so as to bring about the desired result, both in quality and quantity. And why? Because to us things are not dead, but very much alive.

No disease can hang onto one unless he keeps the disease alive by giving it room within his experience. He must supply it with the necessary ingredients, namely, a place to operate, time in which to operate, a state of operation, recognition, admission. He must give all forms of evil, lack, and limitation, a place, a cognition, before they can seem to develop, and he places within them the seed for their own seeming propagation — this all in accord with what has been fed into his computer-mentality via the master robot, a NEVER-ALIVE-theological god!

This insistence that a god so ordered it, keeps the sufferer from questioning too deeply as to whether or not the "claim" is legitimate. Merely to "have" it is sufficient, generally. Who but a dead god could have thought up anything so deadly, so vacuous, so utterly void of Existence that the mind which is NOT can never discover its source or identity?

However, in TRUTH our concern is in no way connected, nor should it even be interested in, what is NOT. We are not to trouble ourselves over the nature of a dead god, or a god who knows death, lack, dust. OUR GOD IS LIFE ITSELF IN OPERATION, WHOLENESS ITSELF IN OPERATION, ACTION ITSELF IN OPERATION, ETERNITY NOW IN ABSOLUTE UNCHALLENGED OPERATION. Herein is naught beside, no other at all, hence no doubt, no call for faith, no application required, no demonstration to be brought about, no fall, no rise, no wait, no penalty, no curse, no time, no source, no outcome — there is ONLY TOTALITY TOTALLY BEING COMPLETE ENTIRETY NOW, HENCE UTTER GOODNESS, WHOLENESS, PERFECTION OMNIPOTENTLY FUNCTIONING TO THE FULL OF WISDOM'S ABSOLUTE SATISFACTION FOREVER. THIS, AND THIS ALONE, IS THE SINGLE IDENTITY-I YOU BE (I AM), AND THERE IS NONE, AND NAUGHT, BESIDE. He who "starts" with THIS FACT, will behold the ACCURACY OF THIS STATEMENT, but he who would begin with intellectualism, will "end up" even as he began, namely, in a whirl.

Only in oblivion can death be found, but where is oblivion? Who has it? Who knows it? Who can actually define the ABSENCE OF EXISTENCE, THE OPPOSITE OF ACTUALITY, THE REVERSE OF BEING, THE STATUS OF NON-BEING, THE IDENTITY OF NO-IDENTITY? Who or what can discuss non-Life, other than to behold that LIFE

PRECLUDES VACUITY, PRECLUDES NON-EXISTENCE, NON-IDENTITY, NON-BEING, or any loss, separation, or tampering with TRUTH.

The only reason we even mention death, and the conditions purportedly dependent thereon, is to show how impossible such can be and is, in the light of TRUTH.

"But," someone will ask, "do you not admit that a body can die, that the soul can depart, that life can go forth from the frame wherein it has operated, lo, these many years?

The answer is an unequivocal NO, WE DO NOT ADMIT ANY SUCH NONSENSE. We do, however, admit that he who begins with nonsense will conclude as he began, namely, with nonsense. He who starts with body instead of LIFE — starts with a mist-conceived "thing" instead of TRUTH — begins with a computerized picture instead of FACT. He who argues for fiction in lieu of ACTUALITY, to him chaos is natural and PERFECTION is impossible.

Do not begin with effect, with the senses, with education, with reaction, with the product of history, if you would know what *IS*. ISNESS, NOWNESS, AMNESS cannot be found in "time," or history. All one will find in history is a hi-story, a tall tale, a supposition, an assumption. As fiction, history is fine, but ONLY AS FICTION. Far too many assume it to be Fact, and thus Truth becomes, to them, mere fiction.

HISTORY IS DEAD, FOR IT NEVER HAD LIFE, ACTUALITY, AMNESS, ISNESS. PROPHECY IS DEAD, FOR IT, LIKE THE OPPOSITE END OF THE MEASURING STICK (THE PAST), IS DEAD, FOR UTTERLY OUTSIDE OF AMNESS, BEING, ISNESS, ALIVENESS!

LIFE IS NOT DEAD, not past, not yet to come into being. LIFE IS TOTALITY ALIVE TO ITS ENTIRETY, CONSCIOUSLY BEING ALL WISDOM, ALL ACTION, ALL

FUNCTION, ALL PERFECTION, ALL AWARENESS, ALL SUBSTANCE OR "STUFF" THAT BEING IS. LIFE IS WHOLLY ALIVE TO THE FULL OF ITS ABSOLUTE POTENTIAL, RIGHT HERE, NOW, EVERYWHERE, AND THERE IS NO DEGREE, NO DIMENSION, NO MEASURING, EITHER IN QUANTITY OR QUALITY, THAT WHICH IS INFINITE ENTIRETY FULLY COGNIZANT OF ITS WHOLENESS, ONENESS, SINGLE PURITY, ABSOLUTE ENTIRETY. THERE ARE NO OTHERS. THERE ARE, THEREFORE, NO SUGGESTIONS OF TIME, AGE, EVOLUTION, CHANGE, CHALLENGE, OPPOSITION, DOUBT, FEAR, SUPERSTITION, SIN, EVIL, SATAN, PAST, FUTURE, WAIT, NEED, REQUIREMENT, PUNISHMENT, REWARD, DUALISM . . . THERE ARE NO ATTRIBUTES, NO CHARACTERISTICS, NO QUALITIES, NO DEGREES OF UTTERNESS, NO COMPARISONS, NO INTENTIONS, NO PLANS, NO COMPLETION, BUT RATHER, ABSOLUTE COMPLETE PERFECTION PRESENT.

THIS DOES NOT MEAN THAT INFINITY HAS AN END, A BOTTOM, OR DIMENSION. FAR FROM IT. INFINITE INTELLIGENCE WILL BE "PLUMBING" THE DEPTHS OF ITS OWN BEING FOREVER NOW, for want of a better way of putting it, BUT never can PERFECTION "BECOME" MORE PERFECT, OR WHOLENESS BECOME MORE WHOLE, TOTAL, SINGLE, ONE, ALL!

No, LIFE IS NOT DEAD! THE BEING YOU BE (I AM) IS NOT DEAD, NOR CAN THIS IDENTITY, THIS LIFE, THIS INDIVIDUAL INFINITE AWARENESS-CALLED-I-AM, EVER "PASS ON INTO A FUTURE!"

To see this, you MUST begin with LIFE ITSELF, FOR IT IS LIFE *BEING* ITSELF THAT IS I, AND THERE IS NONE BESIDE. TO BEHOLD TRUTH, YOU MUST BEGIN WITH THAT TRUTH. ALL ELSE IS BEGINNING WITH FICTION, HENCE ITS SO-CALLED CONCLUSIONS MUST BE

FICTIONAL. WHAT ELSE? TO BEGIN WITH "BODY" OR WITH "PERSONALITY" OR "HISTORY" OR "TIME," IS TO BEGIN WITH FICTION, WITH A COMPUTER, WITH A ROBOT, WITH NONSENSE, AND NOT A SINGLE CONCLUSION ARRIVED AT BUT WHAT WILL BE SUBJECTIVE. EVERY "CONCLUSION" WILL SUBJECT YOU, AS THE "SUBJECT," TO MORE OF THE SAME NONSENSE, UNTIL NOT A GLIMMER OF ISNESS WILL SEEM TO LIGHTEN YOUR DAY!

He who begins with FACT, LIFE AS IT IS, THE WHOLENESS OF SINGLENESS, ALLNESS, ONENESS, PURITY HERE NOW, finds he no longer is subject to the subjective — is not being subjected to the fiction of disease, disaster, dementia, demonology, decay and death — he is no longer being the victim of what seems his own dilemmas, determinations, demands, and demented flounderings — he is no longer a specimen on the table of matter under the knife of time, anesthetized by education, and later on pushed into the recovery room of purgatory!

He who starts with WHAT MIND KNOWS ITSELF TO BE . . . WITH WHAT LIFE IS HERE AND NOW BEING . . . WITH WHAT ISNESS NOW IS . . . WITH THE TOTALITY OF WHAT INFINITY CONSCIOUSLY IS ALIVE TO BEING — yes, he who begins with TRUTH AS THE FACT IT IS, cannot continue to flounder about in the ocean of confusion that passes as present-day society. He must discover that ONLY ACTUALITY IS PRESENT, AND ALL OF IT IS GOOD, SINGLE, UNDEFILED, UNCHALLENGED POWER, AUTHORITY, ABSOLUTE WISDOM. HE DOES NOT TIMIDLY MAKE HIS STATEMENT OF FACT, BUT WITH ALL THE CERTAINTY THAT IT IS SO, BACKED BY THE UNCHALLENGED POWER THAT WISDOM IS!

No one can actually INTELLIGENTLY BEHOLD WHAT

IS WRITTEN HERE, AND HONESTLY ADMIT THAT LIFE IS WHAT IT IS, NAMELY, WHOLLY PRESENT, ALIVE, CONSCIOUS, INFINITE, COMPLETE, HENCE THE SOLE SUBSTANCE, THE NON-SUBJECTIVE ONE INCLUSIVE MIND OR AWARENESS, HENCE THE SOLE IDENTITY, THE INDIVIDUAL INFINITY OF TOTALITY, and continue to be "concerned" with the world as it "looks to be."

No, one cannot be HONEST WITH WHAT LIFE IS, and continue to have It dead in spots, missing in spots, present in a mere degree here and there, nor can he put It out in "time," assuming one must wait for It. Equally, he cannot put It into a body, an organ, a thing, and then be afraid It will go out at any moment and leave him dead!

LIFE IS WHOLLY SPIRIT BEING, AND CAN BE FOUND NOWHERE ELSE, FOR IT IS NOWHERE ELSE, NOWHEN ELSE, NOHOW ELSE, NOWHY ELSE. LIFE ALONE IS ITSELF, AND IS DECIDEDLY ALIVE NOW IN ITS TOTALITY, AND KNOWS IT. THIS LEAVES NO OTHER MIND AT ALL, HENCE NO OTHER THAT "NEEDS" TO KNOW LIFE, NOR THAT *CAN* KNOW LIFE! Are you still trying to behold LIFE with a personal, a computer or sense-mind . . . a gift you received from, or were started out with by biology? Are you still determined to "have-been-born?" Are you still clinging to parents, a date in time when it all "happened?" Are you still clinging to the nonsense that you were a small bark "launched on the sea of humanity" away back somewhere? If so, you are a foreigner to LIFE, YOUR VERY OWN SELF, and it is high time you got to KNOW YOUR SELF AS THE SOLE SELF YOU (I AM) BE!

Every single thought, experience, item that passed as your identity-in-body-as-a-human, is and was, dead throughout. NONE OF IT TOOK PLACE. YOU HAVE NEVER BEEN A

BODY, AN ITEM, A THING. YOU HAVE NEVER BEEN ONE OF THE ITEMS OF WHICH INTELLIGENCE IS AWARE. THERE HAS NEVER BEEN ANY LIFE IN ANY MOVEMENT, MOTION, REACTION, ASSUMPTION, SUPERSTITION, TIME, OR HISTORY, REGARDLESS OF WHAT SO-CALLED AUTHORITY HAS TO SAY TO THE CONTRARY.

Only that which is WHOLLY TRUE OF LIFE PRESENT IN ITS ENTIRETY, IS SO, AND THIS ALONE IS YOUR SOLE IDENTITY NOW. LET US STICK WITH THIS.

CHAPTER III

Indivisibility

While we use many terms for TRUTH, WHOLENESS, ALLNESS, possibly none has a deeper meaning than INDIVISIBILITY, yet no one term is more generally ignored . . . ignored in that the definition of the word seems to carry so little weight.

INDIVISIBILITY is definitive when it comes to ONENESS, TOTALITY, COMPLETENESS, SINGLENESS, PURITY, hence SELF, AMNESS, ISNESS, NOWNESS . . . THE IMMEDIACY OF ACTUALITY, PERFECTION, POWER IN ACTION, AND THE ACTION OF POWER.

INDIVISIBILITY leaves absolutely no possibility of separation, degree, characteristic, qualification, condition. THE INDIVISIBLE ONE means that the SELF YOU BE CANNOT BE PARTED, FRACTURED, BROKEN, LOST, SEPARATED, DIVIDED, SUBTRACTED, OR ADDED TO – IT MEANS THAT THE ENTIRETY OF INFINITY, WISDOM, AWARENESS IS OPERATIVE EVERYWHERE THIS MOMENT – THAT ALL.THE POWER, SUBSTANCE, BEING OF GOODNESS, LIFE, EXISTENCE IS COGNIZED BY THE SINGLE ALL-WISE AWARENESS THAT YOU BE THIS VERY NOW.

THE INDIVISIBLE ONE means that there is no other mentality, point of view, opinion, belief, conviction, notion, obsession, sense, concept, dream, attitude or experience that

exists at all. There is no personal mind possible, hence none
to whisper aught, suggest aught, convey aught or react to
aught. There is no small mind (or large) that can malpractice,
influence, direct, sway, cudgel, drive, draw, tempt, or convey
aught to AWARENESS.

No, there is no dream mind, no evil mind, no lack-or-
man-mind that can belittle INFINITY, squelch OMNIPO-
TENCE, abate TOTALITY, divert CONSCIOUSNESS, blunt
or obliterate SINGLENESS, limit ENTIRETY, minimize
OMNIPOTENCE, or annul OMNIPRESENCE.

LIFE PRESENT IN ITS ENTIRETY CANNOT BE
TURNED OFF, IGNORED, BLOTTED OUT, BYPASSED,
SHUNTED TO ONE SIDE, OR SHUNNED. THE INDIVI-
DUAL INFINITE EXISTENCE THAT IS THE SOLE SELF
OF ENTIRETY, MUST BE THE UNCHALLENGED IN-
SEPARABLE BEING CALLED SPIRIT. WHO OR WHAT
ELSE CAN SPIRIT BE? WHERE ELSE THAN PRESENT?
WHEN ELSE THAN NOW?

Can TRUTH, LIFE, EXISTENCE, SELFHOOD be measured in degree, quantity, quality? We ask this question
repeatedly that the reader not overlook the importance of
NOW, ISNESS, AMNESS BEING WHOLE, PURE, UNCHAL-
LENGED IN THAT IT CANNOT BE MORE OR LESS
THAN PERFECT, ENTIRE, COMPLETE. As we have repeatedly pointed out, THE PRESENT CANNOT BE MORE SO,
LESS SO, NOR EVER BE other than ENTIRE. To in any
manner turn from the Fact, would be to no longer be dealing
in ACTUALITY, but in fiction, nonsense, superstition, hence
outside of INTELLIGENCE, REALITY.

NOW *is*, and all of It *is*. Obviously NOW cannot be "in
part," or parted, divided. And as NOW and the SOLE SELF
THAT ACTUALITY IS, are one and the same, so the SELF
THAT IS, CANNOT BE LESS OR MORE. This IDENTIFI-

CATION leaves nothing hanging in "time," nor waited for via prophecy. Under no circumstances can the sense of "man" behold NOW, hence cannot interpret nor identify the SELF. They speak wholly of themselves because this is the programming that has been fed, via education (both personal and academic) into their self-concocted or dreamed-up subjective instrumentality. The "tape" merely plays back what was inserted, and it does so via the five senses, using body, item or thing as a screen upon and via which to cast its would-be pictures. But to whom, or what mind? To itself only, for ignorance, belief, the dream includes naught REAL, TRUE, GENUINE, PRESENT.

Here is where so many of our readers make a grave mistake. They assume that the pictures are real, that they must be changed, healed, helped, cast out, or recast. They assume the frame within which the picture is cast is their particular identity, body, item, possession, and an absolute necessity to their, and for their, well-being. They assume a personal guilt for the lack, the limitations, the evils that beset the item, either via sins of omission or commission.

None of this theological teaching is true. No devil or evil impulse — an impulse to believe in lack, limitation, a void, a degree of Wholeness — has foundation. NOW IS TOTALITY BEING, AND IS BEING IN ITS TOTALITY, HENCE SINGLENESS, ALLNESS, ONENESS. There is naught missing, naught yet to come, naught waited for or that has passed, gone by, departed, ended.

Either you BE TOTALLY, OR YOU TOTALLY ARE NOT. If NOT, then where is the lack, the limitation, the would-be degree of NOW-PRESENT-IN-FULL? Should you assume you have a choice in this matter, you are again playing along with the nonsense of theology, the religion of cycles, limitation, lack, void, separation, division, degree.

LIFE, to you, is NOT, but in Its stead you have set up a superstition only, to which you bow down and render obeisance, service, worship. This is slavery, and to what? TO LACK, LIMITATION, DARKNESS, IGNORANCE ONLY, but where REALITY ACTUALLY EXISTS NOW, can there be any room left for the theology of division, separation, duality? NEVER!

Do not make the mist-take of assuming you "begin" with TRUTH ALONE in order to take care of things, body, a human sense of plenty and such. Far from it. TRUTH NOW IS, AND IS ALL THERE IS THAT IS TRUE. To look only to things (body, items and such) is to personalize the "pit," or darkness itself, Satan or un-Wholeness in full, hence to non-Exist as Self — to not be SELF, SUPPLY, WISDOM, JOY, BLISS, ALIVENESS!

FACT ALONE BEING, leaves no humanity at all, hence none of the picture just pointed out. We "explain" it that it might be clearly seen as impossible within the scope of TOTALITY. IT IS BEING THAT IS BEING, and not the "things" that education would have us assume to be so important. THIS BEING IS TOTALITY IN THAT IT IS UTTER WISDOM WHOLLY ALIVE TO OMNIPOTENT PERFECT PRESENCE. There can be nothing beside THIS ALLNESS, ONENESS, SINGLENESS, so why try to "use" It in order to attack another mind, another state or condition, or in some way wipe away the sins of the world that have never been? How cleanse that which is not, hence has never been soiled?

We do not ignore evil, limitation, or lack in any manner whatever. We do begin with ACTUALITY wherein no evil can be, and we stay here! This precludes lack from ever making an appearance anywhere, at any time, as anyone. No, we do not ignore it . . . we simply leave it neither root nor branch, history nor destiny. We do not even "leave" it, for it is not there at all! THIS IS POWER HERE NOW. THIS IS AUTHORITY HERE NOW. THIS IS THE INDIVISIBLE FACT THAT REALITY ALONE IS *SO* NOW. THIS IS THE INSEPARABLE ACTUALITY OF THE SELF YOU BE *being* the ABSOLUTE SELF LOVE IS. It (THE AMNESS THAT IS I) NEEDS NO HEALING, HELPING, PURIFYING, NOR DOES IT HAVE TO BE WAITED FOR. NOW IS PRESENT IN ITS TOTAL COMPLETENESS. IT CANNOT BE ABRO-GATED, CHANGED, ALTERED IN ANY MANNER AT ALL, ANY MORE THAN IT CAN BE CHALLENGED, OPPOSED, OR DENIED!

Often those who turn to the Absolute Truth assume they are working correctly in separating the would-be personal identity from INFINITE SINGLENESS, ONENESS, ALL-NESS. If they would but pause long enough to actually define the terms they are using, they would discover that there is not a personal identity *and* a Divine Singleness also! THERE IS BUT THE ONE ALONE ALL, THE SINGLE INDIVIDUAL THAT IS THE SELF-I-AM NOW.

The AMNESS THAT IS I cannot be separated, divided, taken from or added to GOODNESS, LIFE, POWER, NOWNESS, for this is NOW THE SOLE BEING, THE INDIVIDUAL ALL, THE ONLY ONE THERE IS. THIS VERY ONE IS ABSOLUTE, TOTAL, COMPLETE, THE ONLY MIND, AWARENESS, SUBSTANCE, IDENTITY EXISTENT . . . NAY, IS EXISTENCE ITSELF HERE ETERNALLY NOW.

One cannot be of SPIRIT *and* my SELF, but rather, SPIRIT *IS* THIS (MY) SELF, THE SOLE ONE ALL.

LIFE cannot be separated, divided, chopped up, por-tioned out, fractured, fractionalized, for IT IS EXISTENCE, ONE *only*, SINGLENESS IN ITS NUMERICAL ONENESS, INFINITY IN ITS ABSOLUTE UNRELATED TOTALITY.

To separate, or divide — to have another, regardless on what basis, what thesis, what assumption or presumption, or what is used as the would-be mentality devising such a presumption, means there would have to be two or more, duality, adultery, for there would have to be an addition to ONENESS, ALLNESS, SINGLENESS, or a taking away from UTTER COMPLETENESS some of Its SIMPLICITY, PURITY, TOTALITY, ENTIRETY.

As so frequently pointed out in our many books on Absolute Reality, SINGLENESS CANNOT BE SEPARATED, BROKEN UP INTO PORTIONS, DOLED OUT, OR SERVED UP. To what could TRUTH BE PASSED, when TRUTH IS INFINITE, TOTAL, WHOLE, THE ONLY, and there is naught else? From what can SINGLENESS be separated? From Itself? If so, by what, by whom, when, how, why?

No, SINGLENESS IS SINGLE. ALL IS ALL. TOTALITY IS TOTAL. PURITY IS PURE, HENCE UNTOUCHED, UNRELATED, UNCONTAMINATED BY OTHERNESS. LIFE IS NOW ALIVE TO ITS ALIVENESS, ALLNESS. ALL OF LIFE IS WHOLLY ALIVE. THERE IS ONLY THIS THRILLING EXCITEMENT OF UNDIMENSIONAL, UNENDING, FRESHNESS OF INFINITE NEWNESS THAT SINGLENESS IS OMNIPOTENTLY "DISCOVERING" FOREVER IN THE NOW. NEVER A RECURRENCE, REPEAT, RETURN, REVIEW, REMEMBRANCE, BUT ALWAYS GLORIOUSLY NEW, ORIGINAL, NOW. NAUGHT IS EVER IN TIME, IN HISTORY, IN A PLAN, A SCHEME, A PREARRANGED ORDER, A CYCLE, A HABIT.

Time, which is separation, division, limitation, a void within which is all matter, error, evil, Satan, birth-death, hell, creation, theology — all such depends entirely on separation of ONENESS into many, SINGLENESS into multiple fractions, ALL into minuscule portions, and has to have a separate mentality to work its division, maintain its separateness, hence involved reason, cause, purpose, impulse! These cannot be without ignorance of SINGLENESS, NOWNESS, NEWNESS, CHANGELESSNESS, THE PRESENT ISNESS *being!* But by whom or what is this ignorance endowed? Where is it going on? For what purpose? Is there an evil power that will in some manner benefit by destroying SINGLENESS, ONENESS, ALLNESS, NOWNESS?

Just what can Satan (assuming for the moment that there is such!) accomplish by wiping out EXISTENCE? What would be left to follow or serve Satan, death, lack, limitation, void, nothingness, matter? What would there be that knew time, could operate within it, record it, worship or serve it? What would it all accomplish?

No, there is ONLY REALITY, ACTUALITY, THE PRESENT NOW, THAT WHICH IS. THERE IS NAUGHT CONTRARY TO CONTRADICT OR OPPOSE IT. THERE IS NOTHING ELSE. LACK DOES NOT EXIST. HUMANITY (MASS LIMITATION, FINITY, SUPERSTITION, CAUSE-EFFECT, PRESUMPTION, SUBJECTIVE OPPOSITION, OR OBJECTIVE SUBJECTION) IS A FRAUD THROUGHOUT, AND UNKNOWN BY THAT-WHICH-IS, NAMELY, CONSCIOUS INTELLIGENCE, THE SOLE INDIVIDUAL SINGLE COMPLETE SELF YOU (I AM) BE!

All error, lack, humanity, creation, finity, the pictures outpictured by the would-be senses — all these are but focal points within the would-be cycle of zero, sprung from nothingness, going nowhere, accomplishing nothing, and not to be found anywhen within REALITY.

He who would know TRUTH must have FACT AS HIS SOLE INTEREST. He who would try to discover why FACT IS FACT, WHY NOW IS NOW, WHY ISNESS *IS*, will never discover the answer. Why? Because he is still within the throes of intellectualism, reasoning from cause to effect and vice versa — still operating within the adulterous void of nothingness, striving to give his lack and limitations, his ignorance and problems a status they do not have, a respectability they will never know, a place within Existence that precluded them in their would-be entirety.

Yes, he who would try to discover the whys and wherefores of his trouble, analyze "why" thus and thus occurred, is still working in metaphysics, with a second mind, a lesser substance, a sub-state of existence, a fractured, divided, impure singleness, an untrue would-be fact. Such is nonsense. One cannot, simply cannot, intellectualize error into Being, a lie into Fact, a falsity into Reality, time into Now, prophecy into Isness, lack into Identity, disease into Purity, many into Singleness, hate into Love, or a void into Goodness.

One cannot, by reason, or aught else, make creation real, nor have birth and death, a start and a finish, gender, history, futurity, time, multiplicity, part of Intelligence, Individual Singleness, the Amness-that-is-I. SPIRIT ALONE IS THE SINGLE IDENTITY PRESENT AS I, AND SINGLENESS, NOWNESS, ISNESS, I-NESS HAS NO PARENTAGE, NO CAUSE, NAUGHT THAT BROUGHT IT INTO BEING, OR MADE IT OMNIPRESENT OMNISCIENCE, EXISTENCE ITSELF, WHICH IS INCLUSIVE OF ENTIRETY! To presume this Fact can be broken down, ruptured, divided, cast aside, ignored, is too absurd for words!

Never attempt to investigate the whys and wherefores of the trouble. It is always from the same would-be "source," namely, assuming there *IS* a source, cause, beginning . . . that an original void came along somehow and separated the INDIVISIBLE CHANGELESS NOWNESS THAT FACT IS, into portions or particles.

Never spend your time pondering these books in order to discover how to "handle" error, overcome your problems, outwit the human senses, put an end to the ravages of matter, preclude time's prophecy and its mutilating effects on all that you hold dear! No, do not waste any effort looking into error, or uncovering the situations or thinking that purportedly lead you into its toils. Rather, leave all error and its effects, alone. Turn wholly to the ALLNESS THAT GOODNESS IS, THE TOTALITY OF THE UNCHALLENGED NOW, THE FULL PRESENCE OF ISNESS WHICH DOES NOT EVER SPRING FORTH FROM AUGHT, BUT IS EXISTENCE HERE NOW BEING.

This, and this only, is where your entire attention must lie. This, and this only, is what you BE, WHEN YOU BE. THERE IS NAUGHT ELSE AT ALL. WHY? BECAUSE ALL ALONE IS ALL, AND THERE IS NOT MORE THAN ALL, THE SOLE SELF-SATISFIED ONE THAT THE PRESENT INDIVIDUAL-I-AM IS TOTALLY *BEING*.

Stating TRUTH ONLY, and discovering what the statement actually SAYS AND MEANS, precludes any void from which One needs to extricate Itself — any void from which AMNESS NEEDS TO STRUGGLE IN ORDER TO "BECOME." ONE does not need to avoid a void, nor void a void. To ALL there is ALL *only*, so there is no limitation out of which It needs to work Its way. Start with (state) GOODNESS AS IT IS NOW — WITH NOW THAT IS GOOD, FOR THIS IS THE ONE *BEING* — THE SELF-I-AM.

This is ALIVENESS *being*. This is WISDOM *being*. This is IDENTITY *being*, and there is naught else. And remember, GOODNESS does not have to prove Itself to another . . . to anyone, anywhere, anywhen, for any reason, FOR THERE IS ONLY THE ONE INFINITE, HENCE THE ONE INDIVIDUAL ALL, THE WHOLE ONE, THE COMPLETE ONE

PRESENT. This OMNIPRESENCE, THIS ALL PRESENT, PRECLUDES A SMALL (OR LARGE) MIND, hence precludes proof of aught, to aught, for aught, of aught beside! ALL KNOWS ITSELF IN ITS UTTER ALLNESS. There is no "additional mind" to hypnotize, be hypnotized, hence there is no hypnotism of "otherness" existent. It cannot be "handled" or "destroyed," for no such ever is.

THE INDIVISIBILITY OF TOTALITY PRESENT is mighty beyond words to describe or embrace. THE ABSOLUTE UNCHALLENGED SINGLENESS OF THE INDIVIDUAL ONE LIFE, INFINITY ITSELF WHOLLY ALIVE TO ITS ENTIRETY WITHOUT CHALLENGE OF ANY SORT, leaves the nonsense of a would-be metaphysical "proof" without foundation. The alertness of Truth TO THE FACT THAT ONLY TRUTH IS TRUE, precludes the entirety of the "proof-thesis."

All "healing" would be instantaneous if it were not for this silly assumption that "proof" was requisite. The mere assumption that there is aught in REALITY that CAN BE "PROVED," ASSUMES THAT THERE IS EVIL, AND THAT THERE IS A MIND THAT KNOWS IT, AND THAT THERE IS A SYSTEM WHEREBY IT CAN BE HANDLED, DENIED, WIPED OUT, DESTROYED, OR SET RIGHT! All this is a bald denial of TRUTH, SINGLENESS, ONENESS, WHOLENESS, IDENTITY, LIFE PRESENT!

We urge our readers to stay with the ONENESS OF WHOLENESS, AND BEHOLD THAT WHOLE MEANS *WHOLE* — nothing more and nothing less. Yes, indeed, REALITY IS INDIVISIBLE TOTALITY, INSEPARABLE COMPLETENESS, ENTIRETY PRESENT, and there is naught else, hence none to whom TRUTH can, or needs to be, proved. Equally, there is no mind to approve or disprove CHANGELESS INDIVIDUAL (SINGLE) TIMELESS-EN-

TIRETY-PRESENT. This Fact is NOW SO, hence IMME-
DIATE, and ALL THE AUTHORITY OF ITS UNDISPUTED
AWARENESS, is the IDENTITY YOU (I) BE THIS IN-
STANT – NO WAIT, NO DELAY, NO "BECOMING"
POSSIBLE. THE ABSOLUTE IMMEDIACY OF ACTUALI-
TY ALONE IS GENUINE, FOR IT IS ALL, HENCE
CANNOT BE DISPUTED. IT IS, AND ITS ISNESS IS
TOTALITY NOW BEING. HEAVEN (COMPLETENESS,
HENCE, UTTER GOODNESS) IS AT HAND NOW,
FOREVERMORE!

CHAPTER IV

Truth Is Never Under Attack

One of the major superstitions rampant throughout "creation," is that there is a devil, a Satan, an evil power, a void, a second, even if lower mentality, at work trying to cut God down to its level, trying to destroy Life, eradicate Truth, obliterate Reality, overcome Goodness, wipe out Identity, and leave only a void.

All this stems from theology. What theology? The theology of superstition, and there is no other theology extant. All religion, whether faith in a government, in personal power, in time, in a supreme being, personal prowess, intellectualism, evolution, or what, is a SYSTEM OF WORSHIP, a CYCLE OF BELIEF, an ESCAPE FROM ACTUALITY, a TRUST IN OTHERNESS, a FIRM CONVICTION OF TIME, a ROUTINE OF VACUITY, a THESIS OF DUALISM.

One could go on ad infinitum with definitions concerning evil and its would-be results, the void and its would-be creation, a Satan and his would-be victims, matter (the substance-of-lack, vacuity) and its commotion, its reactions, its pretense of victimization. To do so would be a waste, and would in no way prove that evil exists, that a creation has been produced, that cause and effect have validity, that time ever has been, or that birth-death is a certainty, a conviction that is obvious.

ONLY WHEN ONE BEGINS WITH, STATES, DEFINES WHAT ISNESS *is*, is he operating in ACTUALITY. Whatever goes on, purportedly, within the borders of supposition, remains just that — mere supposition without a mind to back it up, know it, experience it or trade in it. No matter how prevalent matter may seem to be, it still has not one thread of Truth within it, for, from its would-be beginning to its final deposition, it is fraudulent, and totally dependent upon its own would-be testimony to bolster its would-be claims to its would-be identity!

Outside of that which humanity proposes, no evil can be found. NOWHERE is there a void. NOWHERE is there Satan. NOWHERE is there an opposition to REALITY, for there is naught BUT REALITY EVERYWHERE.

Humanity itself, the entirety of creation, the argument of time, the would-be substance called matter, the evolutionary thesis — all of this in its entirety is but a theological superstition, as has been repeatedly pointed out. But to see this from the basis of human sense, intellectualism, education, or from studying the pages of Holywrit, books on physiology and anatomy, the course of the stars in their seemingly endless journey through space — to attempt to draw conclusions that will hold up from any such approach, is nonsense.

Only as you begin with EXISTENCE ITSELF — state what LIFE ACUTALLY IS — what ETERNAL INFINITY IS, does the nonsense of materiality become obvious. To the would-be intellectualism of humanity, Life is a total enigma. Existence, to the senses, merely means a series of dimensions computed in time-space via five self-testifying channels. The items that each claims to identify are limited in quantity and quality by the elasticity of the particular "sense" that is doing the identifying. But remember, the identification does not start, nor does it stop, with the sense doing the would-be identifying! The entirety of that chore is taken care of by the superstition which is the whole of creation's warp and woof.

In other words, the whole of the void, and the creation purportedly produced to fill it, is a theological superstition without even so much as a mind with which, or within which, the superstition has origin, or credence. And, as the whole of creation is nonsense, the would-be substance, called matter, of which it is "composed," has no actuality at all. How, then, can there be reliance on the avenues the non-existent superstition instituted as being the purveyors of fact?

In other words, how can one rely on any of the senses when they are merely side issues of falsity, their sole purpose being to testify to superstition as being factual? They are the liar's invention — invented wholly to testify to ignorance, that what ignorance declares is intelligent! The absurdity of this should be patent. It is like saying that darkness is capable of convincing itself via itself, that it is light! But, beginning with Reality, Light, where is there any darkness at all, hence any darkness to testify to or for itself?

Only those who still adhere to seeking things as GOOD, in lieu of GOOD, assuming that those items actually ARE GOOD, displace themselves, discount themselves, discommode themselves, and, at every step, attempt to disprove themselves. The five senses are their sole source of information, dimension, limitation. Those senses are the only manner in which time-space can be measured, doled out, cut off.

Yes, without the senses, no one can suffer pain, age, history, limitation, hate, fear, race, creed, nationality, gender, and all that is summed up between the past and a would-be future — all of it is purportedly passed "under the rod" of material belief, the classifications according to the senses.

But what of REALITY, ACTUALITY, ALIVENESS,

SOUL? According to the senses, the only and all of existence must be measured by, be within the ken of, dimension, duality, that which grows out of the past and extends into a future. In other words, cause and effect, subjectivity and objectivity, supply and demand — opposites!

WE ARE NOT TO TOUCH HUMANITY IN ANY MANNER. WE ARE NOT TO TRY TO SOLVE ITS PROBLEMS, OVERCOME ITS LACKS, CORRECT ITS SHORTCOMINGS, EASE IT INTO NEW CHANNELS, OVERLOOK, FORGIVE, OR FORGET ITS DEADNESS! WE ARE NOT TO TRY TO EXTEND THE INFLUENCE OF MATERIALITY, LENGTHEN THE ATOM'S LONGEVITY, CURE THE WORLD'S INTOLERANCE, DECREASE ITS FLOW OF ADRENALIN, DEODERIZE ITS EFFLUVIUM, OR FEEL PITY, SYMPATHY, OR HAVE A RAPPORT WITH IT. Rather, we ARE TO STATE ONLY WHAT TRUTH IS, LIFE IS, EXISTENCE IS, SPIRIT IS, AND STAY WITH THIS, FOR THIS ALONE IS WHAT YOU ARE, NOW. NONE OF THE MATERIAL SUPERSTITIONS HAVE ANY PLACE AT ALL, OCCUPY NO SPACE, HAVE NO AUTHORITY, NO VICTIMS, NO POSSIBLE WAY OF MAKING GOOD ANY OF THEIR LOUDLY VOICED THREATS.

Yes, there is ONLY EXISTENCE BEING, and that EXISTENCE IS SINGLE, WHOLE, TOTAL, ALL, RIGHT HERE NOW, EVERYWHERE, EVERYWHEN. Naught else is, can be, or has been. No error ever came into being, hence is NOT IN BEING, NOT IN THE SELF YOU BE, and is, therefore, not to be accounted of.

You BE this SOLE ONE YOU BE, NOW. NAUGHT CAN CHANGE IT, NOT EVEN THE SELF YOU BE. TRUTH, YOUR SELF, IS CHANGELESS. IT IS WITHOUT CHAL-LENGE. IT IS NOT UNDER ATTACK NOW OR EVER. IT

DOES NOT HAVE TO DEFEND ITSELF, FOR THERE IS
NAUGHT ELSE, HENCE NAUGHT TO OFFEND, OR BE
OFFENDED.

Should you start with "body" or "thing," you cannot say
this, for every item is but objective, hence is subjective to
that which seemed to have given it origin. He who would
putter along in this gutter can never behold the SELF AS IT
IS, for THE SELF IS NEVER IN A GUTTER.

What we are striving to make plain is — THERE IS NO
EVIL AT ALL, NO SATAN, NO OPPOSITE, NO OPPOSER,
HENCE NAUGHT ATTACKING LIFE, REALITY, ACTU-
ALITY. THERE IS NOTHING HAPPENING TO THE SELF
YOU BE. THAT SELF IS WHOLE, TOTAL, COMPLETE,
ENTIRE NOW, AND WHEN YOU SO STATE THE FACT,
THEN DEFINE WHAT YOU HAVE SAID, AND STICK
WITH THE DEFINITIVE DECLARATION AS BEING THE
SOLE FACT THAT IT IS, THERE IS NO WHERE, NO
WHEN, NO HOW FOR SO-CALLED ERROR TO EVEN
APPEAR . . . NONE TO WHOM IT CAN APPEAR,
NOWHERE FOR IT TO APPEAR. IT SIMPLY IS NOT, AND
THIS IS TRUTH!

Truth is never under attack, regardless of what education,
couched in theological, scientific, emotional or intellectual
terms may declare to the contrary, and endeavor to prove via
its own self-styled evidence, namely, the five senses. Often
education would extend its would-be authority as erudition's
selfhood, by claiming to have a sixth or extra-sensory
perception — a sense that purportedly transcends the
mundane senses of seeing, feeling, hearing, smelling and
tasting. However, no matter what matter pretends to know,
sense, or experience, there is NO MATTER TO MATTER,
NO MATTER TO KNOW, NO MATTER TO BE OR TO
STOP BEING. THERE IS ONLY SPIRIT NOW, EXISTENCE

NOW, TRUTH IN ITS UTTERNESS NOW, AND NAUGHT BESIDE WHATSOEVER.

He who would demonstrate or prove this, is a fool. He who would "put It to the test" is an idiot. He who would try to "understand" or "know" Truth is guaranteeing failure for himself, oblivion for all he assumes exists, darkness forever as his would-be norm. Why? Because there is no such person to begin with, no such mentality extant, no item comprehensible within a non-existent sphere, no identity possible for that which is not.

Truth, Life, Reality, Allness, Wholeness, THE ABSOLUTE PRESENT SELF YOU BE, is not being battled with, nor is It battling aught. Do not try to gird yourself for battle, or try to wear down opposition, disease, time, lack, humanity, falsity, age and the like. Rather, as we continue to point out, STATE THE DEFINITION OF ALLNESS, WHOLENESS, COMPLETENESS, ENTIRETY — see if these words actually have MEANING TO YOU, and if so, WHAT DO THEY MEAN? ARE YOU WILLING TO ACCEPT THE DEFINITION YOU HAVE DECLARED? ARE YOU WILLING TO ABIDE THEREIN, AND ACT ACCORDING TO THE DEFINITION STATED? If so, can you also allow your attention to be focused upon Its opposite, upon lack, fear, worry, dread, disease, hate, limitation, regret, failure, voids of any sort, anywhere, at any so-called time? Can you state FACT PRESENT IN ITS ENTIRETY, YET DEAL WITH A PAST, A FUTURE — WITH A CURSE DUE TO HAVING EARNED SUCH VIA SIN?

Can you honestly STATE FACT AS ALL THAT IS PRESENT, yet be concerned with the consequences of It being absent? Can you STATE REALITY PRESENT, yet flee before a void, slave to cast such out into outer darkness? Can you STATE ALLNESS AS BEING THE ALONE TOTAL

INDIVIDUAL PRESENCE EVERYWHERE, UNDIMEN-
SIONAL, yet have to struggle with nothingness that is not
even a suggestion within the INTELLIGENCE YOU BE?

Is it possible to STATE, THEN DEFINE WHAT NOW,
ISNESS, BEING ACTUALLY MEANS, yet presume there is
a contrary mentality that can and does hypnotize CON-
SCIOUSNESS, AWARENESS, BEING, SELF, ALIVE TO
ITS UTTER ACTION, FUNCTION, so that AWARENESS is
un-Awareness, LIFE is un-Alive, hence dead to Itself? If such
were possible, then what would even pretend to remain, and
how? If there were no Aliveness, no Presence, no Self, no
Consciousness, no Substance, no Existence, there would be
naught at all, so what could pretend what, to what, how,
why, when, and for what reason? How could such suggest
otherness, and again, to what, whom, where, when, or expect
the suggestion to mean aught, or to be carried out?

Hypnotism is impossible, for there is ONLY INTELLI-
GENCE PRESENT, LIFE (EXISTENCE ITSELF) PRESENT
AS THIS VERY SELF, THIS SOLE INDIVIDUAL ONE I
AM. I CAN BE NO OTHER, NOR IS THERE ANOTHER
INFINITY PRESENT THAT COULD BE I! THERE IS BUT
THE ONE ABSOLUTE WHOLE INFINITE EXISTENCE,
AND THIS ONE IS MIND ITSELF BEING UTTERLY
AWARE AS THE SELF IT IS (I AM).

In metaphysics, hypnotism is called malpractice — that is,
the presence of another mind suggesting falsity, error or
otherness, hence duality (sin, evil, Satan, devil, death-birth)
to the one finite mind pretending it has identification. But
the mind pretending, and the pretense of another mind trying
to influence it for any reason at all, is one and the same error
— an assumption without the foundation of a mind to assume
it!

Again, stating FACT, which is but another way of saying

that ONLY EXISTENCE EXISTS, ONLY LIFE IS ALIVE, ONLY THAT WHICH IS HAS VALIDITY, POWER, AUTHORITY, PRESENCE, AND IS THE ONLY IDENTITY-I HERE NOW — stating this Fact and defining the terms used, admitting their full meaning, precludes a personal mind altogether, a sinning mind altogether, a void, a loss, a past, a future, a curse, a theological or physical hell of any sort, even as it also precludes a religionist's heaven, whether that heaven is physical, ethereal, spiritual, or what.

He who would look to body as his dwelling place, or would look to a hereafter as a possible home, is dealing entirely in fiction. He who would dimensionalize THE VERY IDENTITY ONE IS, is absolutely invalid in his conclusions, hence his every premise must be invalid, sick, dis-eased.

In TRUTH we do not deal with any of this, regardless what its would-be source, authority, time-honored reputation, mass acceptance. ACTUALITY ALONE IS THE SUBSTANCE THAT IS THE SELF ONE INDIVIDUAL IS. There is no more, no less. Material evolution, revolution, or resolution will in no way aid the reader to acquire IDENTITY, SELFHOOD, LIFE ETERNAL HERE NOW. REALITY ALONE IS, AND THIS IS ALREADY THE SOLE IDENTITY YOU BE. Stick with this — but not as mere words you can say over and over as if reciting your spiritual beads, saying your prayers, rubbing a rabbit's foot, or depending on some charm, statement, attitude, to get you "safely through" humanity and on to our heavenly rest!

Over and over we urge you to leave things alone — leave body alone, disease, lack, and whatever seems to be troubling you, alone. Leave the argument that you have a separate finite mentality, alone. Don't try to find out why you lack this or that, what the cause of your difficulty is, why you continue to be frustrated, why you do not have plenty of this world's goods and why everything you plan does not go sailing along in a spanking-fine breeze. Do not try to analyze why you appear to have failures in what you attempt, and why Truth does not pour readily into your every waking moment. Do not try to discover why everything does not immediately straighten out when you "voice" Truth, or why some of those who "appear to know more than you do" sometimes seem to go sour, quit the work, give up the ghost, become ill, or whatever.

All such is based on the theological superstition of sin, guilt, that there is a tempter, a Satan, an evil that goes "up and down the earth" tempting the unwary, the undiligent, the idle ones . . . or that there is guilt, and that we all must pay for it . . . or that the troubles we go through are of benefit to us, protecting us, aiding in our evolution, development, lifting us up and beyond what we would otherwise know or attain if it were not for the trouble driving us onward!

None of this is so. He who is disappointed in whatever experience he claims is his, is one who has NOT, repeat, HAS NOT started with the ALLNESS OF ONE SINGLE INDIVIDUAL WHOLENESS WHICH CANNOT BE FRACTURED, OR FICTIONALIZED! Rather, he has outlined THINGS AS BEING DESIRABLE, AS BEING GOOD, AS TAKING THE PLACE OF SELFHOOD, SPIRIT, WHOLENESS, ALREADY AT HAND, AND ALREADY THE VERY SELF HE IS! Had he started wholly with FACT, HERE, NOW, AS THE SELF HE IS, THE GOODNESS HE IS IN ABSOLUTE ACTION, FULLNESS, SUBSTANCE TOTALLY SUPPLIED, he would have no frustration, no disappointment, no worry or upset. How could he?

The frustration, the lack, the disappointment, the resentment, the void, the anger, the blame, the criticism is always based on duality, on otherness, on things. He is upset because he lacks some "thing." He wanted some thing to be thus and so — he wanted not only the quality of some "thing," but also the quantity. He was working "in Truth" wholly for things, and because he did not get them, he is "angry and will not go into the feast" of OMNIPRESENT GOOD, THE WHOLE PRESENT SELF HE IS NOW!

He who looks for GOOD anywhere but as the VERY SELF HE IS, THE VERY LIFE HE IS, THE ACTUAL HEALTH, WEALTH, COMPLETENESS HE IS, will suffer disappointment, frustration, resentment, confusion, blame, guilt, condemnation, and confinement within his limited sense of finity in proportion to its narrowness, falsity, and continued occupancy of his attention. He need expect naught except the fruition of that which he is sowing — lack, lack, and more lack. Yet he is certain to claim it is due to this one or that one, this cause or that! Should he actually behold what is behind it all, he would instantly stop it by beginning with (stating) ACTUALITY ONLY, AND STAYING THERE.

We keep pointing out that we do not mean "staying there" via saying the words over and over, as one would recite his beads of worship, or go through a ceremony via rote. Such a process is worse than folly, for it is invoking ignorance to perform its mystical powers — it is calling evil forth from its so-called confines by incantations. It is total delivery of SELFHOOD into the toils of nothingness, oblivion, the pit, even as Macbeth's witches brewed their evil potion!

ISNESS is not a matter for superstition, supposition, or exploitation. BEING IS HERE AND NOW ALL THERE IS. IT IS LIFE ITSELF ALIVE TO BEING INDIVIDUAL, WHOLE, ENTIRE, COMPLETE, ALL — EVERYWHERE, NOW, WHOLE, GOODNESS, WHEREIN THERE IS

NAUGHT BESIDE, NAUGHT MISSING, NAUGHT THAT CAN BE ADDED, NAUGHT IN OPPOSITION. WITHIN THIS UTTERNESS THERE IS NO CHALLENGE, NO SIN, NO LACK, NO CURSE, NO SECOND-ONE OR SECOND-HAND, NAUGHT SECOND-HAND, HANDED DOWN, OR EVEN HANDLED.

THIS ONE INDIVIDUAL IS ALL THERE IS. IT IS GOODNESS ITSELF, ALIVENESS ITSELF, NOW PRESENT IN ITS ENTIRETY. THIS LEAVES NO CREATION, NO CAUSE, NO RESULT, NO SHIFTING ABOUT FOR ANY REASON, NO ADJUSTMENT TO BE MADE EVER. THERE IS ONLY GOODNESS, FOR THIS IS THE VERY ETERNAL SELF YOU BE NOW. THERE ARE NO OTHER MINDS, LIVES, OR BEINGS ANYWHERE. THERE ARE NO OTHER PLACES, STATES, CONDITIONS, OR "TIMES" ANYWHERE. THERE IS ONLY BEING PRESENT IN THE FULL OF ITS ALIVENESS, CHANGELESS PRESENT ACTUALITY, BODILESS UNDIMENSIONAL ABSOLUTENESS, PURE SINGLENESS.

No, Truth is not being attacked by Its absence, for IT IS ALTOGETHER PRESENT AND KNOWS THIS, NAY, IS BEING THIS RIGHT NOW. This precludes any absence of ACTUALITY, THE PRESENT ALLNESS, so it precludes all disease, poverty, lack, humanity, or minds to know, deal with, or through such. THIS IS THE AUTHORITY LIFE IS, THE AUTHORITY TRUTH IS, THE AUTHORITY THAT ALL IS, HENCE WHEN IT SPEAKS, IT IS ALREADY SO.

Is this how you "work," or do you still declare and declare the wonderous statements of Truth, then wait for time, or nature, to heal or kill your "patient?" Do you abide patiently with the trouble you experience, thinking that you have done your "work," therefore you have a right to expect results some time in the hereafter? Are you, like Job, patient unto death, assuming that patience with error, lack, falsity, a lie, fiction, trouble, humanity, death, is a virtue? What basis, outside of theology, have you for so concluding? True, religion had to invent some gimmick to keep its followers happy in the midst of their vicissitudes, so patience with the nonsense was declared to be a virtue that would bring great reward! Reward of what? Simply more trouble! What utter drivel!

To put up with evil in any way, even for a moment, is a waste, and there is no virtue in it, and equally, it is not a sin. It is merely folly. SIN DOES NOT EXIST AT ALL, even though you may seem to be experiencing what seems to be the results of such. SIN DOES NOT EXIST. GUILT DOES NOT EXIST. TIME DOES NOT EXIST. AGE DOES NOT EXIST. DISEASE DOES NOT EXIST. LACK DOES NOT EXIST. ANOTHER MIND DOES NOT EXIST. HATE, WAR, CREEDS, RACE, HUMANITY, MAN, HISTORY, PROPHECY, DOES NOT EXIST!

Let education, let the press, let the theologian, let the imbecile, let the credulous make of the above what they will, but nevertheless the statements stand. SPIRIT IS ALL, SUBSTANCE IS SINGLE, LOVE IS PURE, WHOLE, ENTIRE, ABSOLUTE, THE ONLY. ALL CANNOT BE DUPLICATED, COUNTERFEITED, SET ASIDE, CAST OUT OR CAST OFF. MIND IS INTELLIGENCE ITSELF, AND THERE IS NO OTHER. INFINITY IS ETERNALLY PRESENT RIGHT NOW, FOR IT HAS NAUGHT TO DO WITH THE DIMENSIONAL, WITH TIME, WITH SPACE, WITH ANY SORT OF MEASUREMENT WHATEVER, WITH SO-CALLED SCIENCE, BELIEF, E.S.P., SENTIMENTALITY, REVERENCE, EMOTIONALISM OR WHAT.

No, TRUTH is forever NOW UNCHANGED IN ITS PRESENCE, ITS WHOLENESS, ITS UNCHALLENGED

AUTONOMY. IT IS NEVER AT THE WHIM OF OTHER-
NESS, SUPERSTITION, BELIEF, SUGGESTION, OR SUP-
POSITION, FOR THERE IS NO SOURCE FOR SUCH, NO
OTHER MIND IN WHICH THESE WOULD-BE NOTIONS
CAN ORIGINATE OR HAVE PLACE, ACTION, OR RE-
SULTS. THERE IS ONLY TRUTH, SO WHO OR WHAT
CAN EXPERIENCE EVIL, SATAN, DEVIL, ERROR OF
ANY SORT? WHO OR WHAT CAN KNOW OR EXPERI-
ENCE LACK, LIMITATION, FEAR, TROUBLE, WANT?
IMPOSSIBLE!

TRUTH IS WITHOUT ATTACK. TRUTH IS WITHOUT
AN ENEMY. TRUTH IS WITHOUT DENIAL, OBSTRUC-
TION, NEED FOR PROOF OR DEMONSTRATION, DE-
FENSE OR PROTECTION. TRUTH IS WITHOUT OTHER-
NESS THAT CAN DOUBT, QUESTION, COMMAND OR
DEMAND. TRUTH IS WITHOUT NEED, WITHOUT BE-
GINNING, WITHOUT END, WITHOUT TIME, WITHOUT
AGE, DETERIORATION, CHANGE. TRUTH IS WITHOUT
DELAY, WITHOUT A DEVIL, WITHOUT A VOID, WITH-
OUT ANY FORM OR SUGGESTION OF LACK ANY-
WHERE, RIGHT NOW, FOREVER. TRUTH IS WHAT
AMNESS IS, I AM!

CHAPTER V

Self-Satisfaction

There is but one "way" to SELF-SATISFACTION, and that is not a "way" at all! SELF-SATISFACTION cannot be obtained, gained, come by, earned. Why? Because It is not a "thing," an item, a possession, an objectification, nor is It a subjective "feeling," experience, attitude, or attribute.

SELF-SATISFACTION is the very WHOLENESS THAT OMNIPRESENCE IS *BEING*. IT IS CONSCIOUS FULL-NESS, ALIVENESS, ENTIRETY FUNCTIONING, PURITY AWARE OF ITS UTTERNESS, ITS UNDIMENSIONAL, IMMEASURABLE, UNCONTESTED, UNCHALLENGED SINGLENESS. SELF-SATISFACTION IS ONENESS IN-FINITELY BEING THE INDIVIDUAL COMPLETENESS THAT SUBSTANCE IS, THAT LOVE IS, THAT AMNESS IS, THAT OMNISCIENCE IS, THAT ACTION IS. IT IS ACUTELY TOTAL, INCLUSIVE OF EACH AND EVERY THOUGHT (IDEA) IT IS FRESHLY NOW CONCEIVING-PERCEIVING. THERE ARE NO REPETITIONS, NO DU-PLICATIONS, NO REMEMBRANCES, NO RECALLS, NO PATTERNS, NO DESIGNS, NO REASONS FOR ANY THOUGHT OTHER THAN THAT INFINITE INTELLI-GENCE HAS THE CAPACITY TO CONCEIVE-PERCEIVE, SO IS DOING SO NOW FOR THE SOLE AND ONLY PRESENT!

We urge you to ponder well the above statement. Do not assume that "things" are what the would-be senses have been computed to identify as "conceptions," or as "that-which-is-perceives." Not a bit of it.

Nothing that the "senses" seem to sense is actual. Not an item is the way it appears to be, or is it what it "seems" to be, nor where, nor when, nor aged, nor the result of aught — not even of belief, dream, assumption, superstition, claim, evil, cause, devil or what! Naught objective, naught subjective exists at all!

No, nothing beheld by the senses is as the senses "sense" it to be. This, however, will not be clear, nor can it be, until you begin TOTALLY WITH WHAT REALITY IS, WHAT MIND IS, WHAT LIFE IS, WHAT AMNESS IS, WHAT THE SELF IS.

Only as ONE BEGINS WITH INFINITY, WHOLENESS, COMPLETENESS HERE NOW CAN THE ABSURDITY OF "WHAT-IS-SENSED" BE SEEN AS AN ABSURDITY. It does not mean that we have to "scrap" all that the senses appear to testify to, or of, nor do we have to destroy those senses, instruct them, evangelize them, or change them in any manner whatever. It merely means that we must begin with WHAT FACT IS, WHERE IT IS, HOW IT IS, WHY IT IS, WHEN IT IS, AND WITH THE TOTALITY THAT IT IS. THIS ALONE IS SELFHOOD, THIS ALONE IS YOUR BEING, THIS ALONE IS YOUR WHOLE SUBSTANCE, EXTENT, DURATION, SUPPLY, WORK, ACTION, FUNC-TION, AND IDENTITY IN TOTO.

SELF-SATISFACTION does not depend upon the secur-ing of items, of things, nor upon their condition, quality, amount, placement, security, endurance, genesis, or demise. SELF-SATISFACTION is merely the NORM OF THE SELF, THE CHANGELESS STATUS OF OMNIPRESENCE BEING

ITS ENTIRE CONSCIOUS ALIVENESS, ALL-INCLUSIVE
ENTIRETY, SINGLE POWER, ABSOLUTE AUTHORITY,
PURE UNADULTERATED SINGLENESS. THIS ONE IS
NOW COMPLETE, WHOLE, ENTIRE, AS POINTED OUT
AGAIN AND AGAIN. IT CANNOT BECOME MORE THAN
ALL, IT CANNOT BE LESS THAN WHOLE, IT CANNOT
BE ANYWHERE BUT HERE, IT CANNOT EXIST ANY-
WHEN SAVE NOW, IT CANNOT GET ADDITIONAL
SELFHOOD, WISDOM, SUBSTANCE, FOR IT IS AL-
READY TOTALITY PRESENT, ACTIVELY FUNCTION-
ING AS ETERNAL INFINITY WHEREIN NO TIME CAN
BE. This is your SELF NOW. This is your POWER NOW.
This is your "work" NOW. This is your ACTION NOW. This
alone is your FUNCTION NOW. No wait is possible, no delay
can take place, no want can be filled, no need can be
overcome, no lack can be removed BECAUSE NO SUCH
EXISTS AT ALL. ONLY THE TOTAL NOW-SELF IS, AND
IT IS I. THERE IS NAUGHT BESIDE, BEYOND, OTHER
THAN, IN ADDITION TO, OR YET TO COME.

SELF-SATISFACTION IS GOODNESS IN ITS CON-
SCIOUS ENTIRETY, INFINITE INTELLIGENCE WHOLLY
BEING ACUTELY, JOYOUSLY, EXUBERANTLY ALIVE
TO AWARENESS BEING SUBSTANCE, THE ONLY
"STUFF" THAT EXISTENCE ACTUALLY IS. And there is
naught to contradict It, or question It. There is naught beside
to doubt, long for, wish upon, need, require, or insist on
obtaining. There is no "other mind" that can pretend aught,
for no such exists at all, hence cannot pretend that it can
understand, comprehend, demonstrate, overcome, manifest,
be led, lay hold on, or "use" SELF, LIFE, EXISTENCE in
any manner whatever.

SELF-SATISFACTION is not the outcome of any
scheme, plan, design, pattern. SELF-SATISFACTION does

not deal in cause or effect, as we repeatedly point out. SELF-SATISFACTION in no way can be "brought about," for all such maneuvering is based on the thesis that SELF-SATISFACTION IS AN ATTITUDE RELATED TO THE PROCUREMENT OF THINGS, THEIR CONDITION, THEIR AMOUNT, DURATION, SAFETY AND SUCH.

He who would *obtain* SELF-SATISFACTION must deny the SELF HE IS, and seek his IDENTITY AS GOODNESS ITSELF, in things, items, ideas, thus guaranteeing abysmal disappointment, continual struggle, total frustration, and ultimate exhaustion, for it is impossible to discover YOUR SELF IN ANY ITEM YOU CONCEIVE! You ARE NOT A THING, A THOUGHT, AN IDEA. NOR CAN ANY IDEA-THOUGHT-THING OPERATE IN LIEU OF INFINITE EXISTENCE, LIFE ITSELF, FOR THINGS ARE BUT PRESENT-THOUGHTS NOW BEING CONCEIVED-PERCEIVED. No item (body-thing-thought) is ever the outcome of cause, time, production, evolution, plan, need, creation. ITEMS ARE SOLELY WHAT INTELLIGENCE IS NOW CONCEIVING ONLY. THEY CONTRIBUTE NAUGHT TO MIND, ARE NOT IMPORTANT TO MIND BEING THE ALL GOODNESS IT IS, ARE NOT NEEDED IN ORDER TO COMPLETE ALL, OR TO MAKE LIFE MORE FULLY ALIVE THAN IT OMNIPOTENTLY IS ALREADY!

If it were not for the foolish and persistent search for things, the devisement of schemes whereby the would-be human can lay hold on things, secure a continuity of things, and personally operate as a thing, he would not maintain and sustain his enslavement to ignorance. Rather, he would drop the nonsense, his labor for nothingness, his servitude to oblivion, his insistence on a past and his fear over the state of his future. No, he would stop trying to see into that future, read the cards, his horoscope, the stars in the heavens, the pages of Holy Writ, or the lines in his hand, the bumps on his cranium, or the number of years he has to his credit or debit!

He who begins with REALITY AS IT IS, must begin with the SOLE INDIVIDUAL INFINITE SINGLE SELF wherein no other at all can be — wherein no contrary mind (his own or that of others) can exist at all. He must state FACT AS WISDOM KNOWS IT TO BE, AS AWARENESS KNOWS ITSELF TO BE, AS CONSCIOUSNESS, SUBSTANCE, KNOWS ITSELF TO BE.

Whatever thing I obey can contribute nothing to me but lack. Why? Because GOODNESS ALONE IS WHAT I ALREADY AM IN TOTO. To turn from THAT WHICH IS MY IDENTITY IN ITS ENTIRETY, and look to a mere thought, idea, thing, as being GOOD, BEING MY SELF, BEING LIFE, SUBSTANCE, REALITY, IDENTITY, POW-ER, WISDOM, ACTION, is to betray my Self, forego Life, quit Love, deny Purity, repudiate Action, stop Function, surrender Authority, and worship a mere item WITHIN Mind, rather than operate AS Mind!

Again, to turn to any "thing" as GOODNESS, SELF, LIFE, SUBSTANCE, is to even ignore IDEA AS SUCH, and to become a slave to what the senses dimensionally claim to be objective substance due to a subjective ignorance — to the processes of a would-be mind of matter, biology, dualism, duplicity, nonsense, and the effects of same. Yes, such turning to things, is to turn from Subtance completely and identify with that which has no identity at all, no place, no stuff to it, not even a dream.

"Things" are to be left entirely to Mind only. The things usually wanted, needed, craved, fought for, claimed as being of value, are invariably the dimensional objectification of the senses. They are considered to be of value only because the one so considering them thinks of himself as being a "thing," hence dependent upon other things for support, sustenance, continuity.

Nothing that the senses claim to sense is existent as it appears. In every case "things" are finite, hence a composition of the would-be mentality "directing" the senses. Under the would-be guidance of that mind, the senses appear to sense only what they are told to sense, how, when, where, and why. Not an item can "appear" contrary to this directive, regardless of what education would claim to the contrary.

All disease, all lack, all creation, all age, all time, all evil, all matter and whatever passes as existent within this framework, is totally false, without Reality, Substance, Power, Authority. Naught it appears to claim for itself or its produce, can do aught to SELF, GOODNESS, NOWNESS, ISNESS, THE IDENTITY YOU ARE THIS MOMENT FOREVER. But to see this, you must STATE FACT, THEN DEFINE WHAT YOU HAVE STATED AND BEHOLD THE FACTUALITY AS IT IS. STICKING WITH THIS, YOU ARE "ARMED" INVINCIBLY AGAINST ANY AND ALL EVIL, FOR YOU BEHOLD THAT NO SUCH EXISTS AT ALL, ANYWHERE, EVER. THIS IS HEALTH (COMPLETENESS) INDEED. THIS IS WEALTH (ENTIRETY) INDEED. AND AGAINST TOTALITY, GOODNESS, PRESENT NOW IN ITS ABSOLUTE PERFECTION, THERE CAN BE NO LAW, NO OPPOSITION, NO OTHERNESS, OR CLAIM THERE-FROM.

To attempt to improve, you must first DISPROVE YOURSELF. To attempt to progress, you must regress from the ALONE PERFECT WHOLE ONE YOU NOW BE. To add aught to your SELF, you must change that SELF into being less than It is — and to do this, you would cease to be!

The above paragraph should make it clear that SUB-
STANCE, SUPPLY, SELF-SATISFACTION cannot be
known, enjoyed, so long as one is seeking for his IDENTITY
where It is not, and never can be. He who would try to
become but one of the many items that human sense
pretends to produce, is attempting to convert from REAL-
TY, INFINITY, to fiction, finity — trying to switch from
THAT WHICH IS, to that-which-is-NOT! Such is impossible.

We are striving to make it clear that the pursuit of
"things" is not a pursuit of "things" as Mind knows them —
not a pursuit of ideas, thoughts, items in Mind, but rather is
the pursuit of the product of insanity, the would-be items in
a dream, the dimensional products of the senseless senses, the
compounds of matter, the compilations of dust, the assumptions of superstition, the substance or "stuff" which purport-
dly makes up the body of fear. He who would seek material
items, physical baubles, gendered objects, time products,
created inventions, is working totally OUTSIDE OF INTEL-
LIGENCE, OUTSIDE OF REALITY, OUTSIDE OF
SPIRIT, OUTSIDE OF LOVE, SINGLENESS, PURITY,
TRUTH, FACT, ISNESS, OMNIPRESENCE, hence has NO
POWER, NO AUTHORITY, NO HOPE OF SUCCESS.
Rather, he is already one with the nothingness he pursues,
already oblivious to Fact, already shut off from SELF-
SATISFACTION. In other words, whatever goes on within
this would-be area is mortal, nebulous, dead already. It has
never been alive, never will come to life, never be actual,
hence never be of concern to the SELF YOU BE.

Material, objective, or even subjective "things" have no
value, for they have no actuality at all. They each and all
spring entirely from assumption, superstition, which certainly
is far from being a life-power, or a life-giver. Because matter
has no place at all, no history, no substance, no selfhood, no

future, no point of reality in Reality, why waste effort an
attention trying to gain more of it, or to salvage any aspect c
it, maintain or sustain it, provide it with a soul, a past, and
future, a place from whence it came and a heaven-hell t
which it will be consigned? Why feel it must be worked fo
with, over, and all the rest of it? Why assume it is one'
Identity? Why look to it, why look for an addition c
subtraction of it, why watch over it, or look out for it?

True, anyone reading these words from the view c
education only, will disagree most strongly. He will assum
the author to be an idiot, the material dangerous, ever
statement that of madness itself, hence not to be accepte
trusted, used in any manner at all.

He who will begin with ACTUALITY, REALITY, EXIS
TENCE AS IT IS, wholly apart from objectification accor
ing to the senses — with BEING, rather than the urge t
"become," or with a subjective state or subconsciou
determinism — will behold the UNDIMENSIONAL STATU
OF INTELLIGENCE, CONSCIOUSNESS, AWARENESS. H
will behold that the thoughts that UNCHALLENGED IN
FINITY, LIGHT IN ACTION, CONCEIVES, IS DECIDE
LY DIFFERENT FROM THE FINITE BABBLINGS O
NONSENSE.

Yes, he will discover that actually there are NO BAE
BLINGS AT ALL IN ACTUALITY — that these appear to b
perceptible only to the finite sense when listened to by suc
He will discover that when he starts with FACT ONLY
THERE ARE NO BABBLINGS, BUT RATHER SOLI
FACT, ACTUALITY, REALITY HERE NOW BEING IT
SELF. Herein is no "becoming," no waiting, no delay, no sir
of omission or sins of commission, no penalties, no curses, n
rewards, no laws, no principles, no rules or regulation
anywhere. Rather, there is ONLY SELF BEING ITSELF

THE INDIVIDUAL ONE BEING WHOLLY INDIVIDUAL AS POWER, INTELLIGENCE, AWARENESS, SUBSTANCE, JOY, SELF-SATISFACTION, MIGHT, WISDOM, BLISS. HE WILL BEHOLD SELF AS IT NOW ETERNALLY IS, INCLUSIVE OF ITS UTTERNESS, HENCE OF ITS UNIVERSE.

CHAPTER VI

Human Success Is Failure

It is impossible to estimate how many billions of words have been written on the subject of good business, but how much of the advice has been accurate?

What is business? What is good business? What is bad business? How does one stimulate business? With whom does One conduct business? What sort of merchandise can and does One handle, and to whom is it distributed? Who or what determines the price to be paid, the net gain, the benefit from the would-be transaction? Is there a tax to be levied, and if so, what determines it, to whom is it paid, what percentage of the gross is it based on?

Is business a personal, a national, a racial necessity? Is there a limit as to who can enter it, or into what specialty he must fit himself? Is his decision his own, or is it due to necessity, inheritance, astrological influence, race, color, creed, education, gender, location, inclination, age, or just what does determine these points?

Does One enter business for profit, for possessions, for influence or control over others, as a power-grab, or that He may live more comfortably than another? Is it because He assumes He is worthy of only the best, and business based on supply and demand, the best way of obtaining that with which He can indulge Himself?

The so-called human approach to business is dealing in things, with things, for things, all based on the notion that One is a thing! This is utterly false — a theological fiction of duality. Nations have come and gone, civilizations have vanished, and the race itself is promised total extinction, all predicated on lack, many, much!

Identity is not a thing. The Individual One, the Sole Self does not need things, does not depend on things, does not deal in things, does not concern Itself with things.

True, Mind conceives, as we have repeatedly emphasized, but not because things are essential for Mind's survival or operation as LIFE ITSELF, ALLNESS ITSELF, THE SINGLENESS THAT BEING IS RIGHT NOW, ETERNAL-LY.

Mind alone is the only GOODNESS there is. It is not being GOOD as a contradiction to "bad," but as GOODNESS ITSELF BEING, there can be no lack anywhere, hence no humanity anywhere, for humanity is but the manifestation, the demonstration or proof, if you will, that less-than-ALL *can* exist! Doesn't education teach you that every "man" is a small piece of Life, a segment of Original Cause, an effect of a void that purportedly exists or existed away back yonder somewhere, sometime, and that a theological Jewish god tried to fill it?

Is not "man" purportedly equipped with a small finite mind, a short span of duration, a given place to fill, a niche that must be occupied if Love's great plan is to be properly executed? Are not all the troubles "man" faces, but part of his development, proof that this god loves him and, in fact, is so crazy about him that he wants to hone him to razor sharpness, refine him to perfection, prepare him for joys untold in a nebulous hereafter? Do not all his "stripes" benefit him, his pains elevate him, his patience in misery lift him up to joy unspeakable? And is not his untimely death, whether in misery or frustration, all a part of the plan to get him to whichever place he is slated for away out yonder somewhere?

Business based on the above premise can thrive beyond one's wildest hopes if he gets in on the ground floor, or if he can bring about a new gimmick and convince the public that it cannot get along without it, or that one never really lived it up till he has come into possession of this particular offering! Even a new type of casket can have them standing in line if the public relations man has done a good job of selling!

But is any of this business, as we use the word in Reality? Is it GOOD BUSINESS, or GOOD IN BUSINESS — THE BUSINESS OF GOODNESS? The answer is an unequivocal "NO!"

Business is not that which is carried on between others. Business is not a commercial development whereby lack can be assuaged, comforts of the body can be augmented, society can be complemented, nations can be arbitrary, planets can be offensive, or souls can be assured of a spot in the orchestra when Gabriel blows his trumpet!

Business is merely the OMNIPRESENT ACTION OF NOW BEING WHAT IT IS IN ITS ENTIRETY, namely, TOTAL PRESENCE WHOLLY PRESENT, LIFE UTTERLY ALIVE, WHOLENESS COMPLETELY WHOLE, ONE UN-DIMENSIONALLY SINGLE, LOVE BEING UNCHAL-LENGED IN ITS ABSOLUTENESS, WISDOM OPERATING FULLY, PERFECTION BEING ALL THAT TOTALITY IS FOREVER, WHEREIN THERE IS NO TIME, NO OTHER-NESS, NO BECOMING, NO CHANGE, NO BOREDOM.

Business is, as just pointed out, WITHOUT CHANGE. This does not mean stagnation, but rather that THE ALL

THAT OMNIACTION IS, cannot be measured, rated, compared, judged, required, needed, or planned. GOODNESS IS WHOLLY GOOD, meaning that PERFECTION IS. Is what? Is absolutely everywhere, infinitely being WHOLE, COMPLETE. It is JOY IN ITS ENTIRETY, WISDOM IN ITS ABSOLUTENESS, SINGLENESS IN ITS FULLNESS OF SELF-SATISFACTION. There can be no breath of finity, impurity, adultery, limitation, change, a void, a need, a requirement, a sufferer, or that which-is-outside-or-out-beyond. There is no possibility of development, growth, change, improvement, gain, acquirement, or ultimate arrival of any sort for any reason. This is why there can be no cause, no effect, for both are predicated on reason, impulse, plan, scheme, design — a whyfore, or an accounting for a stimulus, a purpose, hence that without which there is incompleteness, a state of being unfinished, the need of more, or a "becoming," which is a total denial of ISNESS, AMNESS, NOWNESS! Business, on the human so-called basis, generally, if not altogether, deals in things, for things are its entire premise. In Truth, we do the "reverse." Yes, as we continue to point out, we urge you to leave "things" alone — leave ideas alone — leave "body" alone — leave money alone — leave business alone — leave all forms of prophecy alone, and above all, leave history, the past, relationships, causes, creation, theology and all the rest of human would-be indoctrination, alone!

"But what will be left to talk about?" someone may inquire.

If one has naught better to talk about than trouble, pain, confusion, frustration, insanity, mysticism, and mythical folderol, he had best keep still to begin with! For what possible help or comfort can any of the material nonsense make, either to himself or his listeners?

ONLY GOODNESS IS GOOD, AND ONLY GOOD
EXISTS, NAY, IS EXISTENCE ITSELF, SUBSTANCE
ITSELF, WHOLENESS ITSELF, RIGHT NOW. So, if one
would speak, let him voice FACT, TRUTH, LOVE, SINGLE-
NESS, BLISS, JOY, GLORY, or let him hold his tongue,
even in what appears as our present day routines. Keeping
alive to PURE AWARENESS IN ITS CHANGELESS AC-
TION, will enable one to "do" whatever he seems required to
do, and without all the effort, puzzlement, fear and anxiety
connected with having to make a momentous decision, a
choice that could go this way, that way, and possibly end in
colossal disaster.

In Truth we do not have decisions, choices, to make.
THERE IS BUT TRUTH PRESENT, FOR THAT IS THE
SOLE SELFHOOD THAT REALITY IS, THAT I AM. There
is none beside, naught beside, so no choice comes into the
picture. WHERE ALL IS ALL, what else can there be, and
what would so declare — for what reason, or why? Naturally,
this is nonsense.

The utterness of GOODNESS PRESENT leaves no lack
anywhere, leaves no other mind anywhere. By this we mean,
Truth leaves no additional mind existent, so there is no such
to worry over lack, limitation, dimension, need, frustration,
fear, or humanity. It leaves no small or finite mind that has
obligation, duties to perform, business to attend to, lives to
support, bodies to care for, or a soul which must be
nourished, trained, purified, instructed and ultimately saved
or lost according to how moral or immoral its owner is!

No, not a bit of this is required. Theology requires it, but
we have already shown the nonsense of theology. Education,
in general, requires it, but who or what is educated —
SPIRIT, THE ALONE ONE PRESENT, INTELLIGENCE
ITSELF?

Prophecy and history combine to insist the human exists and will continue, for at least a given time. They both admit that the future of humanity is most insecure, for according to all available information, humanity is determined to destroy itself in one way or another, for such has been its pattern from its seeming start. True, religion points out that Holy Writ is its source of information. Material science says it is so because whatever comes forth from biology finally decays and vanishes as far as its human pattern is concerned. While physics claims that nothing is ever lost, certainly the form or shape undergoes alteration, and the "person" is no more, save as a memory, and that is generally of short duration.

Which are we to stay with — education in its various forms, or are we going to begin with what NOW IS, OMNIPRESENCE IS, TRUTH IS, REALITY IS, ACTUALITY IS, ACTION IS, LIFE IS, AMNESS IS?

If the latter is our basis of daily ALIVENESS, of a certainty we shall find that the mythical assumptions of materiality do fade, and will finally vanish altogether, so the "place (memory) shall know them no more." Why? Because fiction cannot supplant or withhold FACT. Only the FACT IS PERMANENT, UNCHANGING, BECAUSE IT IS SO NOW, WHICH IS PERMANENCY ITSELF IN TOTAL ACTION, BEING, ALIVENESS, ISNESS!

What of business? As we have pointed out, our ONLY BUSINESS IS TO STATE WHAT REALITY IS, WHAT SUBSTANCE IS, WHAT LIFE IS, WHAT AMNESS IS. Then define what we have stated, and stick therewith. Leave things totally alone if you would know SELF-SATISFACTION, that utter aliveness to acute total well-being here now.

Yes, if you would know the joy of LIVING IN THE NOW-FOREVER AS TOTAL UNCHALLENGED GLORIOUSLY BLISSFUL OMNIACTIVE *BEING*, the sole and only

genuine business GOODNESS IS "ENERGETICALLY" EX-
PERIENCING AS THE ALONE INDIVIDUAL COMPLETE-
NESS AMNESS IS, then do not seek ideas, try to procure
them, change them, alter them, or in any way at all depend
on them. Do not deal in things at all. Ideas are only that,
thoughts, if you will, that Mind is "this moment" conceiving-perceiving, but these thoughts (things-items-ideas) are
of no use, no value, no worth to ALLNESS, save that Mind
has the capacity to conceive same, so is doing so.

In other words, TOTALITY IS BEING TOTALLY ALL
THAT COMPLETENESS IS. If Mind has the potential in any
so-called direction, yet is not *being* ABSOLUTELY TOTAL
IN ITS UNCHALLENGED, UNDIMENSIONAL POWER,
WISDOM, ACTION, FUNCTION, ALIVENESS, then It
would utterly vanish. Why? Because the instant INFINITE
WHOLENESS is challenged by less (or more) than Itself, It
would have ceased to be the WHOLENESS IT IS, THE
SINGLENESS IT IS, THE ABSOLUTE SUBSTANCE,
GOODNESS, LIFE, ENTIRETY THAT IT IS. SELF-IDEN-
TITY, SPIRIT, THE SOLE INDIVIDUAL, THE ONLY I
WOULD END, AND THERE WOULD BE NAUGHT.

As pointed out repeatedly, WHOLENESS CANNOT BE
WHOLE, UNLESS IT *IS* WHOLE. The slightest adultery,
whether an adding to, or a taking from, would leave
SINGLENESS nowhere. It would preclude ONENESS, hence
there would not even be a vacuum. Spirit must be THE
ALONE ONE — It cannot *be*, save It is SINGLE, WHOLE,
TOTAL, COMPLETE, ENTIRE, hence COMPLETENESS,
ENTIRETY, INFINITY, whereas humanity can only pretend
to exist via the thesis of two or more, duality, multiplicity.
Humanity's end, abolition, is inescapable in ONENESS, even
as ONENESS would cease to be on the instant dualism is
introduced, if such were possible!

Let us again state, THERE IS NO BUSINESS BUT GOOD BUSINESS — the business of GOODNESS BEING WHOLLY ITSELF, ALL. What else *can* Goodness *be?* Where else can Goodness be save everywhere? When is Goodness being Itself, GOOD? Right here NOW, the present. To Goodness there can be no history, no time at all, no improvement or decline. There can be Itself only, for It is the Sole Substance, the Entirety called Existence.

Yes, It is the Individual Singleness called Self, the only one that Amness *is* — It is I, and there is none beside, so how can It carry on business with another, for another, because of another, or how can another interfere with It, compete with It, use sharp practices against It, or in any manner whatever even come in contact with It?

In other words, there is but one single ONE, one single WHOLE, one single TOTAL PRESENCE, and this one One is I, and there is none else. Where then is blame, where is criticism, where is greed, where is lust for the "things of the flesh?" Where in the whole of WHOLENESS can there be any need, any frustration, any dimension, any comparison? Where can there be an accumulation of "goods," or things? Can ideas accumulate in Omnipresence, in the Mind that is only NOW conceiving-perceiving Its thoughts? Is there "time" in which ideas-now-being-conceived can be stored as though these ideas (thoughts) *were* conceived in the past?

Are we still solely concerned with items, possessions? Are we insistent that Mind is obsessed with props, items with which It bolsters Itself up, shores Itself up, lest It collapse because of a lack of support? Does It demand a multitude of thoughts in order that It *be* Substance, *be* present, *be* alive, conscious, aware — *be* Itself?

We return to these questions again and again to make it clear that REALITY ALREADY IS REAL and there is naught beside whatever, so nothing beside with which One can be concerned.

Whenever you find your attention focused on things, items either present or absent, or their conditions, quantity or quality, rest assured you are indulging Self-denial, Self-crucifixion, Self-sacrifice! You are indulging in fiction, pretending absurdity has the same validity that REALITY enjoys. To assume that non-Existence is the same as EXISTENCE, is to assume that death is the same as Life, lack is the same as Supply, that insanity is the same as INFINITE INTELLIGENCE, that what-you-are-NOT is the same as what-you-BE!

There is no such situation as successful business, to repeat a previous point. One is not in a process of success, for all such is dependent upon evolution, progression, change, an overcoming of opposites, lack, limitation and such. Yes, all such depends upon a certain criterion, a point from which measurement can be made, a goal to be attained and maintained, but above all, the requirement of a standard deficiency! Without lack, a set pattern of vacuity, void, need, requirement, insufficiency, one can never know how humanly "successful" he is, how "much" he is worth, "what" he has secured, what he can claim as his personal possession in comparison with what those about him have, or have not!

TRUTH IS NOT COMPARABLE, NOT IN COMPETITION, NOT STRIVING TO "BECOME" TOTAL, FOR IT IS TOTALITY ITSELF NOW, WHOLE NOW, ALL NOW, AND THERE IS NO LACK EXISTENT AT ALL, NO WANT, NEED, REQUIREMENT, VOID ANYWHERE AT ALL, HENCE NO STANDARD-OF-DEFICIENCY WITH WHICH TRUTH CAN BE LIKENED, COMPARED, EQUALIZED! TRUTH IS NEVER "SUCCESSFUL." TRUTH IS ENTIRETY BEING, COMPLETENESS BEING, LIFE WHOLLY BEING, PERFECTION BEING, and there is no otherness whatever!

That it might be crystal clear what we mean when we say that there is no "success" in Truth, let us point out why, in another way. Success is not what is "granted" you, but is what you *BE*. You are UTTERNESS in operation NOW. This ABSOLUTE SINGLE TOTALITY THAT SUBSTANCE IS, is your FOREVER-CONSCIOUS-IDENTITY THIS VERY "MOMENT." This IDENTITY, this WHOLENESS, ALL-NESS, COMPLETENESS is not an attainment, not a state or thing, situation or condition, elevation or concavity toward which, nor result of which, you wittingly, or unwittingly have striven. In no way is your Identity the outcome of aught personal, racial, a predestined arrangement, or effort.

Success, as used in Truth, is not measured by some changing human standard of evaluation, worth, utility, or desirability — some focal point of a material Utopia, some sub-stance with its would-be code of measurement based on nebulous improbables, or short-termed enjoyment.

Education would have us assume that whatever we attain in a material universe, we "cannot take it with us." It would also have us assume that no matter how much we collect, we are not allowed to retain much of it — taxes, expenses, emotional involvements, obligations and such, filch much of it from us, or, if we have attained a sufficient quantity, we still want more, and what we have seems somewhat tarnished. Rarely, if ever, do the items collected give the joy and sustained happiness, freedom and security, the well-being, peace and contentment we originally thought, when in want, that "much" would grant us.

No, collecting possessions does not assure you of a sense of heaven at hand. Nor do amassed fortunes quell the lust or greed for more. The human never seems to have enough. It is like disease — start out with a little, and worry over it enough, and you will increase it a thousandfold. So with age

— as you begin to collect it, you get more and more of it
until you are surfeited with it and "give up the ghost."
Humanity and its would-be claims never know how to say,
and mean it: "ENOUGH!"

Do not strive to succeed in aught, but rather, begin with
the total perfection of GOODNESS AT HAND, THE SOLE
ONE IN BUSINESS, or, as a friend put it; "Business is to
BE-ISNESS!" What can be more SINGLE, or how can it be
stated more SIMPLY?

He who is busy with, and as, ISNESS has no interest in
"becoming" aught, and that is all humanity ever deals in —
vacuity.

He who states the TOTAL BEING GOODNESS, OMNI-
PRESENTLY, IS BEING, precludes things altogether from
his concern. Naturally, the thoughts (ideas-things) Mind
conceives are this "moment" being preceived by Mind, but
ONLY BY MIND! He who tries to see this via human sense is
trying to see that which ONLY INFINITE INTELLIGENCE
KNOWS, PERCEIVES! In other words, the human would
attempt to outline, outpicture, finitize, dimensionalize, an
INFINITE UNDIMENSIONAL NON-SUBSTANTIVE
THOUGHT THAT INFINITE SPIRIT IS BUT NOW CON-
CEIVING! Such would-be pretense of effort is folly, but no
less silly than the original suggestion that a non-existent
mentality CAN outline, pretend, outpicture, believe in, or
deal with, its own productions. There is no such mind, nor
can what is NOT produce aught, not even nothingness!

Stating TRUTH ONLY, and defining your words honestly, then dealing herein only (for there is naught else existent,
hence naught else One *can* deal with!), there will be no place
left to entertain lack, no lack anywhere to be entertained, no
consequences of either, anywhere, for anyone, for any
reason. What, then, "becomes" of lack? Nothing, for it is not

present at all, so how can aught "happen" to it? ONLY
TRUTH IS PRESENT, IS THE TOTAL OMNIPRESENT
SELF I AM BEING, and sticking herewith will suddenly
"appear" as abundance of items beyond aught you could
have "assumed" when dealing as a mere presumption.

We admit there is a great temptation to try to "handle"
items, things, lack, or to try to "accomplish," work toward,
struggle to escape bondage, but all such merely entangles
you more and more securely within the mess which actually
is not. Sticking with INFINITE ABUNDANT IMMEASURA-
BLE FACT, leaves no lack anywhere, or a mind or minds to
suffer it, or from it.

It is somewhat startling to be told that "success is
failure," or that "success is human, " but such is the case. We
believe it is made clear as to why this is so, but lest there be
any confusion, let us give it a bit more attention.

As we have pointed out, to try to succeed, one must have
a goal to attain, a progression to be made, a completing to be
brought about. He must change, grow, develop, gain, hence
he must begin with less than Wholeness, Completeness,
Allness, Omnipresent Self-satisfied Perfection. He must begin
with the human, the finite, with limitation, a vacuum, a void,
a lack, and must strive to overcome it, lift himself above it,
cause the void to vanish, diminish, shrink, evaporate, disappear. All of which is contrary to Infinite Intelligence at
and as the total Identity that is already the Sole Self you (I
AM) be!

Any success means an adding to, an accumulation, a filling
up or out, and certainly this indicates alteration, improvement, attainment, which purportedly makes for joy, happiness, satisfaction. But what of Perfection here now? What of
Completeness here now? What of Satisfaction here now?
What of the Fact that ONLY TRUTH IS TRUE, ONLY ALL
IS NOW, ONLY THE PRESENT IS?

Can success be brought about without time? Can the void, the need, the lack, the limitation, the dimension, exist without a past in which it resides, has form, is known by its pattern, degree, need, location, and the reasons behind same? Does not the success stem from the overcoming of that "past-condition," or circumstance, by diligent application in what has "passed" as a future? Was it not all brought about due to a struggle or application of "coming events," or a future, an extension beyond the limit? Was it not from using one's purported "tomorrows" that his "yesterdays" grew less and less troublesome, threatening, curtailing?

Yes, he who works as a human, no matter whether he accumulates much and calls it success, or loses much and calls it failure — in both cases he has failed to state Truth, admit his own Identity, be HIMSELF! In both cases he has turned his back on Reality, on Now, on Satisfaction, hence cannot expect to reap aught save more of human belief, human lack, human frustration, confusion, trouble, heartache, and limitation.

To paraphrase Scripture, is it not true that he who gains the whole world and loses his sense of Identity, has naught save the darkness of his own nonsense to comfort him?

Success, growth, addition — these are corruption, an adultering of Love, Singleness, Purity, hence of Joy, Bliss, Power, Selfhood! So, he who is so busy trying for success is actually striving diligently to acquire failure. Frankly, he need not struggle so hard, if failure is what he wishes. All he need do is refuse to be the Self he IS, and he will know all the failure there is! And how much of that is there? NONE AT ALL, FOR THERE IS BUT ONE SINGLE BEING, ONE TOTAL LIFE PRESENT AND THAT ONE CANNOT BE LESS OR MORE THAN IT IS, NAMELY ALL. So, actually there is no failure, no heartache, for there is no One to

experience it. THE ONLY ONE THERE IS CAN KNOW
SELF-SATISFACTION ONLY. This ONE ALL knows no
change, no growth, no adding to, no taking from, and knows
no business being carried on with otherness. TRUTH IS JOY
ITSELF BEING, LIFE ITSELF ALIVE TO ITS ALLNESS,
WHOLENESS BEING WHOLE. And this ONE is I, and there
is none beside.

You cannot succeed, or attain success. YOU ARE
ALREADY PERFECT, ENTIRE NOW, AND THIS FACT
CANNOT BE ALTERED, FOR THERE IS NAUGHT BUT
COMPLETENESS BEING ITSELF PRESENT FOREVER.
Thus, BUSINESS is never human, never bad, never im-
proving, never competing, never dull, never subject to the
flesh in any way, to conditions of any sort, to strikes, unions,
to needs, supply, demands, or what. BUSINESS IS SPIRIT
BEING WHOLLY ITSELF ONLY, EVERYWHERE,
EVERYWHEN, EVERYHOW, AND THERE IS NAUGHT
MORE THAN THE ALL IT IS, HENCE NAUGHT TO
CHALLENGE, CHANGE, ALTER, OR IN ANY MANNER
AT ALL TRY TO SCUTTLE IT. THERE SIMPLY IS NO
SMALL (OR LARGER) SELF EXISTENT TO KNOW, OR
NOT KNOW, THIS. THE ONLY ALONE NOT ONLY
KNOWS IT, BUT IS BUSY RIGHT NOW BEING IT. Against
such ALLNESS there is naught beside, hence no law or laws,
no federal or other type of governments to interfere in any
way. All you "need to do" is to STATE TRUTH AS IT IS,
AND STICK THEREWITH, DEFINING WHAT YOU HAVE
SAID AND BEHOLDING THAT IT IS FACT RIGHT NOW.
THIS LEAVES THE FIELD CLEAR OF REFUSE, AND
LEAVES NAUGHT BESIDE THAT COULD ATTEMPT TO,
OR POSSIBLY REFUSE ALL. ALL IS NOT SUBJECT TO
ACCEPTANCE OR REFUSAL. IT IS ALL, AND ALL
MEANS JUST THAT, A L L.

Do not assume that because we point out what we do concerning success, that Spirit is engaged in failure, want, privation, need, or frustration. Not a bit of it. SPIRIT IS WHOLENESS, COMPLETELY ALIVE TO ITS UTTER POTENTIAL — IS OMNIPOTENTLY BEING ENTIRETY, CONSCIOUS ABSOLUTE JOY, BLISS, FULLNESS, SATIS-FACTION AS ITSELF. THIS IS YOUR PERFECT IDEN-TITY-I NOW. YOU CANNOT ESCAPE IT, AVOID IT, BYPASS IT. Why? Because it is always AWARENESS THAT IS BEING AWARE, and that very CONSCIOUS SINGLE ALIVENESS IS TOTALITY ITSELF, YOUR VERY IDEN-TITY NOW. There simply is no other Identity at all, no other Single One, no other Conscious Awareness, no other Being.

In talking or writing, we use the editorial "we," or "you," but this is not intended to imply that there *ARE* others. There is but the ONE SINGLE INFINITY CONSCIOUSLY BEING THE ENTIRE SELF-AWARENESS SPIRIT IS. This may seem difficult to comprehend by the human. In Fact, IT IS IMPOSSIBLE FOR A HUMAN TO COMPREHEND OR LAY HOLD ON. Why? Because there is no human at all, no finite mind at all, no personal or mass mind at all, no mind in any thing at all. How, then, can "such" behold aught?

Do not let this upset you. Rather STATE WHAT MIND IS, WHAT ALL IS, WHAT ENTIRETY, INFINITY, SPIRIT, LIFE, LOVE IS, and then devote your entire attention defining these terms. Act in accord with the definition you behold, and you will not fail in seeing that there is ONLY THAT WHICH IS, ONLY EXISTENCE BEING, ONLY LIFE ENTIRELY ALIVE TO ITS FULLNESS EVERYWHERE, EVERYWHEN. You will behold there is no other place save ENTIRETY, INFINITY. You will behold there is no when at all, for the very term indicates "time," which is not. There is only ETERNITY, NOWNESS, ACTUALITY in operation.

This cannot be altered, changed, interfered with, or even challenged, for there is naught but THAT WHICH IS, and It cannot challenge or doubt, question or oppose Itself!

Over and over we are under the delusion that things, bodies, people, circumstances and so on can interfere with ISNESS, NOWNESS, BEING, and in some manner pervert It, divert It, persuade or coerce It into altering Its nature, Presence, Power, Intelligence, Operation. This cannot be.

There is no difference, whether it is a person, an animal, a circumstance, a planet, a pre-arranged destiny, time, age, gender or what that puts forth the claim of power and presence, ability and influence, a schedule of its own that is counter to Reality — nay, that ignores Reality and operates wholly as an entity with the ability to enforce its decrees.

Remember, there is but ONE MIND, ONE SPIRIT, ONE SUBSTANCE OR "STUFF," AND THIS LEAVES NAUGHT BESIDE. There is but ONE EXISTENCE, ONE NOW, ONE ISNESS, ONE BEING, and all that IS is going on RIGHT HERE. By "here," we mean, it is not waiting for a future, not dependent on a past, not dealing in time, in commodities, in states or conditions of things, ideas, bodies, trinkets, or a mass of collected items with which It purportedly amuses Itself, plays with, deals in, casts off.

No, Mind knows no such, deals in no such, conceives-perceives no such at all. Mind does not contend with such, protect Itself from such, heal, change, elevate, or rejoice over the saving of such. MIND DEALS WHOLLY AS THE SINGLE TOTAL ONE IT IS, THE ONE THAT IT WOULD CALL "I," IF IT FOUND IT IMPORTANT TO IDENTIFY ITSELF "TO ANOTHER." But, there is no other to whom Mind needs to identify Itself! And surely, It does not need to acquaint Itself with Itself, being that It is already the ALL, THE ALONE, THE ONLY, THE TOTAL, THE ALL!

Mind, Spirit, Life, Love is not under the attack of people, for people do not exist to Mind. The items (ideas-thoughts-bodies-things) Mind conceives-perceives, do not have minds of their own, do not have lives of their own, and have no substance whatever. They are but thoughts in Spirit, Love. Nothing more, nothing less.

The notion that "things," thoughts in Mind, can manipulate Mind, direct It, mist-direct It, hold It up, blackmail It, drive It, pervert It, ignore It, bypass It, is too absurd for words, FOR NO ITEM (THOUGHT-THING-BODY) HAS ANY MIND AT ALL, ANY "STUFF" TO IT AT ALL, ANY FORM, SHAPE, PURPOSE, OUTLINE, DESTINY, AGE, GENDER, OR EVEN USE. Each is but a thought Mind conceives-perceives "on the instant NOW," and that is all there is to it, of it.

Only within theology, the superstition-without-Life-or-Mind-Substance, do the silly notions of otherness, evil, lack, creation, purposeful items appear to have validity, existence, history, or a future . . . and that future is always within the would-be "scheme of things," never within the scheme of Spirit, All, for It has no scheme whereby It will "become" ALL. It is so already, so devises no scheme, plan, or purpose to bring such about!

The notion that people (things-ideas-thoughts) have personalities and minds of their own, is silly. But no less silly than to assume that the planets also have a "will of their own," or an "influence" that cannot be denied! How many assume that age, the mere revolution of our earth on its axis, and its continuous journey about its sun, can influence, nay, control and finally destroy the most hardy of us — can eradicate from the planet even the remains of that which we assumed would "stand forever?"

Every tide, every day and night, every tick of the clock, every changing season, every breath we draw is controlled by time, the movement of the planet, and the influence exerted by other planets in the heavens! Do not be so smug and say that you do not believe in astrology, in prophecy, in time, for you most certainly are manifesting its effect constantly! Not an item transpires on the human basis that is not wholly an "act in time." Not a letter is written, a message sent or received, a transaction brought about, a worry, a bit of pleasure, an enjoyment of any sort, anywhere, regardless of the reason, but what stems wholly from time, within time, and all at the cost of OMNIPRESENT SPIRIT WHICH ALONE IS ALL THERE IS.

We succumb to the prophecy of time more than we admit. We also succumb to the argument that there has been time — a past, a history, a diagnosis, a cause, a reason, a purpose, a happenstance somewhere along the line of time-past, or we would not be in any sort of mess, in a body, in the world, in trouble, in an era, faced with this or that which is peculiar to this particular "year of our Lord!"

No one would be aging, there would be no gender, no Satan, no evil, no lack, no creation at all, hence no hell, pit, birth, death, limitation at all, if it were not for this concept that there is time, and all of it based on the notion that a thing, a body-item-product, has a mind of its own with which to think, act, arrange, disarrange, or be! But not a bit of this is true. It all denies REALITY and once we STATE FACT AND STAY THEREWITH, the mumbo jumbo of theology, superstition, nonsense or nothingness, falls away.

The prophecy of astrology, of time, has no more power to change GENUINE REALITY, NOWNESS, ISNESS, than any other superstition. There is no mind in the planets. There is no power, no planning, no influence, no effect from an idea called a planet, than there is from an idea we may call "body," or "flower," or whatever.

ONLY AS YOU STATE FACT, STAY WITH FACT ALONE, TOTALLY, WHOLLY, CONSTANTLY, will you be free from what passes as prophecy (past or future) from all these would-be minds! Remember, prophecy of the past (called history) is as much a prophetic statement that "it-did-happen," as it would if it said "it-will-happen." It makes no difference which side of the fence-of-time it would speak from, for it is merely chatter that has no place or power at all, for it has no existence in LIFE.

Most of us accept the "has been" as bona fide, whereas we assume we might, given a fair break, outwit that which prophecy claims "might happen." However, they are one and the same! They do not know the one from the other, for they are not two states of pretended being, but all the same pseudo nonsense pretending to be.

Just as there is no other mind to malpractice, think lack-thoughts toward another, or concerning aught, so the planets are void of influence, for any "thing" that exists at all, must be a mere thought within Mind, only. This means that no thought CAN think, for the thought is just that, a mere thought or conception. It never touches or "thinks back" or "against" the Mind conceiving-perceiving it. How can it? And certainly the planets, if they exist at all as thoughts within the Mind conceiving-perceiving them, are equally incapable of thinking aught . . . they are as void of mind, life, substance as any other thought. To bestow power, intelligence, life, purpose, influence upon thoughts, is to totally ignore Self, Life, Love, Purity, Being. To do so would be to exclude Intelligence, Substance, Reality, Nowness, and leave naught but vacuity, hence there would cease to be even a thought — leave no Mind to conceive-perceive such!

The argument that there is treachery following you "all the days of your life," because such and such planet has influence over your daily actions and behavior, thanks to the moment you arrived biologically, is silly. To assume this group or that can manipulate you, control you, have jurisdiction over you because you were born this color, that color, or on this side of the tracks or that, with this family name or that, is equally absurd.

To assume you are this gender or that, are living in this era or that, are so old or so young — this also is totally to ignore REALITY AS OMNIPRESENT ACTUALITY IN ACTION, THE ALONE ONE BEING THE ONLY. To bow down to time, declaring it has jurisdiction over you, plans the food you eat, the activity you engage in, the clothing you wear, the sports you enjoy, the riches you can or cannot indulge, the length of the span in which you can carry on, the type of friends you hobnob with, the cultural pursuits you follow, the likes and dislikes you experience, the date of marriage and the date of your demise (and time alone does all this!) — then to merely brush it aside (while you continue to indulge it by fully practicing in accord with its dictates, continue to grow older, to eat meals, sleep, work, or whatever in the "way that is your custom,") is to prove you do operate entirely within its would-be confines!

There is no mind to believe in time (astrology, prophecy, hence history!), for ONLY INTELLIGENCE IS PRESENT, IS AMNESS NOW, IS I, and there is none beside.

You do not attain success. You do not have to overcome malpractice, whether aimed at yourself by a small personal-ly-possessed-or-obsessed mind, or one equally insignificant called another's. You do not have to deal with general opinions, customs, mores or what. You do not have to succumb to time, age, and all the rest of the nonsense, but

you will do so UNLESS YOU STATE WHAT OMNI-
PRESENT FACT IS, AND THEN DEFINE WHAT YOU
HAVE DECLARED, AND OPERATE ACCORDING TO
YOUR DEFINITION.

To merely cast words at the nonsense will not cause the
habit of time to vanish, the habit of falsification to vanish,
the habit of humanity or manhood, to vanish. It takes more
than words. It takes the honesty of stating FACT ONLY, and
keeping your attention and interest WHOLLY ON INFINITE
TOTALITY AS THE SOLE OMNIPRESENT SELF, THE
COMPLETENESS THAT IS HEALTH, WEALTH, TOTALI-
TY, NAY, THAT IS THE ENTIRE OMNIPOTENT SELF
THAT IS I. And herein there can be no allowances for
otherness, no claiming that Truth is too difficult to stay with,
that Reality is so unrealistic, so abstract, that It is not
practicable. No one can honestly make this claim. These are
but excuses for BETRAYING THE SELF, IGNORING LIFE,
INDULGING IN THE REVERSE OF LOVE, BEING HU-
MAN INSTEAD OF DIVINE!

Who can honestly say that NOW is so difficult to enjoy?
Who can claim that ISNESS is so ephemeral that It is
impractical? Who can claim honestly that the PRESENT is so
abstract that It is folly to stay herewith? Who can honestly
claim that the SOLE SELF HE IS, is too vague and
theoretical to be practiced? Anyone so saying is a fool, a liar,
a cheat throughout, and to whom? To himself only, for there
is no other he can either help or hinder, give birth to or kill
off . . . yet he will vociferously claim he is but one among
many, that he did not start all this, and as a single one he has
little or no influence in putting a stop to it and the troubles
in his world.

However, the FACT IS, WHOLENESS ALONE IS HIS
IDENTITY NOW, AND THE WORLD OF MIND IS AL-

READY WITHIN SPIRIT, THE SOLE SELF, AND THERE
IS NO MORE, NO LESS, NONE BESIDE. PERFECTION
ALONE IS. AS SUCH IT IS SUCCESS – SUCCESS IN
THAT IT MEANS THAT THERE IS NO OPPOSITION, NO
CONTRADICTION, NO REFUTATION, AND NO OTHER-
NESS (NO ONE) STILL WAITING TO "ARRIVE," OVER-
COME, "BECOME" AUGHT. PERFECTION CANNOT BE
IMPROVED UPON, MORE CANNOT "APPEAR," A SENSE
OF NEED, LACK, WANT, DESIRE, CANNOT EXIST AT
ALL. ALL, TOTALITY, PERFECTION ITSELF IS CON-
SCIOUSLY BEING THE ENTIRETY IT IS, THE FULL-
NESS OF THE IDENTITY-I THAT AMNESS IS, AND IS
COGNIZANTLY ALIVE TO THE UTTERLY REAL NA-
TURE OF ITS PURE SINGLENESS, ITS UNDEFILED
LOVE, ITS ETERNAL IMMORTAL INDIVIDUAL SELF-
HOOD WHEREIN ALL CONCEPTION-PERCEPTION IS
"NOW IN ACTION, " NOW "TAKING PLACE" AS FUNC-
TION IN FULL SCINTILLATING JOYOUS ALIVENESS.

It is obvious naught else can possibly be. Equally it must
be obvious that there is no additional, or lesser mind, or
aught beside to know aught, or aught beside to be known,
now or ever.

This ALIVENESS does not mean that what "appears as
success" in our daily round is a sin, wrong, an error, evil, or
contrary to Awareness. Not at all. It but points out, if what is
written here is plain, that ONE CANNOT STATE FACT,
THEN ABIDE WITHIN THE FULL DEFINITION OF WHAT
IS DECLARED, AND REMAIN IN THE THROES OF
POVERTY, LACK, LIMITATION, DIMENSION, EITHER
IN QUALITY OR QUANTITY OF AUGHT THAT WOULD
CURTAIL, CONSTRICT, WALL IN, DEPRIVE, OR
SHRINK ONE'S ACTIVITY. It is impossible to remain a
victim to "Thou shalt NOT," of any sort. It is impossible for

one to be a slave to any "thing," no matter what guise it takes — that is, whether body, organ, gland, person, planet, time, age, gender, prophecy, history, disease, money, circumstance, business activity, the market, government or what. He simply finds he is FREE OF ALL RESTRICTIONS, FOR HE NO LONGER DEALS AS A THING, WITH THINGS, NOR FEELS HE IS DEPENDENT THEREON, OR MUST ASK OR SEEK THE PERMISSION OF THINGS. HE CAN DEAL WITH THINGS AS WHAT THEY ARE, MERE THOUGHTS IN MIND, BUT WILL NOT GIVE THEM POWER, MINDS OF THEIR OWN, NOR PLACE THEM WITHIN THE KEEPING OF OTHER THINGS WHICH CAN USE THEM AGAINST OR FOR HIM!

Things as such, are what they should be, but when one turns to things as though they had taken the place of OMNIPRESENCE, he had best take another "reading" of his would-be mental compass. He had better reset his values, revamp his sense of worth, rearrange his outlook of NOW and see if It has aught to do with history, time, void, theology, creation, routine, cycle of cause and effect, birth and death.

Only when you STATE WHAT ALL NOW IS, WHO IT IS, WHERE IT IS, WHY IT IS, AND THAT IT IS TOTALLY WHAT ABSOLUTE OMNIPOTENT WISDOM IS AS THE ALONE SELF, THE INDIVIDUAL ONE OF TOTALITY, THE IDENTITY THAT IS THE VERY IDENTITY YOU SPIRITUALLY BE (and there is no other identity at all!), then completely operate as this, act in accord with this, hold entirely to this as TRUTH *being,* will what we have pointed out here be clear, and be "usable, practical, inevitable Fact."

In doing your "work" thus, you will behold that ABUNDANCE OF ITEMS (THINGS, MONEY, IDEAS) IS INESCAPABLE, INDESTRUCTIBLE, EVER AVAILABLE, PERFECT IN QUALITY, UNDIMENSIONAL IN

QUANTITY, and you will also discover that you place no value on them, or consider their "possession" something to be desired as giving you what you want, need, or fulfilling a sense of power, authority, prestige, or the right to dominate others, control situations, dictate ultimatums and such. You will, rather, operate as the SELF-SATISFIED ONE LIFE NOW IS, THE SINGLE ALL-INCLUSIVE WHOLENESS THAT IS GOODNESS ITSELF. THIS, AND THIS ALONE IS SUCCESS IN TRUTH, AND IT IS THIS TRUE SUCCESS, SUCCESSFUL TRUTH, YOU BE NOW-FOREVER, AND THERE IS NAUGHT BESIDE TO SAY YOU NAY . . . NO AGE, TIME, OTHERNESS BY ANY NAME OR TWISTED RATIONALIZATION, DEVISEMENT, INSANITY OR VACUITY EXISTS AT ALL. ONLY BEING IS; YOU BE WHAT AMNESS IS. THIS IS TOTALITY NOW, AND NOW IS TOTALITY, SINGLENESS, INDIVIDUAL, WHOLE, AND THERE SIMPLY IS NAUGHT BESIDE. THIS IS POWER, AUTHORITY, LIFE IN ACTION, AND THE ACTION THAT IS LIFE IMMORTAL NOW.

CHAPTER VII

The Immediacy of Light

Who or what waits for what? Do you spend your entire effort in waiting for GOOD to come to pass in your experience — for some lack or evil, want or desire to clear up, be satisfied, go away, or be fulfilled? Are you waiting for the end to come, the trump to sound, a Jesus or saviour to appear, a landslide of wealth to engulf you?

Just what are you waiting for? Is it something bad that you have been assured will catch up with you? Is it a curse you expect to take its promised toll? Is it a wait for your ship to come in, the tide to rise so your ship can take sail? Are you waiting for a loved one, or someone to love, care for, be important to, wait upon?

Are you waiting for business to grow, develop, mature — for a dear one to hit the jackpot, strike it rich, or are you merely so in the habit of waiting that the end alone now is your last hope?

Why wait? Who waits? For what does it (or you) wait?

Can you say that Spirit, your Sole Self, waits? For what?

For NOW TO BE NOW, IS TO BE IS, FOR BEING TO BE? Absurd. REALITY IS NOW REAL, AND THERE CAN BE NO MORE THAN THE ALLNESS IT IS NOW, FOREVER.

Time plays no part at all in NOW, ISNESS, THE PRESENT, ACTUALITY. This may seem difficult to grasp, nay, impossible if one attempts to behold its meaning via the human senses, rationalization, intellectualism, the dust of history, the obscurity of prophecy. But to TRUTH, REALITY ALONE IS WHAT IS, AND IS THE WHOLE IDENTITY THAT IS I. THERE IS NAUGHT TO WEIGH THIS IN THE BALANCE AND FIND IT WANTING, NOR TO COMPARE ITSELF WITH ACTUALITY. THERE IS NO OTHERNESS AT ALL. THE IDENTITY THAT IS THE SELF YOU BE, IS THE ONLY ONE THERE IS, AND THERE IS NO OTHER AT ALL.

The whole of GOODNESS, LIFE, ACTUALITY, GENUINE REALITY, AMNESS, IDENTITY IS PRESENT IN FULL, KNOWS IT, IS THE ACTUAL AWARENESS HERE NOW. No wait for this "event" can be, for IT IS NOT A HAPPENING, AN "EVENT" TO COME ABOUT, A "BECOMING" OF ANY SORT. IT IS ALREADY FACT IN OPERATION, AND TO THIS SOLE MIND THAT IS THE ONE BEING, THE I THAT AM, THE WHOLENESS IT IS IS CLEAR, UNOPPOSED, UNCHALLENGED CERTAINTY NOW. THERE IS NAUGHT BESIDE THAT CAN BE MIND, HENCE NAUGHT EXISTENT BESIDE THAT CAN KNOW, OR FAIL TO KNOW AUGHT. THERE SIMPLY IS NO OTHER AWARENESS, BEING, LIFE AT ALL.

Within what passes as the human experience, no thought is given to ACTUALITY, because to ignorance, INTELLIGENCE is unknown. It is not that stupidity would bypass AWARENESS, or that-which-is-not feels itself superior to THAT-WHICH-IS. Not at all. It is merely that stupidity, ignorance, darkness, that-which-is-NOT does not even exist, so how can it take issue with WHAT IS, defy It, rebuke It, refute It, or in any sense try to oppose It, challenge It, or attempt to outwit or destroy It? Obviously any such attempt is folly, impossible, hence is not going on at all.

Ideas, within the fictional material realm, are the whole of whatever passes as existence. Identity therein deals with things, as a thing, and all concern is with things, over things, because of things, and as things. This is pointed out over and over, but it always bears reiteration lest we forget, overlook, or ignore the seeming platform of the entire nonsense of oblivion, darkness, ignorance, lack, the pit, the grave, death. Remember, all of the above stems wholly from the same premise — a suggestion that there is an opposite to Reality that can and does supplant Actuality!

One never goes into the whys and wherefores of that suggestion — where it comes from, where it does its work, with whom, why, when, how. No, we merely content ourselves by saying there is such — that "they" say so, but no one has ever met up with "them," or "they," nor will they, for such is not.

Ideas are but thoughts in Mind, conceived or thought up right now for the first and only "time." This has been said over and over, but just as evil or lack asserts itself over and over, so we must be alert and not accept any of the nonsense at any turn. No otherness exists at all, but it is not important that this be so. It is totally important that we BEHOLD WHAT IS SO. The negation means naught. THE FACT THAT ONLY REALITY IS REAL, ONLY TRUTH IS TRUE, ONLY LIFE IS ALIVE, ONLY MIND IS AWARE, ONLY AMNESS IS BEING I — THIS IS OF UTTER ABSOLUTE IMPORTANCE, FOR THIS IS SUBSTANCE . . . not a sub-Stance, but SUBSTANCE ITSELF WHEREIN NO

LESSER OR "SUB" STATE EXISTS AT ALL, NO LESSER
"LIGHT" CAN PUT IN AN OAR, DICTATE, QUESTION,
OR EVEN AGREE!

There is ONLY REALITY ITSELF, AND THIS MEANS
THERE IS NO OTHER EVER. THIS LEAVES NO HUMAN
"ME," OR "I," TO DO AUGHT, OR STOP DOING OR
BEING AUGHT. IT LEAVES NO LESSER SENSE,
STANCE, AWARENESS. THERE IS NO sub-AWARENESS,
sub-LIFE, sub-IDENTITY, sub-NOW AT ALL. THERE IS
ONLY THE ONE NOW, LIFE, LOVE, SINGLE PURITY,
IDENTITY HERE.

Whatever is within Mind is being right here now in its
total, its complete perfection, for Mind cannot conceive
aught but what it must be entire, whole, perfect as the
thought it is. It has no outline, no shape, no form, no
"body," no purpose, no value, no dimension. It cannot be
visible to the human eye, nor known by any of the human
so-called senses. To humanity, no thought (idea-thing-body)
in Mind even exists at all. Humanity pretends to know only
that which is material, physical, dimensional, measurable,
molecular, or having some sort of composition that is
detectable to its would-be comprehension.

Whatever is thought by Mind, conceived-perceived, if you
will, by Mind is certainly present to Mind, known by Mind,
real to Mind, but only to Mind. Of a certainty Mind is totally
"satisfied" with what It conceives, knows, thinks. Naught is
missing, yet to come, or capable of being in any way
changed. The idea is, and is satisfactory to its Conceiver.
There is no other to whom the idea can even be, much less
can it be usable or satisfactory to a finite mentality which
does not even exist!

The immediacy of Mind is glorious beyond words. There
is never a delay of any sort. There cannot be, for REALITY

IS. There never can be a promise that It "will be." Isness is
the sole measure of PRESENT FACT. Then of a certainty, as
the idea-thing IS, all of it is, and is "satisfactory" to the Mind
conceiving it for it is, must be, perfect. How much of it? ALL
OF IT IS PRESENT, UNCHALLENGED, WHOLE AS IDEA.
Mind has naught more to do with it, to it, or because of it to
make the thought perfect, make it conform to some pattern,
make it work in some manner to prove its utility, worth,
value, or to finish off some plan for which Mind conceived it.
Mind had no plan in thought, planned no thought, was
pressured into no fulfilling of a scheme which involved the
conception of a particular, or even a general conception
thought-idea-thing.

What we are striving to make very clear is that thoughts
(things) are not the result of aught in Mind, not the
by-product of Mind's incompleteness, not required by Allness
in order to make It *all.* No, Mind is already total in Its
completeness, and things or thoughts-ideas-items are but what
Mind has the capacity to conceive, as pointed out so often
and for no "reason" are they conceived, to fill no need, to
meet with no plan that Mind has for Its continuity, work,
labor, occupation, or just required as a gimmick with which
Mind can keep Itself busy for Eternity so as not to be too
bored with Itself!

One Fact we wish to make clear, however, is that
WHATEVER IDEA EXISTS NOW TO MIND IS COMPLETE.
IT IS WHOLLY PRESENT IN ITS ENTIRETY. NONE OF
IT IS MISSING, DELETED, WORN AWAY, STOLEN,
DISSIPATED, GONE, OR YET TO COME. NONE OF IT
NEEDS REPLENISHING, REPAIRING, OR RECONSTRUCT-
ING — DOES NOT NEED ADDITION, PERFECTING, COM-
PLETING, OR A REPLACEMENT IN ANY MANNER
WHATEVER. It is wholly being the everywhere idea it is, the

undimensional thought it is, and Mind is aware of, or perceives it now in its utterness, perfection, and there is naught or none beside to know the idea, nor is there any idea that can know itself.

We trust this says enough concerning ideas, things, bodies, so that nothing else ever need be brought up about same. We hope that from now on no one will work for an idea, think in terms of idea, try to take care of an idea, assume he is an idea, worry over the state or future of an idea, give an idea any value, place, shape, form, worth, history, place, power, authority, or try to put an idea in the place of being One's IDENTITY, SOUL, MIND, SUBSTANCE, ACTION, SIN-GLENESS, PURITY, LOVE, OR SELF!

The world will surely "appear" to be quite a different spot (or item-thing) when we state TRUTH ONLY, and stick wholly with the definition of what we have declared WHEN AWARENESS ONLY IS OUR ENTIRE CONCERN, OUR SOLE IDENTITY, OUR ABSOLUTE ACTION, OUR ONLY FUNCTION, OUR COMPLETE ALIVENESS WHEREIN NO HISTORY, NO FUTURE, NO FEAR, NO GUILT, NO ERROR, NO OPPOSITION, NO MATTER, NO BIRTH-DEATH OR HELL EVEN PRETENDS TO BE ... WHAT A GLORIOUS ALIVENESS THIS IS, AND THIS IS THE ACTUAL FACT THIS MOMENT. IT IS IMMEDIATELY SO. ALL THE POWER OF OMNIPOTENCE IS OPERATIVE AS YOUR (MY) SELF THIS INSTANT, AND INCLUDES EVERY IDEA (THING, BODY) WITHIN WHAT WE CALL IMMENSITY ... AND ALL IS PERFECT AND UNCHANG-ING FOREVER NOW ... WHAT MORE HEAVEN AT HAND CAN ONE "WISH, " AND HOW CAN THAT WHICH ALREADY IS, BE "WISHED FOR, " AND BY WHAT, WHERE, WHEN, HOW, AND WHO OR WHAT SAYS SO?

The immediacy of *BEING* surpasses "time," leaves no

wait, no unfulfillment. There is no void, hence no theology, or system-of-waiting-for-NOW anywhere. There is no ceremony of worship built on NOW as "being absent." There is no error of thinking, judgment, decision, for there is nothing left in ALLNESS to do any such nonsensical "deciding, wishing, computerizing."

What is LIGHT? Where is LIGHT? When is LIGHT? Of what is LIGHT composed? Where does One go to come in contact with It? How long does One have to wait for It? What is the price to be paid for It? Who has It? What can It do? Why? Who or what says so? Is It fast or slow? With what does It deal, and why? Is It required for Life? Can Mind make "use" of It? For what? What does It look like? Where is It kept when not in use? Just what is It anyway, and how is It to be identified?

Your sole substance is LIGHT. It is Light being Itself that is Amness-I. There simply is naught else existent — nay, LIGHT IS EXISTENCE ITSELF, MIND ITSELF, SOUL, LOVE, ACTION, BEING, FUNCTION ITSELF. Light does not come from some "place," or go to some "place." LIGHT IS ACTUAL BEING, THE ONLY "STUFF" THAT INFINITY IS, THE ENTIRE IDENTITY THAT ALIVENESS IS. It is not a composition, not a "material," not a dimensional composition to which and of which the so-called finite senses can testify, know, experience, talk about, or in some way utilize, make contact with, define, enter into, reject, or even comprehend.

LIGHT IS SOLIDARITY, TOTALITY, ENTIRETY, INFINITY IN ITS FULL IDENTITY, ACTION, FUNCTION, CONSCIOUS BEING. LIGHT IS CALLED SPIRIT, LOVE, SINGLENESS, REALITY, FACTUALITY, TRUTH. Yes, Light is all of these, but not as a separate component of each, but rather as EACH, THE SAME ONE, FOR THE "EACH,"

AND THE "ALL," ARE THE SELFSAME ONE LIGHT *being.*

Light is the Self, is LIFE ITSELF IN ITS UTTER ALL-AWARENESS, ITS CONSCIOUS TOTALITY OF ALIVENESS, ITS ABSOLUTE WISDOM OF SINGLE EN-TIRETY. Light is without body, outline, form, shape, contour, outside-inside. Light cannot be separated, divided, portioned out into small components, packages, parcels, entities, identities, nor can any such would-be compilations have any Validity, any Truth, any Actuality to them. LIGHT IS THE SOLE SELF, THE ENTIRETY THAT CONSCIOUSNESS IS. IT IS THIS LIGHT THAT DOES ALL THE CONCEIVING-PERCEIVING OF THOUGHTS. (Call them ideas, items, bodies, planets, or whatever you will, but it still is Light that alone conceives-perceives, knows, and can identify Its thoughts.)

LIGHT ALONE CONCEIVES, THINKS, BUT NONE OF LIGHT GOES INTO ITS CONCEPTIONS. LIGHT ALONE IS THE ENTIRE SUBSTANCE THAT IS EXISTENCE ITSELF, WHOLENESS ITSELF, ENTIRETY ITSELF, ALL-NESS ITSELF, THE PRESENT ITSELF, NOWNESS IT-SELF. THERE SIMPLY IS NAUGHT BUT LIGHT. So, he who would endeavor to outline Light's thought, see a dimension, a form, a contour, a plan, a scheme laid out like a map, a shade of darkness, grayness, distinguishing mark or shadow between one thought of Light and another, is seeing that which does not exist at all, where it does not exist at all, and with a mind that does not exist at all. Some miracle, if such could be. But can it? No!

Only Light knows what Light is conceiving. Only Light can perceive what Light conceives. Only Light knows what is within Light. Only Light knows that Light is, knows Its ETERNALITY NOW, ITS PRESENCE NOW, ITS POWER

NOW, ITS FULLNESS OF SELFHOOD NOW, ITS SATIS-
FACTION WITH ITS OWN ENTIRETY NOW. There simply
is no "greater Light, nor lesser Light!" THERE IS ONLY
LIGHT, AND THIS IS THE TOTAL ETERNAL JOYOUS
SELF YOU BE NOW.

What of body, item, thing? Well, what of it? Do you wish
to make something of it? Do you wish to elevate it to being
equal with LIGHT? Do you wish it to supplant LIGHT? Do
you wish it to be blessed by LIGHT? Do you wish to assume
that LIGHT does know all about that which is dimensional,
finite, organic, molecular, atomic, fleeting, ephemeral? Do
you wish to still look to finite items with finite vision, finite
senses, finite outlook, finite time-space continuums?

Do you wish to still identify your Self as being material,
dependent on that which is fleeting, nebulous, never present
in any state of durability, substantiality, endurance, as being
who and what you are? Do you wish to slave for things, slave
as a thing, give over all that LIGHT IS, just so you can serve
one of the many items you assume actually has form, shape,
duration, reason, cause, and is an effect within a finite
mentality that is not only not yours, but is not you, and not
even existent?

Do you wish to bypass LIGHT, YOUR SOLE CHANGE-
LESS TOTALLY SATISFIED AND ETERNAL COMPLETE
SELF RIGHT NOW, and claim you are a struggling by-product of biology, so named by superstition, theology, fear,
witchcraft? Do you wish to be hoodwinked by darkness,
overcome by the effluvium of demon's brew, argue that you
are the outcome of animal reaction, composed of impossible
chemical mixtures, operating within a time-space capsule that
has no place at all in LIGHT? In other words, do you wish to
cling to a bag of liquefied "flesh" as your identity, rather
than be the GLORIOUS ALLPOWERFUL, ALLWISE, ALL
INCLUSIVE PURE LIGHT YOU BE?

Can any of the thoughts of LIGHT be seen by human eyes, or contacted by human senses? Can any idea of LIGHT be aught like what the senses of man would dictate, argue for, claim to be genuine, real, necessary, or the identity of aught, anyone, anything, anywhere, anywhen?

Do you not see from the above that ideas are such only to Mind? Whatever the senses testify to are but concoctions of human evolution, the claim that necessity or revolution, time, requirement has brought about. None of this is so. Not that we must destroy what the senses appear to sense, nor do away with things as we now seem to know them, fear them, serve them, and in some cases, enjoy them. Not at all. Leave things alone, regardless of their seeming uses, places, classifications, and all the rest of it. Do not attack, try to improve, save, or lament over aught. Do not damn, condemn, try to evangelize, or otherwise deal with, in, or as an idea from now on.

Rather, let us begin with LIGHT. Let us find out what LIGHT IS TO ITSELF, AND TO DO THIS, WE MUST BEGIN WITH THAT LIGHT, FOR NAUGHT KNOWS LIGHT SAVE LIGHT ITSELF. To try to comprehend Light via the five senses is a waste — is impossible and worse than folly.

LIGHT SHOULD BE OUR SOLE CONCERN. LIGHT IS ALL THE SUBSTANCE THERE IS, AS POINTED OUT MANY TIMES. LIGHT CANNOT BE A COMPOSITION OF ANY PHYSICAL, MENTAL, ELECTRICAL, OR MOLECULAR PARTS OR PARTICLES. LIGHT IS NOT A COMPOSITION, BUT IT IS THE WISDOM THAT IS YOURSELF, IT IS THE CONSCIOUSNESS THAT IS YOUR SELF, IT IS THE LIFE, THE ALIVENESS, THE JOY, THE AWARENESS THAT IS THE ENTIRETY OF YOUR PRESENT PERFECT WHOLE IDENTITY.

LIGHT is what you BE, and there is no dimension to It, no inside or outside thereto. And when LIGHT conceives-perceives thoughts, these thoughts do not in any manner at all fill any "need," or fit into any "plan" to make LIGHT WHAT IT IS, NAMELY, ALL, TOTAL, COMPLETE PERFECTION NOW. LIGHT (YOUR SELF) IS ALREADY ALL. THE THOUGHTS "COME" OR ARE "CONCEIVED" ON THE INSTANT NOW, THE IMMEDIACY OF NOW, BECAUSE LIGHT CONCEIVES THEM. There is no purpose behind the conception, no use for the perception, no adding to LIGHT, no subtracting from LIGHT, and no indication within LIGHT that they even are conceived-perceived.

We have been so indoctrinated by the notion, or with the notion that things have an outline, have a purpose, are filling a need of some sort, have to occupy space, have been brought forth in time, and will finally serve their purpose of existence and be disposed of or wear out due to the passage of time, if not the wear and tear of the work they performed.

STATING LIGHT AS IT IS, THE IMMEDIACY OF ENTIRETY AS WHOLENESS, ALLNESS, SUBSTANCE AS IT IS, leaves naught for "things" to do, no outline for same, no place for such to occupy, no cumbersomeness, no "stuff" of which they are composed. We suddenly are bereft of outlines, purposes, needs, incompleteness, want, anxiety, plots, and that tingling feeling of having made a discovery of the Great Designer's plans for us, and our immediate world!

How many of us proudly claim we have been "called," or that we have "seen the Light," or that a "star appeared in the heavens, and that we followed it?" How many still feel we have been enlightened, that a great burst of light struck us, as it supposedly did Paul when he was on his way to Damascus, and that we were then converted, and also changed our name (our nature) to that which was or is more fitting? How many of us have entered metaphysics, a service for life, wherein we assume we are lifting the fallen, waiting on the needy ones of this world and are thus earning our place in the great hereafter?

Do not all holy pictures show a light behind the head, or over the head of those who have given their all for the world? Yes, and how many of us have had to shell out, far beyond what we feel we should, for the light that comes via pressing a switch on the wall? There are all sorts of light — electrical, spiritual, and solar — but are these the LIGHT OF WHICH WE SPEAK? NO.

LIGHT IS SOUL, SPIRIT, MIND. LIGHT IS THE ONLY SUBSTANCE THAT EXISTENCE IS, AND IT CANNOT BE BLOWN UP BY AN ATOM BOMB, NOR WIPED OUT BY TIDAL WAVES, EARTHQUAKES, RELIGIOUS PHILOSO-PHY OR PROPHECY, THE ARGUMENT THAT THE EARTH IS TILTING ON ITS AXIS, OR ANY OTHER FORM OF DECLARATION, NO MATTER HOW EAR-NEST, HOW SINCERE, HOW ERUDITE THE SPOKESMEN MAY BE.

Light is EVERLASTING BECAUSE IT IS ALL THERE IS OF NOW, ISNESS, AMNESS, SELF, REALITY, GENU-INE ACTUALITY, INTELLIGENCE, BEING, ALIVENESS. LIGHT IS GOD, and this has nothing to do with light that is visible, or with "inspiration," or "hunches." Light is not that which hits the clairvoyant, the "seer," the prophet, the one who sees visions and dreams dreams, or is touched by an invisible hand so that he may foretell aught. It is not that which comes to the holy, or the unholy. LIGHT IS THE BEING THAT IS SINGLENESS, WHOLENESS, ALIVE-NESS, LOVE, PURE ENTIRETY WHEREIN NO FAINTEST OTHERNESS CAN BE, HENCE DOES NOT NEED TO BE DEALT WITH.

To Light nothing less can be. Hence, to the Self you be, there is no darkness at all. Your sole business, attention, concern, should be with ISNESS ITSELF, AMNESS ITSELF, NOWNESS ITSELF, for this IS LIGHT WHEREIN NO WEIGHT CAN OCCUR, NO WAIT CAN INTRUDE, NO "BECOMING" CAN TAKE PLACE, FOR THERE IS NO PLACE OR REASON FOR SUCH, AND NO MIND TO KNOW OR EXPERIENCE IT. LIGHT IS THY SELF NOW, IMMEDIATELY SO FOREVER.

CHAPTER VIII

Function

What is the meaning of the word, "function?"

In Absolute Reality we use the word as a synonym for SPIRIT, LOVE, GOODNESS, SELF-SATISFACTION, IN-TELLIGENCE. But what is meant by function? How do you use the word, what does it signify to you, where, when, how?

What is FUNCTION?

There is a reason for asking the question over and over again. It is one of the most important words in our language, yet, like LOVE, a word that means very little, or a mere personal experience, or one that is so common that it is taken for granted.

What is FUNCTION?

FUNCTION IS POWER. FUNCTION IS INTELLI-GENCE. FUNCTION IS MIND IN ACTION. FUNCTION IS OMNIPRESENCE OMNISCIENTLY ALIVE TO ITS TOTAL BEAUTY, COMPLETENESS, WHOLENESS, SINGLENESS, PURITY. FUNCTION IS AWARENESS ABSOLUTELY ACUTELY CONSCIOUS OF PERFECTION IN ALL ITS

115

GOODNESS. FUNCTION IS PURE SELF WHEREI
NAUGHT SAVE COMPLETE GLORY, CHANGELESS UN
CHALLENGED UNDIMENSIONAL SATISFACTION I
CONSTANTLY NEW, FRESH, SPARKLINGLY THRILL
ING, EXCITEDLY NOW BEING UTTERLY ENJOYED A
JOY ITSELF IN ACTION. . . NOT ENJOYING THA
WHICH MIND IS PERCEIVING, BUT RATHER BEIN(
THE BOUNDLESS UNFATHOMABLE ETERNALLY END
LESS COMPLETENESS IT IS.

What is FUNCTION?

Do you consider function to be the activity carried on b
nature, by glands, by organs, by magnetism, by the laws o
the universe, the result of the sun, the normal product o
cause and effect, the outcome of divine will, the result o
animal natures, the general trend of time, or what? Do yo
look to the body, to the eyes, nose, ears, tongue, nerves o
your physique, or something else, for function? Do yo
consider that function stems from God? Do you connec
function with Action, or is it but the outcome of well-being
or the natural expectation that reaction follows impulse, tha
particular nudge, trend, or urge that has been put int
motion?

How many of our readers have any notion of FUNCTION
aside from things, items, objects? Is it not generally th
"thing" that does the functioning? Do not your eyes, you
ears, and your other senses tell you this or that — as if "they'
functioned? Are you not decidedly alarmed when something
seems to interfere with that "normal function?" But can any
"thing" function? The answer is an unequivocal "NO." An
why?

ONLY SPIRIT IS FUNCTION. Spirit does NOT functio
— rather, SPIRIT *IS* FUNCTION, MIND *IS* FUNCTION
THE SELF *IS* FUNCTION!

No longer look to any item for function. Look only to SELF, LOVE, SINGLENESS, SUBSTANCE, OMNI-PRESENCE, FOR HERE ONLY DO YOU FIND THAT AMNESS THAT IS FUNCTION. It is never in the item which Mind perceives. Function, being Spirit, is NEVER IN WHAT IT CONCEIVES-PERCEIVES — NEVER WITHIN, NOR IS IT THAT OF WHICH IT IS AWARE. AWARENESS AND FUNCTION ARE ONE, THE SAME. FUNCTION IS THE SOLE SELF I AM, I BE, I IS.

He who states what AWARENESS IS, then defines the terms used — defines them to the full — and continues to actually behold what these definitions mean, and continues until they DO HAVE ABSOLUTE MEANING TO HIM, WILL DISCOVER THAT AWARENESS IS ABSOLUTE FUNCTION, FOR ALL OF AWARENESS IS PRESENT, IS AWARE, IS SATISFIED WITH THE ENTIRETY OF ITS ABSOLUTE COMPLETE PURITY, INFINITY, WHOLE-NESS. Nowhere within this AWARENESS can there be the slightest sense of otherness, of a false identity, a smaller or larger "I," nor can there be any sense whatever of possession, or possessions. There can be no sense of "things" as having value, worth, purpose, or being desired for any reason whatever.

Within this TOTAL AWARENESS PRESENT is utter SELF IDENTIFICATION, UTTER FULLNESS, UTTER WHOLENESS, UTTER JOY, UTTER BLISS, UTTER A-LIVENESS, UTTER ALL-INCLUSIVENESS, UTTER OMNI-PRESENCE THROUGHOUT DIVINE INFINITY. Within this AWARENESS, THIS WHOLENESS WHICH IS FUNC-TION ITSELF, THERE IS NO POSSIBLE WANT, DESIRE, WISH, LACK, LIMITATION, FEAR, IGNORANCE, PREJU-DICE, BLAME, DARKNESS, HISTORY, PROPHECY, OR OTHERNESS BY ANY NAME WHATEVER.

Within LOVE WHICH IS FUNCTION, THERE CAN BE
NO HATE, NO EGO, NO LUST FOR POWER, PRESTIGE,
POSITION. THERE CAN BE NO LONGING TO BE TOP-
DOG, TOP-MAN, HEAD OF THE TOTEM POLE, OR
AUGHT ELSE. RATHER, THERE IS ABSOLUTE FREE-
DOM OF ANY PERSONAL SENSE, COMPARISON, COM-
PETITION, OR HUMAN VALUES. There are no "little
people" to push about, or be pushed about. There are no
"big shots" to sound off, or to be listened to.

In LIFE, WHICH IS FUNCTION, THERE CAN BE NO
DISEASE, FOR THE WHOLE OF LIFE IS FUNCTION
ITSELF, LIFE BEING ITSELF, LIFE WHOLLY ALIVE TO
ITS ALLNESS EVERYWHERE RIGHT NOW. THERE IS
NO SPACE, NO TIME, NO HISTORY, NO PROPHECY AS
TO WHEN EVIL, LACK, LIMITATION, DEATH, AN END,
WILL COME, NOR CAN ANY SUCH EVER BE!

WITHIN WHOLENESS THERE CAN BE NO VOIDS, NO
HOLES, NO LACKS, NO LIMITATIONS, NAUGHT MISS-
ING, NAUGHT OVERLOADED, NAUGHT FORGOTTEN,
NAUGHT THAT IS TOP-HEAVY WITH IMPORTANCE!
Why? Because FUNCTION IS WHOLENESS, and that means
that all of WHAT IS — PERFECTION PRESENT, GOOD-
NESS IN ITS UTTER ABSOLUTENESS, POSITIVE HERE-
NESS — IS BEING ALL THAT IT IS. Where in WHOLE-
NESS can one find a hole, a place or spot where there is
un-WHOLENESS, un-NOWNESS, un-ISNESS, un-PRES-
ENCE? Silly, isn't it?

WITHIN AMNESS, FUNCTION, THERE IS NONE OF
ISNESS THAT MUST BE WAITED FOR. But are you
beginning with AMNESS, ISNESS, NOWNESS, PRESENT
TOTAL COMPLETENESS, FUNCTION, or are you waiting
for some "thing" or some "mind" to start to function, start
to act, get busy and bring something more, or something less

to this particular "thing" you call body, money, home, family, country, or self?

Just how do you define your SELF? Just how have you described your SELF, your LIFE, your WEALTH, your MIND, your PRESENCE, your BEING today? Have you looked at the body, felt of its aches and pains, looked in the mirror, into your eyes, your mouth, down your throat, or elsewhere to see how you look, and to discover your present state of being?

How many today have looked into their purse, their checkbook, their newspaper, to see how the stock market was doing, in order to judge how MUCH HEALTH he has, financially speaking? How many of our readers have used their senses to find out the condition of the world, to find out how the weather was functioning, how their neighbors were getting along, and all manner of other nonsense?

How many STATED, FIRST AND ABSOLUTELY, THE ALLNESS OF ALL, THE WHOLENESS OF THE ONE ALONE — HOW MANY "BEGAN" ENTIRELY WITH THE TOTAL AWARENESS THAT SPIRIT OMNIPRESENTLY IS? How many kept at the definition of the words he declared this morning, till he could really declare them and MEAN EVERY WORD, BACKED BY ABSOLUTE CONVICTION, THE POWER OF CERTAINTY THAT SPIRIT ALONE IS, EXISTENCE ALONE IS, THAT AMNESS ONLY IS, THAT THE SELF IS INTACT AND NAUGHT BESIDE EXISTS, HENCE NAUGHT CAN CHANGE THIS CHANGELESS ONE HE IS RIGHT NOW FOREVER?

If this is how you "began" today, then of a certainty you do know that RIGHT HERE THIS MOMENT, THE SOLE AUTHORITY, THE ONLY POWER, ALL POTENCY EM- BRACING THE ENTIRE UNIVERSE THIS MOMENT IS THE FUNCTION YOU BE — THE FUNCTION THAT THIS

INFINITE AWARENESS, THIS ABSOLUTE INTELLI-
GENCE, THIS POSITIVE CERTAINTY OF TOTAL PER-
FECT GOODNESS IN ACTION, IS ALL, HENCE IS
SELF-SATISFACTION FOREVER-NOW. NAUGHT BE-
SIDE CAN BE, NAUGHT IS OMITTED, NAUGHT IS
COMMITTED. ONLY ALL IS FUNCTION, AND FUNC-
TION IS ALL. ALL OF ALL IS IN FUNCTION, AND THE
WHOLE OF FUNCTION IS THE ALL-SELF I BE.

Does the entirety of ALLNESS operate right now as the
SOLE CONSCIOUS IDENTITY YOU BE, INCLUSIVE OF
THE ENTIRETY OF THE UNIVERSE OF INFINITE
MIND? IS THERE AN AWARENESS OF THE TOTALITY
OF COMPLETENESS PRESENT, UTTERLY COGNIZANT
OF AND AS ENTIRETY ALIVE IN ITS ABSOLUTE-
NESS? ARE YOU FULLY CERTAIN THAT YOUR VERY
"WORD" IS ALMIGHTY, EVEN "TO THE PULLING
DOWN OF STRONGHOLDS," AND THAT THERE IS
NAUGHT BESIDE THAT CAN POSSIBLY EVEN RAISE
AN OBJECTION, DOUBT, QUESTION, OR QUERY?

Are you POSITIVE that the mere "conception" of any
"thing," or "item" means that at this very instant you
"perceive" it as present in its entirety, available EVERY-
WHERE for total and satisfying "use" should you so "wish
to use it?" Do you have any doubt that you are the SOLE
ONE PRESENT, THE ONLY POWER, THE ALONE CON-
SCIOUS SUBSTANCE, and there is none beside, hence
naught to question you, obstruct you, doubt you? Or do you
still have a lingering notion that you are also equipped with a
doubting mind, a fearful lack-laden mentality that is afraid,
knows limitation, assumes it is human, mortal, here for but a
short stay, worried over the time it was born, bedeviled by
the aspects of the planets when its first breath was drawn,
hence cursed by ill luck, treachery, disappointments, frustration, a hard time for the entirety of its stay on this earth; or,

perhaps because the date, place, hour of birth was "fortu-
nate," relative to the stars, time, space, ancestry, and such,
that it goes sailing along through its daily round, and
everyone helps it, gives unto it, and it partakes, thanks to
birth data, of the very cream of the land?

Again, do you assume, due to karma, you are under a
heavy spell, with past misdeeds to atone for . . . or that you
come under the religious dictum which says that all of us
"are born into (and due to) sin" and must work, slave, labor,
and finally, if diligent and sincere enough, we shall win
through to a happy time in some distant or nebulous
hereafter?

What of FUNCTION in all this? What of FUNCTION
when it comes to body, planets, animals, prophecy, history,
evolution, nature, or the would-be life-giving properties that
make up our world, sun, light, molecules, energy, and such?

When you consider FUNCTION, are you alive to the
FACT THAT IT IS THE WHOLE SELF, THE ENTIRETY
WE CALL SUBSTANCE, THE ONLY POWER, THE WHOLE
OF ACTION OPERATING, THE ENTIRETY OF COM-
PLETENESS BEING COMPLETE, THE FULLNESS OF
NOW BEING UTTERLY PRESENT IN ITS UNCHAL-
LENGED ISNESS? ARE YOU ALIVE TO THE FACT THAT
NONE OF INTELLIGENCE CAN FAIL TO BE WHOLLY
OPERATIVE HERE AS THE ALONE SELF-I-AM? DO YOU
BEGIN WITH FUNCTION AS A SYNONYM OF LIFE,
hence behold that ALL OF AWARENESS IS THIS IN-
STANT INFINITELY BEING AWARE, HENCE WISE IN
ITS TOTALITY, ALIVE TO THE FACT THAT NAUGHT
OF PERFECT GOODNESS CAN FAIL TO BE TOTALLY
BEING ALL IT IS?

Yes, are you conscious that THE WHOLE OF COM-
PLETENESS IS THE SINGLE SELF, PURE LOVE, ABSO-

LUTE ONENESS OF INFINITY IN CONSCIOUS ACUTE ALIVENESS OF BEING THIS UNCHANGING GOODNESS, PERFECTION, UNOPPOSED SINGLE ONENESS FOR-EVER NOW? Herein is no little mind, or little minds, points of segregation, spots cut off from the Whole, locations where there is a mal-FUNCTION, a mal-OPERATION, a mal-BEING, a mal-ACTION called malpractice, an incompleteness such as hate, bigotry, judgment, blame, fear, disease, shortage of any sort.

Beginning with FUNCTION, you must see that YOU ARE IT, or rather, FUNCTION IS THE ONLY SELF, HENCE THE ENTIRETY YOU BE. There is naught personal, human, mortal, or alien anywhere within THIS SINGLE TOTAL COMPLETENESS. There can be no divisions, diseases, mal-functions of any sort, anywhere, at anywhen. Even in what passes as our everyday round, not a lack can intrude, not a mal-adjustment, a mal-operation, a mal-lady (or malady) can ever be! There is ONLY THE FULLNESS OF INSTANT COMPLETENESS OF THOUGHTS (things, bodies, items in their perfect entirety, changeless fullness), and each and all must be perfect, complete, for MIND CANNOT "FUNCTION" VIA NON-FUNCTION, MAL-FUNCTION, NON-OPERATION, or IMPROPERLY FUNCTION, IMPROP-ERLY CONCEIVE-PERCEIVE.

Infinite Intelligence is incapable of failing to CONCEIVE-PERCEIVE TOTALLY, ANY IDEA, THOUGHT, ITEM, THING, WHICH IT THINKS. THE WHOLE IDEA MUST BE INSTANTLY PRESENT, UNCOMPROMISED, COMPLETE, UTTERLY SATISFYING TO THE PERFECT INTELLI-GENCE-SUBSTANCE DOING THE CONCEIVING-PER-CEIVING. And the SOLE ONE BEING MIND PRESENT, only MIND "USES" THE IDEA, even in what seems our daily round.

This last statement may confuse the unwary. They may assume that we are stating that Mind, which is INFINITE, UNDIMENSIONAL, actually "uses" mortal, material, human instruments in order to accomplish whatever "It" wishes — in other words, that Mind acts as a human, requiring human instruments to do this and that with, through, for, or because of! Not at all. But we do wish to point out that he who states fully what MIND IS, WHAT NOW IS, WHAT OMNIPRES-ENCE IS, WHAT AWARENESS IS, WHAT THE SELF THAT IS LIFE, IS, and then defines these statements in their full and true meaning, if honest, must admit that he would know of no "present existence" at all if it were not for PRESENT INTELLIGENCE, IDENTITY, SELFHOOD. So, staying with the FULLNESS OF WHAT IS, ACTING IN ACCORD WITH THE ONE AND ONLY BEING AS THE SOLE SELF PRESENT, one can then "do" whatever has to be "done" right where he stands, and will discover that BY STAYING WITH REALITY AS *IT* IS, he cannot then operate on the basis of a lesser mind, identity, presence, power, life, substance, assuming that this forces him to be limited, in want constantly, never having what is essential, always void of Goodness, Intelligence, and always in fear of a sudden end. In other words he stops being a slave to his senses, which never fail to testify to lack, limitation, dimension, mortality, time, history, prophecy and all manner of otherness which intrudes in all he seems to experience, whether asleep or awake!

He who begins with TRUTH ONLY, and discovers that THE WHOLE OF LIFE IS PRESENT, FUNCTIONING TO THE FULL, WITH NO OTHER "JOB" IT NEEDS TO CARRY ON, will discover that POWER IS WHAT HE IS, AND HE CAN SPEAK "AND IT WILL BE DONE." HE WILL FIND THAT IT WILL NOT BE "ACCOMPLISHED" AT A LATER DATE, BUT IS DONE RIGHT NOW, IS SO

RIGHT NOW, IS THE FACT RIGHT NOW, AND THAT
LIFE IS LIFE RIGHT NOW, ETERNAL RIGHT NOW, AND
THAT AWARENESS IS AWARE RIGHT NOW, ISNESS IS
RIGHT NOW, NOW IS RIGHT NOW, AND INFINITY IS
HIS IDENTITY RIGHT NOW.

YES, HE WILL DISCOVER THAT HIS IDENTITY IS
DIVINE RIGHT NOW, THAT ALL SATISFACTION IS HIS
RIGHT NOW, THAT SINGLENESS IS HIS RIGHT NOW,
AND THAT THE ENTIRETY OF HIS UNIVERSE IS
INCLUDED WITHIN THIS GLORIOUS GOODNESS THAT
MIND IS, RIGHT NOW.

HE WILL DISCOVER THERE ARE NO OTHERS ANY-
WHERE, NO OTHER NOW AT ALL, NO OTHER LIFE, NO
OTHER BEING, NO MAL-BEING, OR MAL-THING ANY-
WHERE TO FUNCTION, FOR THE WHOLE OF ALLNESS
IS PERFECT NOW, NEVER FALLEN, NEVER SUBJECT
TO IGNORANCE, DEFAULT, DEFILEMENT, DEBASE-
MENT, OR SATAN, BUT IS WHOLLY WHAT IT CHANGE-
LESSLY IS, NAMELY ALL!

This is the IDENTITY YOU BE, AND IT FUNCTIONS
WITHOUT STOPPAGE, FOR IT CAN DO NO OTHER
THAN BE THE WHOLENESS OF ALL THAT ALL IS —
THAT ALL THAT IS BEING ALL RIGHT NOW FOREVER,
FOR THERE IS NAUGHT BESIDE IT CAN BE. THIS IS
FUNCTION. THIS IS THE NATURE, THE IDENTITY, THE
AMNESS THAT IS SELF. IT IS NOT PERSONAL, NOT
POSSESSIVE, NOT AN ENTITY THAT IS SEEKING FOR
THINGS, WANTING TO DOMINATE THINGS, NOT LUST-
ING OVER ITEMS, DESIRING MONEY AND TRINKETS,
CONTROL OVER PLANETS OR PEOPLE, NOT SEEKING
A FARAWAY HEAVEN, NOR FEARING A SUDDEN AND
CERTAIN END. NOT AT ALL. FUNCTION IS MERELY
ALL BEING ALL IT IS RIGHT HERE, NOW, AND THE

WHOLE OF ITS CONSCIOUS AWARENESS ALIVE
THERETO.

When you mention Intelligence as being THAT WHICH
IS, the very SOLE SELF THAT IS THE AMNESS THAT IS
NOW, are you certain that the ENTIRETY OF THIS
INTELLIGENCE IS PRESENT, IS FUNCTIONING TO THE
FULL? As ALL THE INTELLIGENCE THAT INFINITE
WISDOM IS, is absolutely busy being UTTER IN ITS
FUNCTION, there cannot be a possible bit of ignorance, fear,
misgiving, anxiety, lack, dimension, threat, frustration, wish
or finity anywhere. There can only be ABSOLUTE POSI-
TIVE ACUTE ALIVENESS OF FACT, PERFECTION, UN-
CHALLENGED AND UNOPPOSED ACCOMPLISHMENT,
IMMEDIACY, ACTUAL *being* of ACTUALITY IN TOTAL
OPERATION HERE-EVERYWHERE NOW.

Just stop and consider what has been stated above! This
means that there is ONLY TOTAL PERFECTION, ABSO-
LUTE GOODNESS, UTTERLY SATISFYING ACTUALITY
IN OPERATION EVERYWHERE, ALL-INCLUSIVE OF
THE ENTIRETY OF IMMENSITY.

When you use the word LOVE as a synonym of
SINGLENESS, PURITY, AUTHORITY, POWER IN TOTAL
OPERATION, this is FUNCTION, THIS IS THE SELF
THAT CANNOT BE QUESTIONED, REFUTED, SET
ASIDE, BLOCKED, CHANGED, CHALLENGED, BORN,
DYING, HUMAN, PERSONAL, OR WHAT. Rather, it means·
that THE PERFECTION OF ALL THAT MIND, SPIRIT IS
AS TOTALITY, ONE-ALONE, WHOLENESS, SUBSTANCE,
THE ONLY, is in COMPLETE OPERATION EVERY-
WHERE, AND THERE SIMPLY IS NAUGHT AT ALL
BESIDE, HENCE NAUGHT OFFERING ANY RESIS-
TENCE, DOUBT, REFUSAL TO ADMIT, BELIEF OF ANY
SORT, OR FINITY WHATEVER. THERE IS ONLY THE

FULLNESS OF GOODNESS PRESENT. THIS IS FUNC-
TION, THIS IS THE SOLE SELF YOU BE NOW. THIS
FACT MEANS THAT WHATSOEVER, EVEN AS YOU
BROWSE ABOUT IN YOUR DAILY AFFAIRS, YOU
"CONCEIVE" AS BEING "USEFUL" IS INSTANTLY
PRESENT IN ITS COMPLETENESS. There is no reason,
cause, or purpose in waiting for "it." Already "it" is present,
and once you begin with the WHOLENESS OF FUNCTION
ITSELF AS IT IS, you cannot avoid every good-thing you
"conceive."

When you behold FUNCTION AS THE SOLE SELF IN
TOTAL ACTION, ACTION AS TOTAL FUNCTION, you
will also behold that LIFE IS ACTION IN TOTO, IS
FUNCTION IN TOTO, EVEN AS FUNCTION IN TOTO IS
LIFE, IS SELF, IS OMNIPRESENCE BEING THIS CON-
SCIOUS AMNESS THAT IS HERE-I!

Should anyone attempt to "demonstrate" or "conceive"
things only, via turning to the allness of Spirit, he will utterly
fail. Why? Because he is not beginning with ALLNESS,
WHOLENESS, MIND, FUNCTION, but is beginning as the
Bible begins, with a great void that he assumes Spirit will fill
in some manner, and he can spend seven days, or seventy
times seven and still find that he is laid to rest with his
fathers!

Only as one states the WHOLENESS OF ALL, AND THE
ALLNESS OF WHOLENESS, WILL HE BEHOLD THERE IS
NAUGHT BESIDE THE ENTIRETY OF LIFE PRESENT,
THE ENTIRETY OF LOVE PRESENT, THE ENTIRETY
OF INFINITY PRESENT, HENCE THE ENTIRETY OF
THE SELF PRESENT – will he know the meaning of
FUNCTION, ACTION, BEING, POWER, AUTHORITY,
NOWNESS, CHANGELESS ETERNITY WHICH IS JOY,
BLISS, EXCITEMENT, ETERNAL THRILL.

One cannot stick consciously, alively with what THE FULLNESS OF THE PRESENT IS, THE WHOLE OF WHAT EXISTENCE NOW IS, THE PERFECTION OF WHAT ENTIRETY IS, THE ACTION OF WHAT AWARENESS IS, and still assume there is a place where AWARENESS MAL-FUNCTIONS, or where CONSCIOUSNESS MIS-CAL-CULATES, or where dis-EASE, dis-PERFECTION, dis-PRES-ENCE CAN BE.

It is impossible for lack of any sort to even appear when the reader is HONEST WITH FACT ONLY. To give trouble room, a place, a time, a mind within which to operate, a course to follow, a system of decline that it traces, a destructive job to be done, is far from FUNCTION. His failure to begin with WHAT IS, is his downfall, not the disease, the problem, someone to blame, some cause and such. ONLY WHEN ONE TURNS FROM FUNCTION, FACT, TRUTH, ISNESS, WHOLENESS, SELF, does mal-function appear to be real, does dis-ease appear to take its toll, does lack, limitation, misfortune and all the rest seem to take over. But is it the trouble that is the "trouble," the "problem?" Never! It is his own refusal to FUNCTION, TO BE THE FUNCTION, THE ACTION HE IS RIGHT NOW.

This is never a personal demand. This is not a physical call. This is not something that one can gain by study, understanding, by enlightenment, morals, or by being a good and obedient, a patient and contrite sufferer. Never!

Truth is not something to be gained, earned, come by, dug up, discovered, unearthed, or revealed. TRUTH IS WHAT YOU BE, FOR IT IS LIFE HERE AND NOW BEING ITSELF ONLY. THERE IS NAUGHT BESIDE EXISTENT, HENCE NAUGHT BESIDE THAT IS THE AMNESS THAT IS I. Don't ever lose sight of this Fact — don't ever assume TRUTH IS PERSONAL, OR THAT IT CAN BE ATTAINED

BY PERSONAL VIRTUE OR EFFORT, A PERSONAL
GIFT OR VIA PROPHECY. IT IS SPIRIT ALONE BEING
ITSELF, AND THERE IS NO OTHER, HENCE IT IS THY
SOLE UNCHALLENGED SELF NOW, AND TIME OR
SPACE, DIMENSION OF ANY AND ALL SORT, HAVE NO
PLACE AT ALL, ANYWHERE. THERE IS NO SIN, NO
DEVIL, NO HELL, NO PAST, NO HEREAFTER. THERE IS
ONLY OMNIPRESENCE IN ITS FULLNESS FUNCTION-
ING IN ITS ENTIRETY.

This means, naturally, that no lack can function. No
organic, material belief, no error or sin, no fear or otherness
exists anywhere, anywhen, anyhow to do or not to do aught.
Stop messing about with such nonsense and get busy with
FUNCTION, AND BEHOLD THAT THE WHOLE OF
GOODNESS IS, AND ALL OF IT IS FUNCTIONING
TOTALLY, AND THAT IS ALL THERE IS TO FUNCTION,
ALL THAT FUNCTIONS, AND THE WHOLE OF THIS
FUNCTION IS THE SELF YOU BE NOW, WORLD-WITH-
OUT-END! What can be more glorious? And to think, one
never has to wait or wonder if a promise of "better times in
the hereafter" will be actually fulfilled!

Again, as already pointed out, where INTELLIGENT
AWARENESS IS TOTALLY CONSCIOUS, ALIVE, SIN-
GLE, ENTIRE, HENCE ABSOLUTELY FUNCTIONING,
CAN THERE BE ANY FEAR, ANY IGNORANCE, ANY
LACK, ANY LIMITATION, ANY CONFUSION, ANY
DOUBT, ANY DELAY, ANY WAIT FOR AUGHT TO
"COME ABOUT?" Is not the idea-thing-item-thought already
present in its totality?

That is, can Infinite Awareness, being TOTAL FUNC-
TION HERE NOW IN ITS ENTIRETY, conceive, hence
perceive an incomplete thought, item, idea, or thing? And
remember, each of these terms means the same — means

thought Mind alone is conceiving-perceiving, hence the ONLY "PLACE" THE THING-IDEA EXISTS, also the SOLE ONE WHO KNOWS THAT THE THING-IDEA IS, AND ALL CONCERNING IT. It is Mind alone that thinks-conceives-perceives Its thought (idea-thing), and therefore the ALONE ONE WHO KNOWS OF IT, OR THAT IT EXISTS. There is no other mind at all, no other existence at all.

Every item-thing-idea belongs totally to Mind alone, the SOLE CONCEIVER-PERCEIVER, PLACE WHEREIN THE IDEA-THING IS, AND THE ONLY ONE TO "IDENTIFY" IT FOR WHAT OR THAT IT IS!

CONSCIOUSNESS, being ABSOLUTE FUNCTION, AC-TION, AWARENESS, cannot conceive-perceive a mal-Perfect thought, a mal-formed or mal-conceived, hence a mal-per-ceived thought (thing-idea), either in quality or quantity. Every idea (thing-thought-idea) MUST NOW BE CON-CEIVED-PERCEIVED PERFECTLY, FOR INFINITE GOODNESS CAN ONLY CONCEIVE IN ACCORD WITH ITS PERFECT PRESENT UNCHANGING UTTER BEING AS TOTAL TRUTH *BEING!* There can be naught "mal," naught missing, naught deformed, imperfect, incomplete! And Mind is totally SATISFIED WITH THE UTTER PERFECTION OF ALL IT CONCEIVES-PERCEIVES, FOR ALLNESS IS ALL, HENCE IS PERFECTION ITSELF, AND THIS CERTAINLY DOES NOT OMIT ITS UNALTERABLE POTENTIAL OF PERFECT FUNCTION AS CONCEIVER-PERCEIVER, or DIVINE "THINKER-OF-THOUGHTS-NOW."

Over and over we point out that INFINITE AWARE-NESS, LIFE ITSELF PRESENT IN ITS ENTIRE GOOD-NESS, PERFECTION, WHOLENESS, UTTERNESS, ABSO-LUTE SUBSTANCE, IS ALL THERE IS. THERE SIMPLY IS NAUGHT ELSE THAN ALL. THERE IS NO ONE ELSE

BESIDE THIS ONE ALL. THERE IS NO SECOND OR
OTHER INFINITY WHERE THERE IS INFINITY ITSELF,
FOR THIS ONE COMPLETENESS MUST BE THE SOLE
SOUL, BEING, SUBSTANCE THAT IS EXISTENCE IT-
SELF. To this ONE ALL, there is absolute SELF-SATISFAC-
TION, because none of Its ENTIRETY, COMPLETENESS
CAN BE MINUS, MISSING, WAITED FOR, NEEDED,
EXPECTED, DELAYED, OR DEPENDENT UPON OTHER-
NESS, TIME, PROPHECY, PROMISE, PROMOTION, PER-
PETUITY, PROGRESSION, OR PANDEMONIUM.

   TRUTH ALONE IS TRUE, as we point out so often. This
TRUTH ALONE IS ALIVE, PRESENT, ALL. IT IS FACT,
IT IS CONSCIOUSNESS, IT IS AWARENESS. THIS IS THE
SOLE "STANCE," OR STAND, BASIS, FOUNDATION, IF
YOU WILL, UPON WHICH YOU MUST PREDICATE EACH
AND EVERY STATEMENT IF YOU WOULD BEGIN
WITH, STATE, START, OR OPERATE WITH, AND AS
TRUTH. He who begins with some other "STANCE," or
with some "otherness" by any name, nature, reverence for
age, history, respect for those who have voiced the nonsense,
or how long it has been accepted in lieu of Actuality, how
many believe it, and their insistence that they have a
something (called a brain, mind, or what) with which to
believe falsity, error, lack, limitation, duality, impurity,
history and such — regardless of what is presented, should
such be your thesis, your foundation, your "stance," or basis
of operation, or what influences your choices and decisions,
you will remain in hell, darkness, the pit, death.

   There is no sub-"STANCE." There is no sub-FACT. There
is no sub-LIFE, or sub-PRESENT, or sub-AWARENESS, or
sub-I-IDENTITY, or sub-SELF, or sub-INTELLIGENCE-
GOODNESS-GOD! There is but one ONE, and that is THE
ONE PRESENT, OMNIPRESENT, FUNCTION, ACTION,
ALIVENESS.

Only NOW IS. There is no sub-NOW, no sub-IS, no sub-AMNESS! Yet it is this would-be thesis that all religion predicates its concept of God, Life, Reality, Action, Substance, Eternality, Being, Wealth, Health, Identity, Heaven upon. The whole of education is based on lack, on limitation, on dimension, on littleness, on a shortness of duration and a longness of "everlasting."

All education depends upon the senses (which are but the product of the thesis of otherness), to testify and prove that evil, lack, dimension, ignorance, doubt, fear, disease, birth-death, genesis, cause-effect, exists, and that whatever points to the contrary is altogether nebulous, ethereal, abstract assumption. For what passes as eons this has been going on, but has it helped what appears to be your world into a better, a safer and more serene state, a surety of harmony, protection, joy everlasting, a sense of peace and plenty and the harmony of unity, oneness? Most emphatically just the reverse!

Our "work" begins with FACT, REALITY, NOWNESS, ISNESS, BEING, THE PRESENT ALONE WHICH IS ETERNALLY NEW, FRESH, WHOLE, HENCE WHOLESOME RIGHT HERE NOW, INCLUSIVE OF THE ENTIRETY OF THE UNIVERSE. It leaves no otherness to contend with, no assumptions and presumptions to deal with, no regrets of the past, no fears of a future, no pictures to change, alter, or feel responsible for or to, no wars or the rumors of war to battle, no ignorance to beat down, no devil to beat off, no Satan to blame, or aught else, including yourself, your times, your neighbors, or those high (or low) in office in any and every field.

No, we do not even have a devil upon whom to blame aught, nor a God that needs blaming, or who is accused of putting up with a devil, with another, an opposite, regardless of what "reason" is given as a matter of rationalizing!

No, our "work" begins with FACT ALONE, PRESENT IN ITS UNSULLIED, UNCHALLENGED, UNOPPOSED SINGLENESS. What can challenge NOW? What can refute AMNESS? What can possibly find a foothold to battle ISNESS? Where can an-absence-of-Reality-Goodness-Presence-Being go to find a safe battleground upon which to wage war against OMNIPRESENT OMNIACTIVE OMNISCIENT OMNIPOTENCE? Where can impurity find a suitable spot where it can safely challenge PURITY, SINGLENESS?

Where can hate, malice, prejudice, bias, bigotry discover LOVE in order to flank It, overpower It, destroy It, and for what purpose? Where are the minds doing all this, the soldiers carrying on such nonsense, LIFE BEING SINGLE, WHOLE, TOTALLY SATISFIED WITH ITS OWN INFINITE ALL-SATISFIED GOODNESS, INCLUSIVE OF EVERY "ITEM-THING-BODY" IN ITS UNIVERSE? How can ONE ALONE fight Itself when It is never divided against Itself? How can WHOLENESS wage war against Itself when IT IS FOREVER NOW, WHOLE, COMPLETE, CHANGELESS, AND EXISTENT ONLY IN THE NOW AS ALL, BESIDE WHOM THERE IS NO OTHER?

Is this the SOLE "STANCE" (STAND, BASIS OF DECLARATION), THE SOLE WAY YOU "BEGIN" EVERY THOUGHT CONCERNING YOURSELF AND WORLD? Is this how you STATE THE TRUTH, declare FACT, and are these the terms you are defining? If not, then you but continue the lie with which you pretend to begin, but that lie was never aught that "you" began . . . it is the lie that says "it" *BEGAN YOU!* It is the lie of cause and effect, the lie of a void that a god "tried" to fill, the lie of a need for *more*, because ALL IS NOT ENOUGH! It is the lie that says duality, impurity, need, necessity, privation are the goads that push one onward and upward, that growth is required, and that the only proof you have that there is a loving god off up in the sky somewhere is thanks to the troubles he supposedly heaps upon you here to make you "grow in grace," for "god loveth only those whom he chastens!" What utter nonsense! Not a bit of Truth in it, so do not take this as your "stand," for of a certainty it is a sub-STAND, and all that you accept of it is not SUBSTANCE, but totally a sub-STANCE, meaning an "under" statement, under-Truth, under-Supply, under-Health, under-Completeness, hence forever under trouble, lack, limitation, falsity, error, nonsense. Is it any wonder then that whatever is "born" of such nonsense, that is, taken in by it, will find his days full of dust, nothingness, until he finally turns from it to Truth?

Is it any wonder that anyone who is under this cloud of falsity is in a constant void, constant demand to struggle, strive, overcome, climb, and try to attain, only to finally fail and "be laid to rest with his fathers," even as King Asa? Is it any wonder that this false, sub-stand, means taking less than Truth as your FOUNDATION OF NOWNESS, WHOLENESS, POWER, AUTHORITY, MIGHT, AWARENESS, CONSCIOUS ALIVENESS RIGHT HERE NOW THAT IS TOTALLY SATISFIED WITH THE FULL OF ITS FUNCTION EVERYWHERE, HENCE INCLUSIVE OF THE PERFECTION OF ITS ENTIRE UNIVERSE — is it any wonder if such a sub-stand is the foundation for your every move and reaction, that you grow more and more weary, discouraged, hopeless, and even faithless? He who seeks money is working from sub-Stance, so will always be short. He who stays with Substance only, leaves money and things out of his thought. He, if honest, cannot avoid Infinite Supply for this is his actual Identity *now* — All in total present Function. But, do not try to fool your Self, declaring the word, "All," but "wanting" money, a healthy organ, a healed body, or some other material or sense-thing!

There is but SUBSTANCE which means ONE WHOLE TOTALITY PRESENT RIGHT NOW, FULLY FUNCTION-ING IN ITS ENTIRETY THIS MOMENT, AND IS SATIS-FIED THAT ITS EVERY THOUGHT-IDEA-THING IS TO-TALLY PERFECT, FOR ONLY THIS GOODNESS-THAT-IS (THE AMNESS THAT IS I) CONCEIVES-PERCEIVES THE ITEM, EVEN RIGHT HERE NOW WITHIN WHAT PASSES AS OUR DAILY ROUND.

This ONE MIND IS FUNCTION ITSELF, and there is no limitation at all, no mal-formation, naught missing whatever, and none beside existent, hence none upon whom LOVE must wait, or depend. ALL IS HERE NOW, AND IS SATISFIED WITH THE PERFECTION OF "EVERY DE-TAIL" OF ITS PERFECTLY CONCEIVED-PERCEIVED IDEA (thing-body-item). If it were not for MIND, LIFE, SELF PRESENT, NAUGHT WOULD BE KNOWN, HENCE WHAT NOW SEEMS TO "APPEAR" IN MY DAILY ROUND IS THANKS TO MIND BEING ITSELF, EVEN THOUGH INFINITE GOODNESS, SPIRIT, INTELLIGENCE, SINGLE-NESS IN ITS ABSOLUTE INFINITY KNOWS NAUGHT OF THE "ITEM" OR "THING" AS IT NOW "APPEARS" TO ME PER SE!

In other words, as MIND IS ALL, ACTION IS ALL, FUNCTION IS ALL, AND ALL OF LIFE IS FUNCTION-ING, ALL OF AWARENESS IS FUNCTIONING, ALL OF GOODNESS IS FUNCTIONING EVERYWHERE, AND THERE IS ONLY MIND BEING, ONLY THIS ONE IS THE VERY ETERNAL LIFE I NOW AM FOREVER AND THERE IS NONE OTHER, THEN I "STAY" HERE, ACTIVELY DEFINING MY STATEMENT, STAYING WITH IT TILL IT MEANS WHAT IT SAYS, AND IT HAS ABSOLUTE MEANING TO ME, THUS SHUTTING OUT PRECLUDING, IF YOU WILL, ANY SENSE OF OTHER-

NESS, IMPURITY, CHALLENGE, VOID, TIME, GENESIS, EXODUS, AND SO ON — as I do this, I dismiss totally any problem, error, fear, sense of body, whatever the senses would proclaim, disclaim, or claim for myself or another, anywhere, any time, anyway.

Yes, AS INFINITE INTELLIGENCE IS ALL, here is "where" I state, define, dwell, NOW, AND CONSTANTLY "WITHOUT CEASING" NOW. Naught else is, hence naught beside should, or could concern you or me. Is this how "you" work, or are you still determined to begin with body, with problems, with time, age, history, hate, bias, ignorance, physique, organs, senses, the world at large, prophecy, aches, pains, financial distress, race, color, creed, gender, and all the rest of it? Are you still holding up a picture and trying to change it, alter your thinking, correct your morals, improve your outlook, learn, study, advance, evolve, pay the price of karma, follow the horoscope, keep "God's commandments," and such? If so, your lot will continue a sorry one, and you will go the way of all flesh, for such is your mal-Vision, your mal-Now, your mal-Function, mal-Action, mal-Identity.

Remember, your "mal," and your "sub," both have the same meaning in actual practice. Both mean falsity, error, that which is wrong, that which is beneath or other than Fact, Actuality, hence PRESENT REALITY, TRUTH, FUNCTION, ISNESS, BEING! If you wish to malfunction, then you wish to improperly function, or fail to function, to be, for FUNCTION IS SINGLENESS IN ITS ENTIRETY, AND CANNOT BE SEPARATED, DIVIDED, BROKEN DOWN, CHANGED, ALTERED, BUT IS WHOLE, COMPLETE, PRESENT AND IN ABSOLUTE TOTAL OPERATION, ACTION.

The same holds good for "sub" — if one wishes to be sub-normal, sub-jugated, sub-merged, then he is seeking to be substituted for the Real, the Actual, the Genuine, the Whole, the Complete. WHERE COMPLETENESS IS, IT CANNOT BE BROKEN DOWN, DIVIDED, SPLINTERED, BUT MUST REMAIN SINGLE, ENTIRE, INDIVISIBLE, INSEPARABLE.

Waste no more effort to "overcome" handicaps of any sort, whether for yourself or another, or your world at large, but rather begin with the ONE INSEPARABLE NOWNESS, THE WHOLE NOWNESS, THE INDIVISIBLE ISNESS THAT OMNIPRESENCE IS, AND DEFINE YOUR TERMS TILL THEY HAVE MEANING TO YOU AND YOU CAN ACTUALLY MEAN WHAT YOU SAY WHEN YOU SPEAK OF FUNCTION, ACTION, BEING, ALIVENESS, WHOLENESS CONSCIOUSLY AWARE, SELF-SATISFIED WITH THE PERFECTION OF ITS WHOLENESS OF WISDOM, BEING, PURE LOVE, ALL-INCLUSIVENESS, INFINITE SUBSTANCE, TOTALITY, wherein no genesis or exodus can possibly be, no change can take place, no challenge exists at all, no time or otherness even crosses the threshold of INTELLIGENCE, and you will know HEAVEN AT HAND NOW, AND YOU WILL BE THE ABSOLUTE UNCHALLENGED PURE AUTHORITY OR GOODNESS IN ABSOLUTE OPERATION, TOTAL FUNCTION . . . and against such there is no law, no rebuttal, no time, no coming or going, but WHOLENESS, BLISS, JOY IS AT HAND AND IS THE ALL-INCLUSIVE IDENTITY-I. This leaves no person, personality, matter, materiality, creation — THERE IS BUT GOODNESS, LIFE, WHOLLY FUNCTIONING AS LOVE ITSELF "wherein there is no evil or accuser of another at all!"

This is your SELF NOW . . . TOTAL TOTALITY FUNCTIONING WITHOUT CHALLENGE! Can there be aught beyond (or less) than ALLNESS? YOU ARE JOY

ITSELF NOW, INCLUSIVE OF YOUR ENTIRE UNI-
VERSE. GET BUSY AND *BE*, rather than pretend!

As already stated, if there is any item or thing you seem
to need, or that is in need of any sort, do not struggle over it.
Do not try to acquire aught, do not try to hold aught as your
personal possession, do not try to defend aught or in any way
deal in or with things. Rather, as we constantly state, begin
with the ALLNESS OF ALL and actually discover what
OMNIPRESENCE IN ITS FULLNESS HERE AND NOW,
REALLY MEANS, and then act in accord with this Fact.

One cannot do this honestly, not at all, so long as he is
clinging to things, to their condition, to the lack or need for
things, or so long as he assumes he is a thing, requiring all
manner of additional things to keep this "personal-body-or-
ganic-material-finite-human-thing" in business!

Whenever lack of any sort seems prevalent, or there is
aught which one feels is essential for well-being, turn from
such altogether. How? By beginning, starting with, STATING
THE PERFECTION, THE ALLNESS, THE WHOLENESS
OF LIFE PRESENT (or whatever other statement you wish
to make concerning Truth, Reality, Wholeness), but be
certain that your statement is totally TRUE, PURE, SIN-
GLE; that it is concerning the ONE OMNIPRESENT PER-
FECT LIFE, THE SOLE SELF, THE SINGLENESS OF
LOVE. Then, by "digging" to discover the full significance of
what you have declared, its totality, its immediacy right here
now, you must behold there can be naught beside present,
nor any lack of WHOLENESS IN OPERATION, TOTAL
ACTION — in other words, FUNCTION WHOLLY FUNC-
TIONING AS ALL OF GOODNESS FULLY BEING.

Where, then, can one find lack of any sort? Where, within
this AWARENESS THAT IS WHOLENESS *being*, is there
any other mind, one that is diseased, malfunctioning,

reacting, desiring, afraid, overwrought, under tension, aging, falling apart, drugged, addicted, afflicted, etc. Lack simply vanishes, another mind is precluded, matter is not, a troubled person, relative, world, past, turbulent future, time, and all the rest of the nonsense of insanity, fiction-taken-as-Fact, and so on, no longer can trouble, or be a trouble, for trouble has no place in NOW.

The "way to plenty" is not via the stock market, via labor, via creation of some sort, or any of the get-rich schemes that are so prevalent in any society. The only "way" is not a way at all, not a system, not a method, a belief, a maneuver, an inheritance, the course of the stars, the trends of time, morality or what. There is but one way, and it has naught to do with one "doing" aught!

PLENTY is not enough. A lot is not enough. A great deal is not enough. NAUGHT BUT TOTALITY IS "ENOUGH" FOR ALLNESS TO BE ALL. IT NEVER STOPS SHORT OF BEING TOTAL WHOLENESS, TOTAL PRESENCE, TOTAL LIFE, TOTAL ABUNDANCE, TOTAL CONCEIVER-PERCEIVER OF EVERY AND ALL "THINGS" WITHIN ITS UNIVERSE, AND THERE IS NAUGHT BESIDE.

Spirit is ALL. There is no other SUBSTANCE, SUPPLY, PRESENCE, MIND, ACTION, FUNCTION. SPIRIT IS WHOLE, AND IS YOUR VERY IDENTITY RIGHT NOW. DO NOT LOOK WITH THE SENSES TO DISCOVER "HOW MUCH," OR "HOW FAR," OR THE "CONDITION" OF ANY "THING." As the item can only be because Mind here and now CONCEIVES-PERCEIVES it as a thought, idea, thing within Its AWARENESS, that item exists, but ONLY AS A THOUGHT TO MIND. THERE IS NONE BESIDE TO WHOM AUGHT CAN EXIST, FOR THERE IS NAUGHT BUT INTELLIGENCE ITSELF THAT IS EXISTENT AS EXISTENCE ITSELF.

The lack of "things" is ALWAYS, and let us repeat, "A L-W A Y S" the effect, or outcome of starting with the senses — starting as a second mind — starting with duality, belief, void, cause, and judging in accord with personal or mass-induced standards of littleness, of fiction, of non-Fact — starting with and as mal-function, mal-adjustment, mal-practice, mal-conception, mal-perception — always starting with fiction in place of Truth, having more than WHOLENESS, or rather, rejecting WHOLENESS, NOWNESS, ISNESS, AM-NESS, BE-ING-NESS!

To so-called "cure" any ailment, be it diseased, be it lacking, be it in too much evidence, be it mal-formed, or de-formed, is to leave it alone and begin entirely, and only, with ACTUALITY, SPIRIT, THE ENTIRE SELF PRESENT, THE ONLY FUNCTION THERE IS, THE ABSOLUTE ACTION OF TOTAL GOODNESS IN ITS COMPLETE INTELLIGENT AWARENESS AS THE SINGLE ONE THAT ISNESS IS! One simply cannot stay with TRUTH and consciously behold the WHOLENESS OF THE PRESENT, AND THAT ONLY THE PRESENT IS PRESENT, IS WHOLE, IS COMPLETE, IS ENTIRE, AND FULLY FUNC-TIONS AS THE ENTIRETY IT IS, and still have a past, a future, a genesis, a prophecy, a fear, a regret, a material form or aught else as IDENTITY, AS I-AMNESS! It is impossible.

Again, one cannot begin with WHOLENESS AND BE-HOLD WHAT HE IS STATING, REALLY BEING ALIVE TO ITS MEANING, AND MEAN IT FULLY WHEN HE STATES IT, AND STILL HAVE HIS THOUGHT AND EXPERIENCE FILLED WITH LACK OF ANY SORT, WITH DISEASE OF ANY SORT, WITH STRIKES, WAR, HATE, MALICE, RACE, COLOR, CREED, AND SUCH. Impossible!

One cannot be honest with TOTAL ACTION PRESENT, ABSOLUTE FUNCTION AS THE COMPLETENESS OF

THE IDENTITY GOODNESS NOW IS, RIGHT HERE-
EVERYWHERE-AS-THE-AMNESS-THAT-IS-I-IDENTITY,
AND CONTINUE TO FRET OVER BODY, MONEY, GOV-
ERNMENT, STATE, EMPIRE, GALAXY, HELL, HEAVEN,
OR THINGS! He cannot begin with WHOLENESS and still
worry over friends, relatives, the weather, astrology, the
trends of the market, gender, teen-age activity, and such. He
simply cannot begin with the Fact that ALLNESS IS ALL,
WHOLE, THE SOLE MIND, POWER, ACTION, FUNCTION,
ISNESS, TOTALITY, SUBSTANCE, IDENTITY and still
have others, a variety of conditions, things with which he
relates, or many to whom he cares to "re-late" or "tell" all
the nonsense of matter, insanity, fiction. Should he mention
fiction, he will do so as fiction. He will not act as if he
thought fiction is Fact, and vice versa.

Equally he cannot fail to include the whole universe
within this AWARENESS THAT IS ONE'S SOLE PRESENT
AND ETERNAL IDENTITY. There is naught more, naught
less, naught outside ALLNESS, HIS ACTUAL BEING NOW.

This, and this only, is the would-be "cure" for any and all
sorts of lack, limitation, dimension, and the way whereby all
laws of restriction, constriction, addiction, prediction, and
their threats, vanish altogether, and the place "thereof shall
know them no more." Why? Because, as so often pointed
out, NO EVIL WAS EVER "THERE," OR "HERE" TO
THREATEN AUGHT. ALL THAT IS PRESENT IS WHOLE-
NESS, AND IT FUNCTIONS TOTALLY, FOR IT IS
INVINCIBLE, INDESTRUCTIBLE, INVIOLATE, UNDI-
MENSIONAL, IRREVERSIBLE, UNCHALLENGED, INDI-
VISIBLE, INSEPARABLE TOTALITY NOW, and there is no
time at all, no space at all, no otherness at all, and never was
or will be!

ONLY PERFECTION IS, AND IT IS THE IDENTITY

YOU BE THIS INSTANT. DO NOT PUT OFF "BEGIN-
NING" WITH NOWNESS IN ITS TOTAL UNSULLIED
PURITY, SINGLENESS, AFFLUENCE, PERFECTION.
ETERNITY GOES "ON AND ON FOREVER" BECAUSE IT
IS ETERNAL ALREADY, NOW. SO BEHOLD AND BE
THE BLISS, THE JOY THAT IS THE SOLE SELF THIS
INSTANT. Waste no more time or effort with what is not
even a dream, for it never is at all! BE THE FUNCTION
THAT IS UTTER GOODNESS IN ACTION, UTTER WIS-
DOM IN OPERATION, ABSOLUTE LOVE, PURITY, SIN-
GLENESS, SATISFACTION THAT PERFECTION IS THIS
MOMENT. This TRUTH ALONE IS TRUE, and you cannot
escape It if you would, and, BEGINNING WITH WHAT
TRUTH IS, YOU WILL NOT "TRY" TO ESCAPE WHAT
YOU BEHOLD AS INFINITY IN FULL, FOREVER-NOW
PLUMBING THE DEPTHS OF ITS OWN GLORIOUS
I-IDENTITY-SELF!

CHAPTER IX

Letters

Every letter in this chapter is an actual reply to some request for "help," or from some question sent in pertaining to our exposition of Reality. Each letter makes a point. Many include similar or exact statements of Truth made elsewhere in our work, but this repetition is of importance, for it always relates to fundamental Fact.

All "personal" reference is deleted from the letters, and the names used are not the actual names of those to whom the letters were sent.

It is hoped that those reading the letters will gain a broader sense of the magnitude of the Self they be — will awaken to an outlook of Infinite-I, the Single Individual-I-that-I-Am, that shows them Heaven is at hand and not afar off, that Life is present to be enjoyed to the full, that Power cannot be set aside, that Intelligence cannot be hypnotized into assuming It is ever human.

Dear----------

So thrilled that you intend to come to the Seminar out here. Regardless of how the picture "seems," it is important to you that you attend — for what except TRUTH can clear away the seeming cobwebs of humanity, the nonsense of that which never is, was, or will be?

So many of us are tempted to wait "for a more convenient season" which will never arrive. Why? BECAUSE NOW is all there is! There will never be more of N O W — NEVER MORE OF THE PRESENT present, and It can never change into a past or a future. So let us get busy WITH NOW ONLY, and stick with NOW ONLY, and never allow ourselves the evil-intent of thinking of a tomorrow, planning for a future and such, based on an "IF" so and so happens or doesn't happen.

Planning, in a sense, to attend a Seminar, is not the "planning" I'm speaking of, for WE KNOW ALL GOOD IS PERMANENT, UNCHANGING, UNCHALLENGED NOW AND ETERNALLY NOW. SO WHEN WE SAY WE "WILL ATTEND," IT IS ACTUALLY A STATEMENT THAT NOW IS BEING WHOLE AND THAT WHOLENESS IS OURS NOW, AND NAUGHT ELSE CAN BE, HENCE NAUGHT CAN CHANGE IT, ALTER IT OR STOP IT — quite a "different" sense involved, you see. Human planning is always based on the "if" of evil, lack, disaster, unwholeness — "if" lack doesn't stop me, then I'll do so and so. I stick with the ALLNESS OF PRESENT GOODNESS BESIDE WHICH THERE IS NAUGHT, HENCE I CAN SAY WITH CERTAINTY I "WILL" HOLD THE SEMINAR, FOR I THINK OF IT IN PRESENT TENSE, EVEN THOUGH I HAVE TO USE THE WORDS OF SOCIETY TO MAKE THE

POINT. I NEVER SAY: "NOW, 'if' evil, satan, devil, lack, humanity, time, etc. permits me, I'll do so and so!" No, I KNOW NOW IS ALL, SO I KNOW GOODNESS IS NOW ALL, AND THUS AND THUS IS SO, AND THERE IS NAUGHT EVIL, NO VOID THAT CAN PREVENT OR EVEN TALK BACK, FOR THERE IS ONLY, YES, ONLY REALITY, GOODNESS, THE SOLE SATISFIED SELF *BEING* RIGHT NOW!

So, be determined and BE SURE YOU DO COME, for ALL THIS GOOD IS YOURS NOW, FOR IT IS THE SOLE SELF YOU BE NOW. Naught has "happened" to IT. THIS SELF IS YOURSELF NOW, CHANGELESSLY WHOLE, AND THIS MIND KNOWS IT. THERE IS NONE OTHER, SO DON'T KEEP "GOING BACK TO THE FLESHPOTS OF EGYPT," DARKNESS, A PAST which never was, is, or will be – ONLY NOW IS!

Please ponder in THE UNCHALLENGED SELF, 38:10-13, and dig at it until you know what it says, and then operate therefrom. SPIRIT NEVER HAS HAD ANY "EX-PERIENCE" OF ANY SORT, NO ACCIDENT OR WHAT-EVER, AND AS SPIRIT IS THE SOLE SELF YOU BE THIS VERY MOMENT AND ALWAYS, WHO OR WHAT HAD AN "ACCIDENT" OR AN "EXPERIENCE" OF ANY KIND? THE ANSWER MUST BE, "NO ONE," SO DON'T TALK ABOUT IT, SERVE IT, OR KEEP REMINDING YOURSELF OF A LIE! STATE FACT AND BE TRUTH-FUL. DON'T LIE TO YOUR SELF, OR ABOUT YOUR SELF. AND DO NOT ASSUME YOU HAVE THE POWER TO CHANGE THE CHANGELESS PERFECT PRESENT ONE YOU BE. YOU CANNOT PRODUCE EVIL OR LACK, A VOID, ANYWHERE FOR ANY REASON. THERE IS NO

SUCH ANYWHERE SO DON'T EVEN PRETEND YOU
CAN GET RID OF THE PERFECTION YOU BE.

AND THIS IS ALSO TRUE OF MARY. I HAVE GIVEN
HER THE "BOOST" YOU REQUESTED. REMEMBER,
THERE IS ONLY TRUTH BEING, SO ONLY TRUTH IS
OPERATING, AND IT IS NOT HAVING TO "OPERATE"
ON ITSELF FOR THERE IS NAUGHT WRONG WITH IT.
IT IS WHOLENESS NOW, SO STICK WITH THE FACT,
FOR THIS ALONE IS LOVE, SINGLENESS, PURITY,
WHOLENESS, THE FACT RIGHT NOW. THERE IS
NAUGHT MORE, NAUGHT BESIDE, HENCE NAUGHT TO
EVEN PROTEST OR CONTRADICT IT.

Must dash for now.

Love to you both.

Dear----------

Yours came this morning, and I have given your son a
'boost," as you requested.

Do NOT watch him — do NOT ask about him — do NOT
'judge after the seeing of the eye or the hearing of the ear,
for all such judgment is unrighteous." Any inquiry about
error, any questions pertaining to matter, physiology and
such, is TRYING TO CHANGE THE PICTURE — LOOKING
FOR "RESULTS" — HENCE, FOR EFFECTS, all of which
is based on cause-and-effect, or DUALISM, IMPURITY.

In our work, we "begin" solely with WHAT OMNI-
PRESENCE IS, WHERE IT IS, WHY IT IS. This leaves
utterly nothing to be evil, nothing to be in lack, nothing to
be in matter, trouble, a problem, or a state of transit!
WHERE *ALL*, ONE, IS TOTALLY PRESENT, where can
you find LOVE (SINGLENESS, TOTALITY) absent, and

what would you be using as a mind to detect Truth's absence?

We are so glib in "saying" that Love is ALL, but we immediately begin to act, or continue to act, as if our statement were a lie! When we go out to inquire, "How is he?" — do we not imply there WAS (and maybe STILL IS) some lack, somewhere where TRUTH IS NOT ALL?

We say that this work is so difficult. That is false. The only place and time you find it hard is when you try to make that-which-is-NOT, become REAL! It simply cannot be done. ONLY TRUTH IS TRUE. ONLY GOODNESS EXISTS AND IS THE AMNESS THAT IS I. There simply is no other, none beside. Let us stay with this Fact, regardless of what the senses claim to sense. We are NOT IN THE SENSING BUSINESS — WE ARE IN THE *BEING* BUSINESS — so let's stay busy herein, and not go "down to the plain of Ono" to find out all about what is NOT!

NOTHING CAN BE HEALED. WHY? BECAUSE NO-WHERE IN OMNIPRESENCE IS THERE AUGHT SAVE OMNIPRESENCE BEING PRESENT, WHOLE, ENTIRE, ACTIVE, ALIVE, EXISTENT. THEN WHAT IS LEFT TO HEAL, WHO AND WHAT SAYS SO, AND BY WHAT AUTHORITY? TO WHOM DOES IT TALK — UPON WHOM DOES TRUTH CALL TO GET A HEALING? Of course, this is nonsense. WHERE REALITY *IS*, no lack (appetite, desire, uncontrolled lust or yearning) can be. ONLY WHEN WE BEGIN WITH THE WHOLE SELF HERE NOW, do we see there is naught but SELF-SATISFACTION IN ITS FULL-NESS. TRUTH KNOWS NAUGHT BESIDE, CAN BE NAUGHT ELSE THAN WHOLE! This, and THIS ONLY, is the MIND YOU BE, AND IT INCLUDES EVERY

THOUGHT (IDEA-BODY-THING) AS TOTALLY COM-
PLETE RIGHT NOW WITHIN THIS MIND, WITHIN THIS
TOTAL SATISFACTION. It leaves no THOUGHT (IDEA-
BODY) "out there" filled with appetites! Such is absurd.

In our work we do not put ANY IDEA "OUTSIDE" OF
SPIRIT. ALL IDEAS ARE WITHIN MIND NOW, AND
EACH AND EVERY ONE IS PERFECT,, WHOLE, EN-
TIRELY THE COMPLETE, HENCE SATISFACTORY I-
DEA, IDEAL IDEA, IT IS. BUT ONLY MIND INCLUDES
THE IDEA, ONLY MIND KNOWS THE IDEA, ONLY MIND
KNOWS THAT THERE IS SUCH AN IDEA! The idea (body)
does not know anything, for IT IS NOT MIND, NOT LIFE!
Idea is WITHIN LIFE, BUT THERE IS NO LIFE, NO MIND
WITHIN THE IDEA! IDEA IS BUT A THOUGHT! MIND
ALONE IS THE I-AM-IDENTITY, THE SOLE SUBSTANCE,
LIFE, AWARENESS, AND ALONE INCLUDES IDEA,
THOUGHT! So don't see him as having a small mind of his
own, taken over by appetite, or aught else! Stay with the
ONLY MIND WHEREIN THE THOUGHT (IDEA-BODY) IS
ALREADY WHOLE, PERFECT, COMPLETE, AND SATIS-
FYING TO THE MIND THAT CONCEIVES-PERCEIVES
EVERY IDEA! (In NOW, ponder 117:3-28; 95:7-14 on next
page; 81:3-30; 82:20-28 next page.)

Cordially,

Dear----------

Thanks for your letter. I do wish you could and would
attend our forthcoming Seminar in London. The last night of
the Seminar we leave on a sleeper for Edinburgh for a
12-day tour of Scotland, England and northern Wales. Each
night I give, gratis, a one-hour talk to all those who go along

on the trip and have been with us at the Seminar. To many, this is a real inducement for it amounts to a 9-day Seminar! Just when I may be in London for another Seminar I cannot say at this time for there are more and more demands being made upon my "time" for lectures, Forums and Seminars in other places. I am sure you'll "see through" the nonsense that appears to be nibbling at your coattail! Do give it serious thought, and do make it if possible! Nothing you EVER do will be as "helpful." You owe it to yourself to "take advantage" of this opportunity to quit forever the "mess" of human sense! I'm sure you CAN make it if you wish, above all, to KNOW ALL AS IT IS. Whatever would suggest you cannot do it, is but an argument of human sense striving to convince you to remain human, in lack, in fear and burden! TRUTH NEVER REFUSES, NEVER WITHHOLDS, NEVER FOREGOES THE GOODNESS-IN-TOTO THAT IT IS RIGHT NOW! There is no "other one" to say unto Reality: "What doest Thou?"

As to the situation you mention — the nonsense of trying to "patch up" a marriage affair that has "gone on the rocks" is foolish. Just as I cut off the nonsense that I must cling to the Bible, must belong to a church, or that I am a member of the human race, so I cut off all the junk that says I must be "legally tied" to human sense that seems determined to remain and act humanwise! There are times when I feel divorce is decidedly right and proper. Do not feel a sense of moral-guilt! That is a hangover of society via religion, especially metaphysics! On the same basis you do not have to remain "loyal" to a political party, once you see Reality! It is difficult to put this in a letter so that my exact meaning is not misunderstood, but I think you do get what I am trying to point out here.

Starting with OMNIPRESENCE, AND STAYING HERE *ONLY,* precludes any other mind and hence all the junk dredged up over the centuries by that mind! Staying with REALITY you will see what is "sensible" to do in your daily affairs, and will find it easy to do it without having to battle a sense of personal guilt or failure! In REALITY we do not concur with the platitudes of emotionalism and sentimentality, but we DO ACT IN ACCORD WITH THE SINGLENESS, THE PURITY OF ONENESS, JOY, BLISS, ACTION, BEING. Herein are only ideas, but no idea is "wed" to another idea, regardless of how it may seem according to education! THE JOY THAT YOU BE CAN NEVER BE DIVORCED FROM ITS SINGLENESS, WHOLENESS, HENCE NEVER HAS TO RETURN *TO* WHOLENESS — AND THIS MIND BEHOLDS EVERY "THING" AS AN IDEA ONLY, PERFECT FOREVER, BUT WITHOUT A MIND OF ITS OWN. HENCE, NO IDEA CAN ACCEPT OR REFUSE, OPPOSE OR CONCUR. ONLY MIND IS, AND IT IS ETERNALLY COMPLETE WITHIN ITSELF, HENCE FOREVER SELF-SATISFIED. This leaves no little mind filled with appetites, misgivings, frustrations, accusations.

You see, the "problem" is never what it seems, but merely the assumption that there is another mind, and that that other mind has the capacity and ability to hatch up all manner of trouble, lack and otherness, always telling you it is the "other fellow" — that there is a "they," etc.

There is nothing wrong in getting a divorce, any more than there is anything wrong in changing your gown, or the spot where you "live." But remember, the real culprit is but a suggestion of another mind that is casting the pictures of humanity upon the wall of what seems your daily experience. Turn off the projection camera and you've ended the pictures.

As to "teaching one a lesson," you have no right to do this for it implies another mind, and thus whatever you may say or do is based on self-righteousness, and is fraught with evil! WHERE ONE MIND IS ALL, WHO OR WHAT NEEDS "TEACHING," AND WHO WOULD PRESUME TO DO THIS "TEACHING?" You see the error in such a premise!

Clear your own sense of having a small human mind and you will see clearly what is sensible to do right now. In "working" thus, there will be no accusation, no excuses, no incriminations, etc. AS THERE IS BUT ONE MIND, THE VERY WHOLE ONE YOU BE, NO OTHER MIND EXISTS, HENCE NONE TO TEACH OR DO THE TEACHING. I am sure you see this.

In SUPPLY please ponder 40:9-6 on next page. In NOW 67:20-24, 117:10-15, 235:4-24. In POWER, 83:3-1 on next page.

Cordially,

Dear----------

Please ponder well in BACHELOR GOD page 162:5-10. Just stick with this, really "going to town" on what the words MEAN. There's no use just saying them or trying to "know what they mean" on a human basis. WHAT DO THEY "MEAN" TO INFINITE INTELLIGENCE? THEN, THIS IS WHAT THEY MEAN TO YOU, THE I THAT IS, THE SOLE IDENTITY YOU *BE*. No wait, no delay, no change. Particularly note that last — *NO CHANGE!*

You see, we are so prone to look for a change, and that is

always the personal, the man or human mind doing it! TRUTH (YOUR SELF) IS CONTENT TO BE WHAT IT PERFECTLY *IS*. THIS MIND YOU *BE* DOES NOT LOOK FOR CHANGE OF ANY SORT, FOR IT HAS NEVER CHANGED IN ANY WAY.

You can seem to have a growth ONLY BY STARTING WITH A HUMAN MIND, WHICH MUST HAVE A PAST, A HISTORY WHEREIN A CAUSE OPERATED TO PRODUCE THE CONDITION, THE EFFECT THAT THAT MIND NOW IS STUCK WITH, LABORS WITH, SUFFERS WITH, AND SUFFERS (PUTS UP WITH!) – all of it within another mind which never *is*. All history is a painful growth, an evolving development, an "accumulation" of vacuum or void! It is not growth, but merely an enlarged void that troubles and is painful to the human mind. It is merely the human's sense of objectified void, lack, is-not-ness! So, we, in our "work" waste no time or effort over the lack "within" the human mind, but behold in the Light of FACT, ISNESS, OUR VERY BEING, EXISTENCE, that there is no human mind existent within THE EXISTENCE WE BE, hence no place to harbor or develop an accumulation of lack – no place to "grow" limitation, vacuum, nothingness, lack! You cannot destroy lack (a growth or accumulation-of-what-is-not-REAL- ITY) because IN REALITY THERE IS TOTAL REALITY ONLY – AND REALITY IS EVERYWHERE REAL!

I beg of you, dig more at WHAT LOVE IS, and leave all else, including the so-called human sense, entirely alone, out of thought! Don't try so hard to heal it, overcome it, see it as nothing, see that it does not exist and all the rest of it, for this is all metaphysics only! Be so busy "discovering" the glory and FULLNESS OF REALITY that you cannot mentally "run back into history, or remembrance" to mess around with folly, humanity, time, physicality, body or whatnot!

I've given you another "boost." Truth cannot be side-tracked, opposed or accepted — IT MERELY *IS!* There is naught to oppose or deny It! It (MIND, YOUR SELF) KNOWS THIS, AND THIS LEAVES NONE BESIDE, HENCE NONE ELSE TO "KNOW" IT — NONE THAT COULD OR WOULD NEED TO! This is Fact. Do you still "assume" you can doubt it, oppose it, or keep Truth from BEING ALL IT IS, RIGHT HERE NOW? If you say there is a growth, you are denying TRUTH, HENCE INSISTING ON A HUMAN! Do you have this power? Where does such a mentality come from, who says so, where, when, how? It is this simple!

As to your niece, the above is still ALL TRUE, leaving no neice-mind, alcoholic-mind, frustrated-mind, guilty-mind, fearful-mind or what! Don't "treat" aught — SPIRIT IS ALL! Stick here, with Mind's INTELLIGENCE, and this precludes aught else, even a false mind, or error!

Cordially

Dear----------

Just returned from a lecture tour of Canada and the Eastern Seaboard and found your letter waiting for me.

As to helping you, have done so. As you must have found from reading THAT WHICH IS, we do not stress healing. Our SOLE INTEREST is in the ALLNESS OF OMNIPRESENT LOVE, ONENESS, SINGLENESS, PURITY. Where OMNI-PRESENCE IS, naught beside can be, so where is evil, suffering, or a human mind to testify to such?

I urge you to get all of my books and read them, keeping your thought off body, and find out what manner of BEING LOVE IS, FOR SPIRIT BEING ITSELF IS THE SOLE I-IDENTITY YOU BE RIGHT NOW! Your only "problem" is dishonesty with LOVE, due to not knowing LOVE, SPIRIT, BEING AS THE ALLNESS IT IS. To ignore LIFE OMNIPRESENT is to ignore HEALTH, WEALTH, PERFECTION — IS TO DENY YOUR SELF ALL THE GOODNESS THAT BELONGS TO YOU RIGHT NOW. TO IGNORE SPIRIT IS TO PLAY PRODIGAL, to assume "body" is your home and identity! This is wholly false, hence is dishonest with OMNIPRESENT TRUTH, CHANGELESS PERFECTION.

In the book FORUMS, please ponder well: 130:2-20; 131:6-17; 162:12-28; 242:25-13 next page. Please "dig" at these citations and you will find you are ALREADY WHOLE, COMPLETE, WELL! It is this simple.

Do not keep looking with the "feelings" to find how much of GOOD (GOD, LOVE) IS PRESENT, for the "feelings" cannot tell you aught concerning REALITY.

Do get the other books and read them to discover what manner of God Love *is*. Herein is only GOODNESS, for LIFE IS GOODNESS ITSELF, *now* — there is no wait, no curse, no guilt anywhere where God is, and there is nowhere God is not!

In the book, NOW, please ponder well page 81:3-30; 111:10-22; 225:18-1.

So glad you are listening to the tapes which I made — they deal with REALITY ONLY wherein no "other mind" exists at all.

My best wishes to all the folks there who attended our

work.

                    Cordially,

Dear----------

Just completed talking with you and "doing my work" of
STARTING WITH THE ALLNESS OF ALL – STATING
ONLY THE ALLNESS OF ALL, THE OMNIPRESENCE OF
ALL, THE SUBSTANCE THAT IS ALL, THE ONLY THAT
IS ALL, THE ONE THAT IS ALL, THE AMNESS THAT IS
ALL, THE LIGHT THAT IS ALL, THE SUBSTANCE
WHICH LEAVES NO DARKNESS, NO CHALLENGE, NO
OPPOSITION EXISTENT – FOR WHERE ALL IS *ALL*,
THERE IS ONLY THE ALLNESS THAT *IS* THAT ALL,
AND THAT IS I. There is naught more, naught less, and this
leaves no little Joan or Alfred-mind anywhere, for any
reason, hence no such to try to defy Truth, excuse itself
because it is in error, or in any way to try to explain away
REALITY, THE WHOLE BEING THAT IS THE INFINITE
ONE THAT IS I.

You appear to always be SO SURPRISED that I am so
"severe" with you when you call. No matter how often you
go through this, you simply insist on VOICING YOUR
PHYSICAL AILMENTS, as though you were reciting your
troubles to a doctor. You could not possibly be more
complete if you went to the hospital and gave them daily
your complete physical history. WHY, JOAN, do you INSIST
ON DOING THIS, KNOWING AHEAD OF TIME THAT I
WILL CUT YOU OFF, WILL NOT LISTEN – BUT YOU DO
IT EVERY TIME WITHOUT EXCEPTION! WHY? It is for
this that I call you sharply to account, but it seems to roll off
you as if I did not say it! I have naught to do with GOD

BEING ALL, THE WHOLE IDENTITY YOU BE, so do not assume God is being "called down." NOT A BIT OF IT. TRUTH IS WHAT YOU BE. NO MATTER WHAT, TRUTH WILL FOREVER BE WHAT YOU BE. NAUGHT CAN OR WILL EVER CHANGE THIS. WHY KEEP TRYING TO FORCE GOD TO RELINQUISH HIS ALLNESS, JUST SO A JOAN-MIND CAN BE SOMETHING?

Now, in all honesty, if it is medical attention you want, I'd advise you to go to an endocrinologist and put yourself in his care! It is better to do that than to merely recite words, and go totally opposite to what OUR "WORK" URGES, INSISTS ON, DEMANDS, NAMELY, STATING THE SIN-GLENESS OF REALITY, AND NEVER, BUT NEVER, TALKING OF BODY, DISEASE, CONDITIONS, OR TRY-ING TO HEAL BODY, CHANGE THE PICTURE, ETC. I do not think it wise to merely "talk" words and let the house burn down when you CAN turn a hose on it. I feel you should either get down to the business of there being ONE ONLY, HENCE ALL PERFECTION PRESENT AS INFIN-ITE AWARENESS, BESIDE WHOM OR WHICH THERE IS NO OTHER, or take whatever "steps" seem to be demanded by a matter-sense-of-body. It is not right to sit half-way between, doing nothing but tolerating a slow or rapid decline! I do hope this is taken as it is meant. As you know, I am happy to help you whenever you need that help — but I am not yet where I can eat your meal and have your stomach filled with the food!

Fondly,

P.S. I do *not* advocate doctors, but I equally do not advocate the "continued complaints of disease" — either clear your decks as Mind-alone-*being* ALL, One, or else do what "seems" required if you assume "body" is your residence!

Dear----------

Yes, instead of keeping active, there does sometimes seem to be a great tendency to slow down when things do not go as they should, and one gets slower and slower, until he finally assumes he must stop. All this is due to assuming one lives IN AN IDEA, IS SURROUNDED BY THAT IDEA'S SHELL, AND IS DICTATED TO BY THAT IDEA! None of this has aught to do with FACT! But so long as we LET BODY, PHYSIQUE, DICTATE TO INTELLIGENCE, ACTION, FUNCTION, MIND, SELF, telling Consciousness "what It can do," when It can do it, how, where and with what limitations, then rest assured one is listening to body-material-physique, and not STARTING, STATING, AND STAYING WHOLLY ALERT *AS* MIND, ACTION, BEING, FUNCTION, ALIVENESS WHOLLY ALIVE TO BEING ALL, THE ONLY, THE ALONE, THE ALL-ONE SELF that knows no otherness, is touched by no otherness, is dictated to by no otherness, and is not transferred to a "thing" by some sort of witchcraft or belief in otherness!

Should aught argue you are within it, and that FREEDOM OF ACTION, FUNCTION, is threatened, curtailed, stopped, then AS MIND, OPERATE AS THE WHOLE UNCHALLENGED ONE THAT BEING IS! Do not sit down and "wait" for a healing of some sort, or for a change of an optical or sense picture! ACT AS ACTION ITSELF WHICH IS UNCHALLENGED, UNOPPOSED, UNRESTRICTED! Do not give in to restrictions, whether of one cane, two canes, a wheelchair, a physique, a specific spot in a specific room, or

what! MIND IS UNCONTAINED AND FREE TO BE
ABOUT ITS BUSINESS OF ALLNESS. THIS IS YOUR
IDENTITY, AND THE SOLE IDENTITY FOREVER! It
cannot be put aside, sidetracked, challenged or stopped!
There simply is naught to argue back when we STATE FACT
AND STICK THEREWITH — not just "saying the words."
CONSCIOUSNESS IS NOT CURTAILED, AND CON-
SCIOUSNESS AWARE OF ITSELF IS THE TOTAL IDEN-
TITY I AM. THERE IS NONE BESIDE!

The item we term "body" is ABSOLUTELY UNRELAT-
ED TO MIND! Life is unrelated to "body." Mind is what I
am. Life is what I am. "Body" has nothing whatever to do
with Life, with Consciousness, with Mind! Frankly, I never
do any work with "body," for "body," or because of
"body." I leave "body" wholly alone, for IT HAS NO
RELATIONSHIP TO AMNESS, ISNESS, AWARENESS,
CONSCIOUS LIFE, IDENTITY. "Body" has no Substance,
no Action, no Function, no Value, no Worth, hence why give
"it" so much attention, service, thought, adoration, alarm,
panic, or consideration? IT IS SPIRIT THAT IS ALL, IS
LIFE, IS MIND, IS CONSCIOUSNESS, IS IDENTITY, IS
SUBSTANCE, IS OMNIPRESENT OMNIPOTENCE WISELY
BEING ITS ENTIRE SELF! This, and THIS ONLY, is where
I "work." I give no more "consideration" or "thought" to
"body," than I do to a teacup, a violet, a fleck of dust
blowing across the desert! "Wherein is "body" to be
accounted of?" It is SPIRIT ONLY THAT IS MY SELF, MY
ALLNESS, MY IDENTITY, MY INFINITY, MY ETERNAL
SELFHOOD. Just because Mind can this moment, this NOW,
think a thought, so what? It does not MAKE MIND
BECOME MIND, ALL, LIFE, SELF, for Mind is already the

WHOLENESS OF THE WHOLE ONE INDIVIDUAL I THAT IS ALL, and there is naught beside, none beside, nowhere beside, nowhen beside! Therefore, I CAN AND DO ACT IN ACCORD WITH WHAT I AM and not as a "body" for I AM NOT BODY. I AM TOTAL PERFECTION IN ACTION, AND I ACT IT! I will not, do not, and CANNOT "LISTEN TO BODY," FOR NO "THOUGHT" CAN TALK! (See BACHELOR GOD, pages 99 and 100).

Fondly,

Dear----------

Thanks for your letter and will try to answer it briefly. To quote from your letter, you say: "In Reality I am Lois, all that she is, is me, etc., etc." Rather, you should begin always, let me repeat, *ALWAYS* with the ALLNESS OF LOVE, LIFE, MIND, AWARENESS (or whatever term you wish to use for Spirit, All!). AS ONLY *ALL* IS ALL, THE ONE ALONE INFINITE OMNIPRESENT INTELLIGENCE, then of a certainty that very LIFE MUST BE I, FOR THERE CAN BE AND IS NO OTHER! The very ALIVENESS, CONSCIOUSNESS, AWARENESS YOU NOW KNOW, EXPERIENCE, BE, is the SOLE INFINITE ONE BEING ITSELF! There is no otherness at all possible. Then, of a certainty, EVERY THOUGHT (thing, item, idea, body, or whatever term you wish to call a CONCEPTION) is conceived BY MIND, IN MIND, AND IS KNOWN TO NO OTHER THAN MIND. As with an author, whatever that idea (thing, body) appears to do, is it not the author who is really "doing" it all? There is no stuff to that idea, thought, is there? There is no life, no substance, no purpose within that idea, is there? Of course not! And so, even in our daily round, thanks to

AWARENESS, we include many ideas, things, including the body you've been calling Lois — but each of these items is but an idea, a conception, a thought within the MIND THAT IS I-AM! Nowhere else can it be found! And if it were not for CONSCIOUSNESS, there would be no AWARENESS OF THE IDEA-THING AT ALL!

There is no Life in the character-item-idea-body-thing-thought. Each thought is IN LIFE, but never the other way around — and no thought EVER changes into some-other-item-thought! To Mind a thought is existent, real, to It! But this does not mean there is any stuff to the idea. If you were not CONSCIOUSNESS, you could not be aware of music, yet music is abstract — but it is REAL TO INTELLIGENCE, is it not? However, if you were un-Conscious, would there be music to you? It is not the ears that "hear" the music, but INTELLIGENCE, AWARENESS, CONSCIOUSNESS!

THAT CONSCIOUSNESS CALLED SPIRIT, MIND, LOVE, ALIVENESS, IS YOUR SOLE IDENTITY, THE ONLY I-OMNIPRESENCE EXISTENT, INCLUSIVE OF ITS UNIVERSE OF THOUGHTS — UTTERLY UNDIMENSIONAL, WITHOUT BORDER, MEASUREMENT, LIMITATION, AND TO THIS ONE AWARENESS, THIS ABSOLUTE INFINITY, THERE IS NO OTHERNESS AT ALL. Hence, one of Mind's thoughts-ideas is NOT MIND, NOT THE INFINITE ALL-INCLUSIVE AWARENESS, INTELLIGENCE THAT IS DOING THE CONCEIVING-PERCEIVING, *BEING.* An idea is just that — idea. I urge you to stop confusing a thought with the INTELLIGENCE YOU BE, THE ONE CONCEIVING THAT THOUGHT AND INCLUDING IT!

Your husband is but an item of which you are aware, even

right now! But the INTELLIGENCE WHICH YOU BE is the ONE INCLUDING THAT IDEA. That same MIND THAT IS I, INCLUDES THE BODY-ITEM CALLED Lois.

Hope the above proves "helpful" to you.

Sincerely,

Dear----------

It was good to hear from you. Yes, I also wish you might be at the Hollywood Seminar this fall.

Now, Margaret, I have given you some help "on the house" — on this witchcraft situation. It should totally disappear.

Please look up the following: BACHELOR GOD 96:1-13. THAT WHICH IS 120:15-25; 180:1-2, 6-9, 15-24.

Remember, all witchcraft or devil, evil, void, influence, possession, obsession, comes wholly and only due to theology, religious teaching! It all is a matter of church, and there is no such. You have no mind to believe it or to have such a belief. SPIRIT IS THE ONLY MIND THAT YOU BE — IT IS NOT EVEN A MIND YOU POSSESS — IT IS WHAT YOU BE!

Also, please look up: THAT WHICH IS 219:8-22, 26-28; 221:25-6; 223:1-17; 225:1-9. Dig at all of these till they have genuine meaning to you, then when you declare them, you WILL MEAN THEM, FOR THEY ARE POWER — YOU "SPEAK" AND IT IS DONE, FOR YOU (MIND) ARE AUTHORITY ITSELF, AND THERE IS NAUGHT TO DENY OR CHALLENGE THIS. Let's get busy with Fact!

Sincerely,

Dear----------

So good to hear from you and have given you the boost.

Please, in BACHELOR GOD, ponder well the citations below. Read them out loud if you can, and then define each term used, and dig at the definition until what you state has meaning for you. You will then find there is no room anywhere, no place anywhere, no mind anywhere, and no lack anywhere to give trouble, have trouble, know trouble, talk trouble, claim a history for trouble, or even a "healing" of trouble — for where IN THE WHOLE OF OMNIPRESENT WHOLENESS, NOWNESS, THE PRESENT TOTALLY ALIVE TO BEING ABSOLUTELY SATISFIED WITH ITS OWN ALLNESS EVERYWHERE (AND THERE IS NAUGHT ELSE AT ALL) — WHERE WITHIN THIS AWARENESS, THIS I-IDENTITY YOU BE, CAN THERE BE OTHERNESS? WHAT CAN IT SAY? TO WHOM CAN IT SAY IT? WHY SHOULD IT SAY IT WHEN "IT" ITSELF DOES NOT EVEN EXIST — AND THAT TO WHICH "IT" PRETENDS TO "SAY IT" DOES NOT EVEN EXIST?

Guess that'll hold "lack" for a spell, eh?

Here are the citations: BACHELOR GOD 214:13-27; 223:8-20; 229:5-24; 129:12-7; 66:24-1; 131:10-29 on next page. Also, go over the August, 1967, Monthly Letter carefully.

The length of time has naught to do with any problem. Can you say that because folks believed 2 plus 3 made 100, and they believed it for centuries, that would make it so, or make it harder to start with Fact RIGHT NOW? FOR REMEMBER, ONLY — YES, *ONLY* TRUTH IS TRUE, so any disease is a lie now and forever, therefore, it is not real, so it is not present, so don't try to do anything to it, but keep thought centered WHOLLY ON REALITY AS SPIRIT KNOWS ITSELF TO BE.

Do drop me a line — know you will find ALL IS ALL
ALREADY, RIGHT NOW — AM IS, AND IS AM RIGHT
NOW, AND NOW IS AM, IS IS, IS ALL, IS THE SELF YOU
BE, AND THERE IS NONE BESIDE. Don't try to see this by
way of the senses, the table leg, the street bus, etc. The senses
have no sense to start with, so can't make or know sense.
Only TRUTH IS TRUE, AND IS SO NOW.

Love always to you all,

Dear----------

Your letter just reached me. Now, concerning the "seeming problem" — do not start out with a daughter, a runaway
child, or with any blame for anyone, or anything. That is
merely aiding error! Rather, FIRST STATE THE ALLNESS
OF THE ONE OMNIPRESENT MIND, THE WHOLE OF
WHOLENESS, THE TOTALITY OF WHAT LOVE IS! Then
begin to define what your statement MEANS in its deep
sense. Behold that WHERE ALL, WHERE GOODNESS,
WHERE LOVE IS TOTALLY PRESENT, there cannot be
any trouble at all. The difficulty is never what it seems — it is
merely that you turn your back on WHAT SPIRIT *IS* —
WHAT LOVE, PURITY, SINGLE GOODNESS *IS*, and then
you seem to have two minds. You no longer operate AS
POWER ITSELF, PURITY ITSELF, WHOLENESS ITSELF,
which is the ONLY AUTHORITY. You find yourself merely
repeating words, meanwhile looking for "results" which
never come!

TRUTH, THE WHOLENESS OF PURE LOVE, IS TO-
TALLY PRESENT RIGHT HERE NOW. WITHIN THIS ONE
AND ONLY MIND, THIS ONE AND ONLY IDENTITY
YOU BE THIS VERY MOMENT, THERE CAN BE NO

LITTLE MIND OR MINDS, NO FEARS, NO LACK, NO TROUBLE AT ALL. You must DISCIPLINE YOURSELF TO STICK WITH WHAT YOU STATE LOVE TO BE, NAMELY ALL, WHEREIN THERE IS ONLY THE INFINITE ACTION AND FUNCTION THAT IS GOODNESS ITSELF, SELF-SATISFACTION ITSELF, HAPPINESS ITSELF, JOY AND CONTENTMENT ITSELF. This shuts off any error, for it leaves it no place, no identity, nowhere to do its would-be "work," no victim of it, no need to try to get rid of it, or to overcome it, or to try to "demonstrate against it," for WHERE LOVE, GOD, IS ALL, THERE IS HEAVEN AT HAND, HENCE NO HELL AT ALL, NO LACK AT ALL, AND NO WOULD-BE MIND TO DENY LOVE! It is not your daughter that you need "think" of, but it is WHOLLY THAT YOU MUST KEEP YOUR *ENTIRE* THOUGHT AND *ATTENTION* ON THE ALLNESS OF PURE UNCHALLENGED LOVE RIGHT HERE NOW. Don't do this to "bring about a change in the picture," for then you are only fooling yourself — you are still working with, and for, evil, error, lack! IT IS ONLY TRUTH THAT IS TRUE, SO STICK WITH TRUTH WHOLLY — DON'T JUST SAY THE WORDS, BUT REALLY GET DOWN TO BUSINESS AND SEE THAT WHAT YOU "SAY" CONCERNING *ALL*, IS REALLY SO RIGHT NOW. This leaves you with no problem. Don't try to "outline" *HOW* it will "work out," for that is still sticking with the error! WHERE ALL IS ALL, there is no error to "work out." Let us be HONEST WITH LOVE, and there can be no contrary mind or minds anywhere, anywhen, anywhy! If you really "love," you will DO THIS AS WE POINT OUT HERE. To keep on worrying, is to hate LOVE, refuse LOVE! In BACHELOR GOD,

ponder well 127:15-25, and really "use" it!
Cordially,

Dear----------
Was amazed at what you wrote about the "happenings" at
your house — witchcraft, and nothing else — the superstition
that ails us all of believing another power can be! It has
nothing to do with a "you" or "me," but is all due to the
"time-track" which has no existence at all. We must really
"dig" at what REALITY IS — HERE, NOW, AND ALL OF
IT. There is no prophecy to be filled, Bible-be-hanged! There
can be no upset of NOW, operating as physical states,
conditions, whether as body physical, or nature, inventions,
etc. There is ONLY ONE PRESENT MIND IN OPERATION
NOW, AND THAT IS SELF-SATISFIED FOR THERE IS
ONLY GOODNESS, AND NAUGHT BESIDE CAN BE. How
I have to stick with this. Sometimes it seems as if the lid was
going to blow off something — and sometimes it seems it has
— but sticking with ONE ALL, where, what, why, how can
there be aught but GOODNESS PRESENT! This is not
chatter — it is FACT ONLY.

You see, it is this argument that electricity, the so-called
"vapid fury of mortal mind," and all the rest of it, has
become an actual part of religion, daily belief, general
opinion on the part of present-day humanity. We fall heir to
this if we are not constant with the Fact that there is ONLY
THE IMMEDIACY OF NOW, ISNESS, BEING ONLY,
WHEREIN NAUGHT IS STIRRED, OR CAN STIR, FOR
THERE IS ONLY GOODNESS, HENCE NO LACK (MAN) —
NO EVIL (ABSENCE OF SPIRIT CALLED HUMANITY) —
NO LOSS OF NOW (CALLED TIME — THIS YEAR). I hope

to bring more of this out in the Seminar in Hollywood and have notes already made on it. We are being pushed about too much by strikes, color riots, inclement weather, politics, and such — all part of the same would-be evil (absence of NOW!). Let us really get down to business! There are times when it seems that I know a lot of things without being in anyway "told," but never for any "wrong" purpose. It is never "personal," but to me it is like being proficient at the piano — suddenly you are acutely aware of a discord somewhere that your so-called "inner ear" picks up, even if you do not "locate it geographically," but it is never personal — merely a suggestion that there can be TOTAL HARMONY *and* discord at the same spot, and you know this is not true, so you may mention it out loud merely to clear your own thought. Sometimes people give you credit for being super-sensitive, or think you have peeked into their innermost thoughts, but that is not so. You merely are alert to it for it is contrary to Fact, and music-wise, you clear the decks by being like the conductor in an orchestra — he hits the stand and says, "Folks, let's play that over, and remember, in the clarinet section there is someone making a noise he calls music — watch it, please!"

There is nothing supernatural, nor overly bright as a human about me — and I'll be thrilled when there is not a seeming vestige of humanity here at all — for right NOW THERE IS ONLY SPIRIT AND THAT IS THE GOODNESS I BE. Yet, I still "seem" to breathe, eat, travel, talk, sleep and so on, but THE SELF DOES NONE OF THIS, AND THE SELF ALONE IS WHO AND WHAT BE-I.

I'm so thrilled you both love the new book. That has "helped" me more than you know, and I know you'd tell me the fact. I do not want to merely rewrite my older books. I want this to be new, fresh, filled with "guts," and all to the point.

Love to you both.

Fondly,

Dear----------

I urge you, do not keep looking via the senses as to how "well" or "active" or "good" INFINITE INTELLIGENCE "FEELS." It can't be done, and if you use the senses as measuring rods whereby to discover the degree of perfection, or lack of perfection, of THE ALONE SINGLE MIND THAT LIFE IS, THE VERY MIND THAT IS THE WHOLE SUBSTANCE YOU BE, you are certainly confused and working with metaphysics — an attempt to "improve" or "progress, grow, develop, evolve," and all such nonsense!

We urge you to STATE WHAT INFINITE TOTALITY IS, then begin digging at the definition of the words you have voiced, and find out if they mean aught to you, what they mean, why, how, where, when, and if they are so — and if so, what else can there be, where else can there be, who else can there be, and with what is all the non-knowing taking place in a non-place, by a non-One that is non-Existence?

Leave your waterworks alone, leave the whole body alone, leave your worries alone, leave your education alone, and GET BUSY WITH ANY STATEMENT OF THE ALLNESS OF ALL, THE OMNIPRESENCE THAT IS EXISTENCE ITSELF, THE WHOLE OF ACTUALITY, TRUTH, REAL-ITY, AS IT IS. Find out something concerning FACT, and stop being so concerned with all the junk that denies Fact, is not Fact, knows no Fact, deals in not-Fact, and in Fact is

NOT FACT AT ALL! Our sole concern is with WHAT IS, WITH TRUTH, WITH REALITY, FOR THAT ALONE IS LIFE, IS NOW, IS AMNESS, IS BEING, IS ACTUALITY, IS THAT WHICH IS! All that the senses pretend to sense via a sack of liquid called a physical shape, is nonsense, and deals totally with a history, time, guesswork, a past, or that-which-is-NOT!

Stop trying to lay off the old so you can put on the new. THERE IS ONLY THAT WHICH IS, HENCE IT IS SO NEW THAT NAUGHT CAN BE "NEWER!"

What can be more new than N O W! And when you deal ONLY IN NOW, you cannot mess about in "was," will-be, and all the junk that "body" as a physique wholly depends on. Leave "body" alone. You'll do with it and for it what has to be done, but aside from that, leave it out of your thought, and you can do this only by STATING FACT, AND DIGGING AT INFINITY. This leaves no time, and it leaves you with no idleness with which to ponder aches, pains, stiff joints, stumblings, bumblings, worries over shapes, forms, contours, or waterworks and such! TRUTH IS MUCH MORE WORTHY OF YOUR THOUGHT than aches, pains, squeeks and squawks! When you weigh the ALMIGHTY in the balance of NOW, do you find your pains are so much more entitled to your attention than INFINITY, REALITY, GLORY, WISDOM?

In BACHELOR GOD, ponder well 63:3-2 next page; 58:14-28 next page; 158:6-1. These will give you something worthwhile to chew on.

Cordially

Dear----------

Yours arrived yesterday and I am giving you the "help."

Please ponder well in POWER 155:2-11; 121:4-7; 67:1-6; 66:13-33. In FORUMS, read 155:15-20; 154:5-21; 138:15-21; 126:19-26; 115:6-9 on next page; 102:24-8.

I am sure these will "help" you see what the so-called *real* "problem" is, namely, another mind, of which there is none! We become so upset over the difficulty that seems to interfere with our free movement, that we begin to hack or kick at it, rather than sticking to EXISTENCE. Existence MUST BE SINGLE, WHOLE. There can be no holes in It, nor any "mind" to testify to Its absence! If EXISTENCE WERE ABSENT, THERE WOULD BE NAUGHT!

YOU ARE NOT YOUR BODY! You have to cling to "another" mind to assume "body" to be your identity! Certainly SPIRIT, YOUR SOLE SELF, DOES NOT CLAIM ONE OF ITS THOUGHTS (BODIES) TO BE IT! So, you must forsake, deny, your I-IDENTITY (LIFE, AWARENESS, INTELLIGENCE) IN ORDER TO ARGUE, HENCE "SENSE OR FEEL" VIA A BODY! Starting with ONE INFINITE EXISTENCE, LIFE, BEING, INTELLIGENCE OR OMNI-PRESENCE, you simply cannot *be*, nor *have* a contrary, an ABSENCE-SENSE (dis-eased sense) of Existence. To REAL-ITY, ALL IS REAL AND THERE IS NAUGHT MISSING FROM ITS WHOLENESS. IT IS UNCHANGED IN ITS ENTIRETY, INSEPARABILITY, COMPLETENESS!

If I could only make it clear to you that you do NOT SUFFER *FROM* A "PROBLEM" OF BODY OR AUGHT ELSE — BUT RATHER YOU *SUFFER* (PERMIT, ADMIT, ACCEPT, CLING TO) ANOTHER MIND! This is your "only enemy" — but in REALITY there is no such at all. ONLY REALITY IS REAL. Where then do you come by another mind which testifies wholly to what is NOT Real? There

annot be two of you, each being INTELLIGENT, EXIS-
TENT! If One is not THE SOLE ONE, there is naught — for
he "false" one is not one at all. It pretends via assumption,
o be — but to Intelligence? NEVER! So, all you "need" do
s to state any FACT OF REALITY, then begin digging and
pull the statement apart to find out if YOU REALLY
ACCEPT IT AS FACT. IS IT TRUE, REAL, PRESENT,
AND IF SO, CAN THERE ALSO EXIST A CONTRADIC-
TION THERETO? And soon you'll be so thrilled at what you
are "discovering" concerning BEING (YOUR ACTUAL
PRESENT FULL CHANGELESS IDENTITY) that you are
no longer listening to nor enacting an "if" or a "refusal" of
Truth! Sooner or later you'll be forced to admit Truth, for
TRUTH *BEING*, is your PRESENT IDENTITY! You can't
change it. Like the prodigal, the nonsense is nonsense NOW,
so why admit it into a place it cannot occupy, and then try
to rid yourself of it, when in REALITY IT IS NOT THERE
NOW?

KEEP THOUGHT ON REALITY, NOT ON "BODY"
AND BODY'S CONDITIONS! Body has NO CONDITION,
NO STATUS, NO PLACE — IT IS BUT A "THOUGHT" IN
MIND!

My best to you, as always,

Dear----------

Will try to briefly answer some of the questions you have
raised. (The answers are all in the books, as I'm sure you
know, but sometimes pointing them out makes them stand
forth more clearly.)

It makes no difference how long a lie has been around, it
is still a lie. No matter how long dirt has been on your

windows, it washes off the moment you wash them. No matter how long you assume 2x2 equals 50, the discovery that it is 4 ONLY, precludes it ever WAS 50! And so it is with those in your household!

THERE IS NO CAUSE, NO EFFECT. THERE IS ONLY, I REPEAT, ONLY INFINITE OMNIPRESENCE BEING. This ONE MIND PRECLUDES any other mind, hence any of the "junk" therein! And certainly SPIRIT IS NOT "SUF-FERING" FROM OR WITH ANY OF THE CONDITIONS YOU MENTION. So, if not Spirit, who or what other mind exists TO suffer? NONE! To argue "yes," you must first deny TRUTH, CONSCIOUS FACT!

SPIRIT BEING THE ONLY MIND, cannot know fear, for fear is but ignoring the ALLNESS of All! And as there is NO OTHER MIND EXISTENT, what, who or whatever knows fear, and who or what is saying so? By what Authority? Certainly not by DIVINE AUTHORITY, for REALITY BEING REAL, PRECLUDES UN-REALNESS, IM-PERFEC-TION!

You cannot "drop duality" for IT DOESN'T EXIST TO BE DROPPED, HANDLED, OVERCOME, WIPED OUT, SIDE-STEPPED, OR AVOIDED! All there is, IS LOVE, SINGLENESS, ALLNESS, EXISTENCE BEING WHAT IS! As for being backward, retarded, slow, "different," not "normal," etc., you must start with something other than ONE ABSOLUTE REALITY, hence you "suffer" because you are being prodigal, robbing Self, denying Truth, going without, or outside of Reality! Such is impossible, really, but it seems to operate so long as you insist on seeing lies instead of Truth. THERE IS ONLY SPIRIT PRESENT, OMNIS-CIENTLY BEING ITSELF, I, AND THIS ALONE IS

'NORMAL," THE STATUS QUO, and Intelligence has never been elsewhere! No "brain" has an I.Q. — no human has such for SPIRIT BEING ALL, THERE IS NAUGHT HUMAN ANYWHERE, AND NO MIND TO CLAIM, ARGUE, SEE, OR REACT AS SUCH! This is Truth, Fact, RIGHT NOW, HERE, ALWAYS.

You are so right, REALITY ALONE BEING ALL, there can be NO "FATHER" OR "CHILD," FOR SUCH WOULD MEAN DUALITY! So, religion and its devil-curses are out the window! And Spirit does not say, "Thank you, Spirit!" This is also a hangover of gratitude from a child to a father for goodies received! GOODNESS ITSELF IS SPIRIT BEING, THE VERY SOLE IDENTITY YOU *BE*! LIVE THE LIFE THAT YOU BE — DON'T MERELY BABBLE WORDS OF SO-CALLED THANKS, FOR THEY ARE TOTALLY HOLLOW, VOID OF SINCERITY AND GENUINENESS SO LONG AS ONE OPERATES AS "OTHER-THAN-WHAT-HE-IS!" SUPPLY is who and what MIND IS, YOUR ACTUAL SELF NOW, INCLUSIVE OF EVERY GOOD IDEA (thought-body-thing!) But none of these "think" or know aught any more than the letters of the alphabet! You include those bodies (family) WITHIN MIND!

Ponder in NOW 211:8-14; 197:21-26; 193:12-5 163:17-23; 157:3-23; 104:23-6. These are sure to "help" you. Read them aloud, pull them apart, then LIVE THE TRUTH YOU UTTER!

Cordially,

Dear----------

First, I'd like to correct a slight error — I am NOT a D.D. My title of Doctor is because I hold a degree as a dentist, as well as a medical doctor. I am not a theologian. Thought you would prefer to know.

I have given you the "help" you requested. If you are very familiar with my writings, you know I never give more than a single "treatment." If further assistance seems required, it must be requested. You see, as I have tried to point out, INFINITE INTELLIGENCE ALONE IS THE SOLE PRESENCE, THE ONLY MIND THERE IS, THE ACTUAL LIFE YOU BE THIS MOMENT! Does Truth, CHANGELESS SPIRIT, require assistance, "healing," or is it an assumption of something beside Spirit that seems ailing? You see, we are either trying to "heal" God, or we are trying to heal something beside God, and in both cases we are starting out by robbing God of HIS PRESENT, UNCHANGING TOTAL ALLNESS!

The trouble is not with a body, not with the eyes, not with organs, but always due to our ignoring the ALLNESS OF OMNIPRESENCE!

Where SPIRIT IS, Heaven is. There is nowhere SPIRIT (GOD) IS NOT, SO THERE IS NOWHERE HEAVEN IS NOT. Where, then, in HEAVEN do you find evil, lack, Satan, hell, the grave? You see, to try to find evil (lack) anywhere, one must first DENY SPIRIT ITS ALLNESS, ITS TOTAL AND PERFECT PRESENCE! In other words, to have sickness anywhere, one must first ROB GOD OF HIS OWN ALLNESS, DENY TRUTH, REFUTE FACT, AND THUS PLAY PRODIGAL TO HIS OWN IDENTITY!

Remember, the prodigal did not suffer because it was necessary, but because HE REFUSED TO BE COMPLETELY HONEST WITH GOD'S ALLNESS, OMNIPRESENCE, SOLE TOTALITY! He started off by denying THE SOLE SELF,

ignoring OMNIACTIVE LOVE, PURITY, SINGLENESS.
Instead, he insisted on otherness, an ALL that was less than
ALL! And it was this very DENIAL OF LOVE'S ALLNESS,
PRESENCE, SINGLENESS, POWER, AWARENESS, that
caused him to wander about "in far lands" seeking for the
WHOLENESS THAT WAS ALWAYS WITH HIM! And as
soon as he "came to HIMSELF," he was free! He could have
been free from the very start had he been TOTALLY
HONEST WITH THE OMNIPRESENCE OF SPIRIT! But
rather, he insisted on "judging after the seeing of the eye and
the hearing of the ear" — insisted on judging "after his
senses" and that made no sense at all!

I urge you to please take the book, "THAT WHICH IS,"
and turn to page 144:8-24 on page 147. Especially note
144:17-20. When you read it, please use the word, "ALL," in
place of the word, "GOD." And then ask yourself if you
HONESTLY ADMIT, WHOLLY, WITHOUT RESERVA-
TION OR EVASION, THAT SPIRIT, LOVE, PURE SIN-
GLENESS IS TRULY ALL, THE ALONE ONE, THE ONLY
"BESIDE WHOM THERE IS NAUGHT ELSE!" Or do you
still go on thinking of a body as your identity, your self, and
thinking of a "god" way out yonder somewhere upon whom
you can call? Just HOW MUCH HONOR, GLORY, GOOD-
NESS, PRESENCE, POWER, AWARENESS, WHOLENESS,
TOTALITY, INFINITY, SINGLENESS, do you admit GOD
TO ENJOY RIGHT HERE NOW AS THE ONLY PRES-
ENCE?

Cordially,

Dear----------

It was so good to hear from you. Yes, I can well see why

you might miss your friend — such a dear and so in earnest. Far too often, though, a personality plays an important role in one's search, and there appears to be too much "person" and their human point of view rather than attention to REALITY, SPIRIT ALONE, PURE SINGLENESS. As you so well know, OUR WORK IS CONSCIOUS AWARENESS IN ACTION AS THE ONLY, THE ALONE, THE ONE PURE UNCHALLENGED SELF-THAT-IS-I *being*, wherein no human, no history, no dream or otherness has identity or place.

At times in this work, going about as I do, I find again and again where a "person" who develops a following, insists on personal plaudits, recognition as a leader, and they would force others, if possible, to follow where "they lead, read what they are told to read, attend Spirit only as the 'director' instructs, etc." Truly it is a case of the blind leading the blind, all in a mistaken sense of "doing God service," (or so they claim). Yet, starting with FACT HERE NOW, THE ONLY ONE, I cannot even say that "such" exists anywhere where Spirit IS (AND THERE IS NOWHERE SPIRIT IS NOT!) — so where is even the pretense? Nowhere, ever!

Am interested in your trip to Africa. Many of our books are now being sold in Nigeria and I understand a few are being translated into the local language.

Nice to hear from you!

Sincerely,

Dear----------

In answer to your recent letter — instead of reciting the various errors about the body, IN TRUTH WE DO NOT CARE A HOOT ABOUT THE BODY, HOW IT ACTS OR REACTS, WHAT IT DOES OR DOES NOT DO, WHERE IT

IS LOCATED, HOW IT SMELLS, TASTES AND SO ON —
BECAUSE ONLY REALITY IS REAL, AND IS OUR SOLE
IDENTITY RIGHT HERE NOW!

WHERE IS TRUTH TO YOU? WHAT IS REALITY TO
YOU? WHAT ARE YOU? WHO ARE YOU? WHAT IS
LIFE? WHAT IS MIND? WHAT IS SUBSTANCE? IS
REALITY ONLY WORDS TO YOU? DO YOU NOT STOP
TO DISCOVER WHAT THE WORDS MEAN WHEN YOU
DECLARE THEM? ARE YOU SPEAKING TRUTH? IF SO,
FOR WHAT POSSIBLE REASON DO YOU THEN DELIB-
ERATELY AND CONSISTENTLY DENY THE MEANING
OF THOSE WORDS? IF WHAT YOU SAY IS FACT, THEN
ANY REFERENCE TO "BODY" IS FICTIONAL, UNTRUE,
AND OF NO POSSIBLE CONCERN TO YOU AT ALL!

SPIRIT IS THE SOLE SUBSTANCE OF THE IDENTITY
YOU *BE*. Body is a mere thought right now being conceived.
How then can you constantly talk only about "body" when
it is brand new to Mind Itself? Where do you get another
identity with which to "foresee" what idea-body is "going to
be like," and begin to fore-tear it to pieces, disease it, groan
about it, declare it physical or organic, aged, disintegrating,
material and so on? THE SOLE SUBSTANCE IS MIND,
INTELLIGENCE, AND IT CANNOT BE ILL, WOBBLY,
WEAK, INSECURE, LAME, TROUBLED — AND AS
THERE IS *ONLY* CONSCIOUSNESS-SUBSTANCE, WHERE
ARE YOU GOING TO FIND SOME "OLD" MATTER TO
WORRY OVER OR CLAIM IT BELONGS TO A BEV-
ERLY ? What you still persist in doing is practicing
Christian Science! You haven't gotten away from the old
grind of latching onto the "trouble," pinpointing its exact
location, declaring how it forces the body to react, and how

that, in turn, influences your "thinking and acting!" You are not PUTTING REALITY, ACTUALITY, FACT, BEFORE YOU AS THE SOLE BEING THAT IS THE IDENTITY-I-AM! If you say you do, then let me ask you, IS SPIRIT ILL! IS IT WOBBLY, IN PAIN, DISCOURAGED, UPSET, ARGUING WITH ITSELF?

As for repeatedly asking yourself, "since Spirit is all, where is there a mind apart from Spirit that thinks it can have difficulty?" — this also is quoted, but it is NOT TRUTH, AND HAS NO MORE AUTHORITY THAN ASKING WHERE THERE IS A MIND TO HAVE 2x2 equals 40! You are still right down there on the Plain of Ono, debating, talking back to the error, rationalizing, trying to convince yourself via argument that there is no reason for trouble or difficulty, and always in connection with body! I am not "scolding" you, but am trying to wake you up as to why you do not manage to help yourself! You do NOT start with CONSCIOUS INTELLIGENCE *ONLY*. If you did, you'd not be still trying to heal a body. HE WHO STARTS WITH FACT ONLY (AND AS FACT ONLY IS FACT), CANNOT KEEP TALKING ABOUT A FLAT EARTH, A MISTAKE IN MATH, OR THAT THERE IS A SAVIOR, A GUILT, A BIRTH, A DEATH, A HEAVEN, A HELL, OR ANGELS AND DEVILS! To keep these items before you in your daily affairs is to believe in them, to operate within superstition.

AS ONLY WHAT ONE-ALONE IS, why talk about what is not THE PRESENT FACT CONCERNING THIS ONE SINGLE TOTALITY? Do you mean to tell me that you HONESTLY STAND BY THE FACT THERE IS ONLY SPIRIT PRESENT, ONLY WHOLENESS BEING, ONLY ALL HERE AS THE SINGLE IDENTITY CALLED"I?" Or do you still try to reason this out, see it as Beverly, apply the Truth, thus healing her?

You write, "I have asked myself over and over again," etc. This has nothing, repeat NOTHING in common with REALITY! You are asking a little mind, a personal sense, to agree concerning REALITY, INFINITY! It simply cannot, repeat, CANNOT do aught for you! But when we declare that SPIRIT IS ALL, and then dig this apart to see what the statement says, finding out the exact and full meaning of those words, and beholding that we have stated FACT AS FACT OMNIPRESENTLY IS, then this is what is so here, now! This precludes any would-be discussion with aught, concerning aught, in relationship with aught — no time, no when, no where! WE, FROM THIS MOMENT, ARE SPEAKING TRUTH AS TRUTH, FACT, *IS*, FOR THIS IS ALL THERE IS, SO HOW CAN WE "TALK OR CONSIDER, AFFIRM OR DENY, REPULSE OR CHANGE AUGHT BESIDE?" There simply is ONLY SPIRIT, MIND, INTELLIGENCE, SUBSTANCE, ACTUALITY PRESENT! Either this is thy IDENTITY, or you be not! Whatever you say concerning body, matter, physicality, physiology, fears, pains, and efforts, IS SHEER FICTION, and is at the expense of GLORYING IN THE JOY THAT BEING IS!

STARTING WITH ONLY REALITY AS REALITY IS, leaves no place for self-pity, discouragement, remembrance of a past, the collection of garbage down the years, hence, precludes any guilt, sin, trouble, or a recall of habit of any sort. SO LONG AS YOU STILL "REMEMBER THE PAST," AND RECALL HOW "LONG" YOU'VE BEEN STRUGGLING, HOW OLD YOU ARE, and such, YOU ARE NOT, REPEAT, NOT "STARTING WITH FACT," but are still trying to validate fiction!

In this work, we are not even remotely desirous to hear anything concerning body, for BODY IS ONLY A THOUGHT MIND IS NOW CONCEIVING. IT IS NOT IDENTITY, NOT MATTER, NOT ORGANIC OR PHYSICAL, NOT THE DWELLING PLACE OF A BABY SOUL! As Intelligence is not concerned with "body," HOW CAN YOU, THE AMNESS THAT IS I, SAY YOU ARE CONCERNED, AND THEN TRY TO PROVE YOUR CONCERN BY LOOKING TO BODY, AT BODY, TALKING ABOUT BODY, WATCHING BODY, DECLARING THAT IT IS BODY THAT CONTROLS YOU AND IS YOUR MASTER?

I have given you the "help" you requested. See NOW, 225:13-1; 239:7-10; 241:6-11; 249:15-19, 21-30; 173:11-23.

Am sure if you really dig at these, finding out what you are saying when you read aloud — seeing it as FACT, and sticking with FACT (for you ARE STUCK WITH IT!) — of a certainty you'll see that you have nothing else left with which to complain, suffer with or for error, physicality, humanity, the-product-of-biology-and-gender, that would-be reproduction of mortals, or any of the nonsense that fiction would present in the realm of make-believe! From now on, WORK WITH FACT and leave fiction alone. It's only when you try to substitute fiction for the FACT that you appear confused!

I must get at all my other work now — but sticking with FACT, we just keep LIVING NOW ONLY, and soon the jobs are done!

Fondly,

Dear----------

In answer to your last letter — regardless of what the

picture seems to be, one cannot "launch forth" therefrom. To do so means that we accept the picture as a REALITY, as a FACT, hence as TRUTH! To assume any picture of trouble, no matter by what name called, is to assume that trouble is one and the same with TRUTH, FACT, hence with GOD, SPIRIT, LOVE, SINGLENESS, *INFINITE BEING!* It must be obvious to you that "trouble" and TOTAL JOY, UNHAMPERED INFINITY are NOT THE SAME! So which is UNCHANGING TRUTH, FACT, REALITY — WHICH IS FACT and which is fiction? The "picture" is the fiction! And what does one have to do with fiction? NOTHING AT ALL except to stop accepting it as the FACT in place of WHAT THE FACT ETERNALLY IS!

What I am trying to make clear is — we do not "monkey" with the picture that your five senses testify to. Remember, I told you recently about a fellow being hypnotized into thinking he is a dog — does he not immediately appear to have four paws, a tail, fleas, mange, and talk with a bark? Does he not "see" a bone on the floor, a saucer of milk and such? BUT HOW CAN HE SEE WHAT IS NOT THERE? Because he does not stick with WHAT *IS* THERE, NAMELY, FACT, TRUTH, REALITY — ONE MIND, ONE LIFE, ONE TOTAL I-IDENTITY WHICH IS SPIRIT BEING ITSELF! Don, do you assume SPIRIT, GOD, LIFE, AWARENESS (the ACTUAL SELF OF YOU) is in trouble, in jail, under sentence, resentful, falsely accused? Or is SPIRIT ALL, WHOLE, THAT WHEREIN NAUGHT BESIDE CAN BE? Would you try to "heal" or set God "free?" NO! Why? Because THE SINGLE ONE ALONE IS NOT BOUND, NOT FACING OTHERS, NOT SHARING OR COEXISTING WITH ITS OWN LACK, ITS OWN ABSENCE OF ITSELF.

How can It when IT IS NEVER ABSENT, NEVER DIVIDED
INTO MANY, NEVER BESET BY A DEVIL, EVIL, LACK,
LIMITATION, FEAR, IGNORANCE AND THE LIKE?

So long as you cling to the argument that you are what
your senses tell you, namely, "man," a human, a mortal,
one-among-many, you will find that trouble is closer than
your skin! But the moment you turn WHOLLY, HONEST-
LY, ENTIRELY to LIFE, SPIRIT, GOODNESS ITSELF
PRESENT AS THE ONE ALONE ALL, then you no longer
judge by what you see, feel, hear and so on! Even when these
senses try to overwhelm you, stick with what GOODNESS,
LOVE, SINGLENESS knows Itself to be, for this is YOUR
SOLE IDENTITY NOW AND ALWAYS! Spirit cannot be
jailed on any charges — how could Intelligence be thrown in
jail? If you assume you are either that dog, or that you are
the bone the dog is told to "see, chew on, then bury," you
are in jail mentally, believing every whim of nonsense that
blows!

There is no one in the world who assumes he is a body,
and that life is within it along with a small mentality, but
what is IN JAIL! I know of naught that can so imprison one!
And the church says he must serve out a whole lifetime
within that flesh, subject to all sorts of restrictions! But this
is merely the picture — merely that painting done by
ignorance, painted in utter darkness.

But Don, we are NOT TRYING TO CHANGE THE
PICTURE — rather, start with WHAT SPIRIT IS HERE AND
NOW, FOR THIS IS THE SELF ALREADY. This PERFECT
SELF YOU BE does not need help, for it is LIFE ITSELF IN
ACTION. Don't confuse this SELF with a body-sense, for
that is what the whole world is doing, and all of them are in

he prison of fear, greed, ignorance, darkness, frustration, oneliness and all the rest of it. ONLY AS YOU START AND STICK WITH WHAT CHANGELESS TRUTH, FACT, OMNI-PRESENCE *IS*, are you out of the prison of humanhood, physical bondage, time, age, decay and frustration!

I am sure you'll have to read this letter several times to really "get" it. The words are plain, but when it comes to sticking with ALL, WHOLENESS, PRESENT HERE NOW, WHEREIN THERE IS NO HISTORY, NO PAST, NO FUTURE, BUT ONLY ETERNAL WHOLENESS, HAPPI-NESS — well, that's not so easy because totally contrary to education, and most of all, contrary to what the senses say! But keep at it, for it not only will set you free of jail, but also from believing you are caged inside your body, subject to all sorts of appetites, hungers, fears and despair.

Please borrow the book, "NOW," and read carefully the following, then put it into practice without stopping, and you'll "be out of jail" because you'll discover YOU AC-TUALLY NEVER WERE IN JAIL, ANY MORE THAN YOU EVER WERE A DOG AND HAD TO BE SET FREE OF SUCH IMPRISONMENT.

NOW 193:12-5; 194:22-14; 207:3-209:26; 212:20-7; 216:28-8; 217:22-28 on 219; 227:27-21; 232:27-19; 237:2-17 on 238; 239:7-29.

Yes, it's a lot of reading, but you have the time, and nothing can be of greater assistance to you if you REALLY, HONESTLY are sincere. If it's not worth "working for within your Self," then it isn't worth having. One must BE WHAT HE IS, or he is in constant bondage to what he assumes he is. A prodigal jailed within ignorance, fear, superstition, matter, and all such is sentenced to death by

time, if not by something else! So let's "get with It!"
                                                    Cordially,

Dear----------

Please, in "NOW," read and ponder well the citations
given below — "dig" at what the words say, what they mean.
Do you accept what is stated as TRUTH, FACT, ACTUAL-
ITY HERE, NOW? Is CHANGELESS PERFECTION consciously operative NOW, or is EXISTENCE absent, REAL-
ITY false, CHANGELESS ACTUALITY out of business? Is
ONE now two or more? Is SINGLENESS double, adulter-
ated, contaminated? Is INTELLIGENCE intelligent, or is It
stupid? Is the SELF I AM actually here, or is my SELF
absent, missing, off on a wild goose chase, out somewhere
else looking for itself?

In the book NOW, please look up: 174:6-11; 184:3-10,
28-4; 191:1-1 on next page; 193:23-5; 205:28-5; 209:18-22
on the next page. Then, for other reading, do browse through
the chapter on GUILT in NOW.

Don't battle with error. Don't try to "forget" error for
such merely makes you remember it. Rather, so fill every
moment with INFINITE GLORY, PERFECTION, WHOLE-
NESS, LOVE, SINGLENESS, AWARENESS, INTELLI-
GENCE, JOY, ALIVENESS, that naught beside can even
tempt you to give attention thereto! Who, beholding ALL-
NESS IN ITS UNDIMINISHED GLORY, WOULD WISH TO
GIVE ATTENTION TO NOTHINGNESS, VACUITY, VOID?
Not One! And One is all there is — the VERY ONE YOU BE,
RIGHT NOW!

I'm sure this will keep you so busy that you'll no longer
waste effort over "body" or any "thing." IT IS REALITY

THAT WE BE, THAT IS THE ACTUAL SUBSTANCE I AM. "Things" are of no import at all, save that Mind only NOW conceives-perceives them, but never re-thinks them, never "thinks about" them. To do so would mean that Mind "re-produced" them, "re-conceived" them, and that is totally contrary to NOW ONLY BEING. There is no time, no history, hence naught growing or stemming therefrom!

Cordially,

Dear----------

I have given you the "help" requested. Please BE SURE to hear the lecture tape from New York which I made dated June 26, 1966. It is entitled, "SELF-SATISFACTION." I am sure it will give you a "boost."

There is no substitute for COMPLETENESS, SINGLE-NESS, WHOLENESS. No matter what we do, where we look, what we seek, what we claim to have found, IF IT IS NOT COMPLETENESS, PURE WHOLENESS, we have NOT found our SELF! What can possibly take the place of your IDENTITY, ALIVENESS, CONSCIOUSNESS, AWARE-NESS! Without ALIVENESS, what real good can you find in any "thing?" Can dope help to comfort a corpse? Can dope give pleasure to that which has no LIFE? Can any sort of compromise give you a "charge" if you are un-CONSCIOUS, un-ALIVE?

As ALIVENESS, AWARENESS, COMPLETENESS, WHOLENESS IS WHAT YOU BE, why look to dope to *make you AWARE*, ALIVE, WHOLE, COMPLETE? Do you have to take something to knock you OUT, in order to let you know what you CONSCIOUSLY BE? Just so long as you are "out," you are NOT CONSCIOUSNESS IN ACTION, HENCE YOU ARE *NOT* BEING YOUR SELF, NOT BEING

ALIVE, NOT BEING! You are as dead as a doornail! He who is moving about DEAD, is a long, long way from being ALIVE, being the SELF HE IS, being CONSCIOUS, being WHOLE, COMPLETE.

To deliberately "take" something which will make you, not half-ALIVE, but totally DEAD, UNALIVE, UNCON-SCIOUS, UNAWARE, UN-SELF, UN-PRESENT, UN-IN-TELLIGENT, is being far from very bright, isn't it?

He who starts with WHOLENESS, finds he is JOY ITSELF, LIFE ITSELF, POWER ITSELF, WEALTH IT-SELF, SATISFACTION ITSELF, SO DOES NOT HAVE TO "TAKE" AUGHT TO MAKE HIM MORE THAN HE IS, namely ENTIRE AUTHORITY, BLISS.

Naught can act as a substitute for LIFE, IDENTITY, SELF-AWARENESS! Why then listen to such suggestions? They cannot "tempt" you, for things cannot talk — and when we are AWAKE TO WHOLENESS, THE SELF WE BE, we will not talk "for" the suggestion! ONLY YOU CAN BE YOURSELF. NO ONE ELSE CAN DO THIS FOR YOU! ONLY YOU CAN BREATHE FOR YOURSELF. NO ONE ELSE CAN DO IT FOR YOU, OR TAKE YOUR PLACE. THIS PLACE IS ETERNAL RIGHT NOW. GET BUSY AND BE WHAT YOU BE, AND DON'T TRY TO FIND HAPPI-NESS, WHOLENESS, IN UNCONSCIOUSNESS, STUPID-ITY, OBSCURITY, DREAMS, NIGHTMARES! These are not any kind of a substitute, and they can't attack YOU, and you do not have to embrace THEM! ALL POWER BE-LONGS TO THE SELF, AND ONLY TO THE SELF, FOR IT ALONE IS AUTHORITY, THE ONE UNCHALLENGED BY ANOTHER, FOR THERE IS NO OTHER WHERE THERE IS ONE ALONE, COMPLETENESS! The WHOLE-

NESS IS THE SELF YOU BE, not to be found in a "thing" you INCLUDE!

Stick with our books. BE THE SELF YOU BE! Don't sell your SELF for less than a mess of unconsciousness, false dreams, false hopes, false sensations and illusions! THE SELF IS INFINITE WHOLENESS AT HAND, AND IT IS ALL YOURS ETERNALLY NOW. TAKE IT, BE IT, "USE" IT!

Cordially,

Dear----------

Gave you the "boost" requested. Please look up in NOW, reading out loud, then pulling each sentence apart as you again talk aloud, to find out what IS SAID HERE. This will really "help" you greatly:

NOW, 101:1-30; 105:1-13 next page, especially 13-30 on 105: 111:10-16.

You see, Marie, we do not accept anything, anyone, any situation, any law, reason, cause, effect, circumstance, etc., of the "picture." 100% WE START OUT WITH THE FACT OF WHAT CONSCIOUSNESS IS, WHERE, WHEN, HOW, WHY. THERE IS ONLY SELF *being*, so why try to "meet" aught that is the dictate, assumption or superstition stemming from otherness, when obviously, THERE BEING BUT ONE INFINITE LIGHT ONLY, THE ACTUAL AND ONLY ONE EXISTENT, THE SELF-SAME ONE READING THESE WORDS — there can be naught beside. STARTING WITH THE SINGLENESS OF FACT, THE ONLY PRESENCE, ALL THERE IS — any contest is precluded; any opposition is precluded; any challenge is precluded; any picture, no matter how framed, is not to be taken seriously, BECAUSE ONLY WHAT AWARENESS IS AS ITSELF, is

WHAT IS.

You see, FACT, TRUTH, LOVE, PURE TOTALITY WHEREIN NO CHALLENGE OR QUESTION CAN BE, is not dealing with or in things, not trying to do aught with thoughts (items, bodies, etc.), but IS BUSY BEING UTTER-LY TOTAL, UTTERLY AWARE AS FULL ALIVENESS, CERTAIN OF ITS COMPLETENESS! (Hope this doesn't seem abstract to you. It won't, if you begin with OMNI-PRESENCE AS INTELLIGENCE WHOLLY CONSCIOUS. Herein there can be no concern for lack, void, absence of thoughts-things-items-ideas, because THIS CONSCIOUSNESS IS WHOLLY ALIVE IN ITS UTTERNESS OF ABSOLUTE-NESS. But "things" have no worth, value, place — they are being conceived-perceived because Mind has this capacity-potential-function. There is no time, no past, no-when within which a "need-for-things-on-a-physical-basis" ever came about, or "when" ISNESS "learned" to "depend-on-and-re-quire-such" in order that NOW CAN BE NOW!)

"NOW" DOES NOT NEED A PAST TO BE ITS FOUN-DATION — OR SO NOW CAN *BE* NOW! "Was" has no place in NOW —so all this picture of a developed human economy, the how's-and-why's for "money" never got started, so can't hamper or influence, bedevil, or irritate, annoy or frustrate MIND-SELF! Waste no effort trying to "work out"such a problem, for it cannot be done. Beginning with FACT, YOU HAVE NO PROBLEM OF A PAST (money) TO WORK OUT. ISNESS IS FACT *being*. This IS POTENCY IN ACTION. THIS IS POWER THAT IS AUTHORITY AND VICE VERSA! HEREIN NO OPPOSITION OR CHAL-LENGE, NO WAIT, GROWTH, ADDITION OR SUBTRAC-TION CAN TAKE PLACE. NO CONTACT IS SOUGHT, NO

CONTRACT "WAS" MADE, OR "WILL BE" MADE! SNESS IS FREE OF ALL SUCH SUPERSTITION – THE SUPERSTITION OF OTHERS "SCRATCHING" YOUR BACK SO YOU WILL IN TURN SCRATCH THEIR BACKS –this is nonsense of "service" and thus being "serviced!" REALITY IS SINGLE, TOTAL, WHOLE! Let's stick with THIS FOR IT IS FACT, AND THERE IS NO MARIE-MIND AT ALL – HENCE NO MARIE-WORLD WHEREIN THIS OR THAT IS REQUISITE OR PRE-REQUISITE, FOR THIS OR THAT REASON, RESULT, etc. No sin, no guilt, no evil, no devil, no time, no impurity (void, vacuum, lack, ig- norance!).

Fondly,

Dear----------

Sorry to be so slow in answering your letter, but just arrived back in New York from my tour, and am taking off for the Seminar on Friday to be gone two weeks.

You state: " . . . the only 'I' includes All . . . which certainly does not exclude Wealth . . ." This statement is decidedly wrong. Don't "work" after this manner.

Wealth and Consciousness, Spirit, God – these are absolute synonyms. All mean the ONE OMNIPRESENT ALL. It is this ALL that is I – never an "I" being All! (That would be the teaching of metaphysics!)

Again, "I" could not "include" All! As INFINITE ALL and I are ONE AND THE SAME TOTAL INDIVIDUAL BEING, inclusive of EVERY THOUGHT (thing-body-item – call Mind's thoughts by any name you wish, for THOUGHTS ARE IDEAS TO MIND, but to Mind only, within Mind only, known by Mind only, and existent nowhere else, ever, for

there is NO OTHER SUBSTANCE OR BEING AT ALL,
hence "nowhere else" to be!) — ONLY MIND CAN HAVE
"THOUGHT" or "IDEA."

Sure hope you plan on attending our work in September
and bring along your friends.

Sincerely,

Dear----------

Now, please do not think that I am trying to influence
you one way or the other with this letter. I'm merely trying
to point out what I feel is most important. Do we DEMAND
OF OURSELVES THAT OUR FIRST AND TOTAL ATTEN-
TION, OUR FIRST AND TOTAL IMPORTANCE, BE ON
THE SOLE SELF, THE ONE ALONE COMPLETENESS,
WHOLENESS, SINGLENESS — or are we making our FIRST
demand that of relationship, relatives, our human desires and
outlines — and then, if there is any time, money, or
opportunity left over, we can toss that toward SPIRIT, THE
SINGLE ALL-INCLUSIVE SELF?

I find in my work that the ALLNESS OF ALL, THE
SINGLENESS OF THE ONE ALONE has to come FIRST. I
do not start out with human plans, outlines, obligation,
desires, and then try to rationalize as to how I can "do" what
I-as-a-human-Alfred-mind "WANT TO DO!" If I did, none of
this work would exist at all.

In the sessions given at the Evansville Seminar, we gave a
lot on relatives, relationship, and we pointed out that ANY
AND ALL HUMAN RELATIONSHIP IS BONDAGE, THE
INSISTENCE THAT WE ARE BORN, HENCE THAT WE
MUST DIE, AND WE INCLUDE OUR WORLD WITHIN
THIS FRAMEWORK SO LONG AS WE PERSIST — ESPE-

CIALLY IS IT SO WHEN WE "SERVE" THE HUMAN
RELATIONSHIP IN PREFERENCE TO THAT WHICH IS
WHOLLY SPIRIT, INTELLIGENCE, CONSCIOUS AWARE-
NESS, SELFHOOD — when we think we are "being good to
our loved ones, doing them good, bringing good to them,"
rather than by BEING GOODNESS, ITSELF, WHICH IS
ETERNAL, ALL-INCLUSIVE HEALTH, WEALTH, HAR-
MONY.

Of course, I'm sure all manner of reaction will greet this —
blame (our dearest friend as a human) will rise up and
condemn, accuse, rant and snarl around to make its desires
appear virtuous, legitimate, and in many cases, obligatory or
binding upon us because we've promised!" Well, if we fall for
that, it is because we really wish to — we really have a
preference, because we truly wish to be human, have a
human world of lack, trouble, birth, time, servitude, disease,
death — prefer to have a little world "out there" we can feel
obligated to, for, and can have it look to us for comfort,
pleasure — that we can be emotional and sentimental over,
for thus WE CAN CONTINUE TO ASSUME WE ARE
PHYSICAL BODIES, THAT WE ALSO HAVE BEEN BORN
OF RACIAL STOCK, ARE GENDERED, ARE AGING,
ARE FULL OF WOE AND KINDNESS, OF GOOD DEEDS
AND MURDER, OF A FORM OF HONESTY WHICH IS
DISHONEST, etc.!

To me, the FIRST AND ONLY POINT TO BE CON-
SIDERED IS THIS: WHAT DO I CONSIDER TO BE THE
MOST IMPORTANT — SPIRIT, INTELLIGENCE, LIFE,
LOVE, PURE SINGLENESS, POWER, WEALTH, HEALTH,
THE ACTUAL WHOLE SELF THAT IS I — or relatives,
relationships, being one-among-many, obligations, duty, ser-

vitude, being sweet, kind, obliging, aging, dying — allowing my world to go hang and all because "i" as a human, "want this, have planned that, have promised something else," and then, if all my outlining has worked out and there is time left, then, AND ONLY THEN, will Truth come in for the balance of my attention! In other words, WHAT COMES FIRST — TOTALITY or humanity? And surely, in what you told me this morning, you do have the answer. And you know, time being wholly human, celebrations are often shifted from one date to another, and there is time to do that, if it was IMPORTANT ENOUGH FOR YOU TO SEEK SELF, REALITY, *FIRST!* No one has ever suffered or lost aught WHEN REALITY COMES FIRST, have they?

You assume, perhaps, that "others" will be disappointed — but you'd rather allow them to be sick, human, die, merely because you wish to be human — whereas by HAVING SPIRIT AS FIRST AND ALL, ALWAYS, LEAVES NO HUMANS ANYWHERE AT ANY TIME, HENCE YOU INCLUDE TOTALITY AND PERFECTION AS THE SOLE RESIDENCE OF ALL IDEAS. Which of the two "approaches" is being LOVE insofar as these ideas are concerned? Is it not like giving a violent poison to a little child who likes the color of it, and you wish to be so sweet and loving, so you pass it over so the child can die a horrible death?

Yes, those dear folk can hold their celebration a bit ahead or a bit later, if necessary, can't they? And they gladly will if YOUR FIRST LOVE IS FOR REALITY — but if you begin with relationship, and thus toss TRUTH ASIDE, NO MATTER HOW YOU TRY TO SLICE IT, EXCUSE YOURSELF, rationalize, connive, think up "reasons against it", and ALL THE REST OF IT — TO HOLD "THEM" TO TIME, IS TO

ALSO DAMN THEM IN HELL, THE GRAVE, AGE, DEATH! So, to stay home in honor of TIME, AGE, CREEPING DEATH, in preference to LIFE, JOY, BLISS, REALITY — you "figure" that one out, and in genuine honesty, wholly apart from BLAME, CHARGES OF PERSONALITY, TRYING TO HOOK YOUR FRUSTRATIONS, ANNOYANCES, DISAPPOINTMENTS AND THE REST OF HUMAN TRAITS ONTO "THIS ONE," or "THAT ONE!"

I beg of you, DO NOT GIVE VENT TO BLAME! Or try to hide behind that old bromide: "Well, but I thought — I understood — well, but I imagined — for all such is merely holding still to a determination to be human — still is an attempted escape from FACING UP TO IT THAT WE REALLY PREFER HUMANITY TO REALITY — THAT WE REALLY WISH TO DO AS WE OUTLINE, RATHER THAN TOTALLY DESIRE FACT, TRUTH, BEING! Oh, yes, when we are in pain, and trouble, then we'd like Truth only, but when it comes to our "wishes, desires, plans," let Truth take a back seat and we'll "CALL FOR IT WHEN IT IS A MORE CONVENIENT SEASON!"

This latter is why so many have withdrawn from this trip! They have been THRILLED to find what they are trying to kid themselves into believing is a legitimate, valid "reason" FOR NOT GOING! They actually DO NOT WANT TO GO! THEY ACTUALLY WANT TO SAVE THE MONEY, and are so tickled to find a way out so they CAN SAVE THAT MONEY! And don't you be blind to this! I am POSITIVE IF I OFFERED THEM EACH $10,000 for going, NOT ONE OF THEM WOULD LET EVEN HELL ITSELF KEEP THEM FROM BEING THERE! You know that as well as I do! And therein lies the answer! So, IS YOUR "FAMILY" TO BE

FIRST, AND TRUTH CAN WAIT "TILL A MORE CON-
VENIENT SEASON," OR IS REALITY THE WHOLE OF
WHOLENESS TO YOU RIGHT NOW? IS YOUR WHOLE-
NESS, YOUR ONENESS, ACTUALLY WHOLE, COM-
PLETE — or are you waiting for GOODNESS to get filled up
at some later date? If so, don't complain about any of the
"troubles" you and your world seem to experience betwixt
and between — WHEN THE FEAST IS SET, THE EXCUSES
COME: I HAVE A FATHER-IN-LAW WHO MUST BE
BURIED; I HAVE A DATE TO CELEBRATE A CERTAIN
SPOT IN TIME; I HAVE A PROMISE THAT MUST BE
KEPT; I HAVE A DOLLAR I WISH TO PRESERVE FOR
SOME GADGET I WANT TO BUY, LIKE A PLEASURE
TRIP, A NEW GOWN, A PRESENT FOR A LOVED ONE;
SOMEONE SAID SOMETHING NASTY AND I DON'T
LIKE IT, SO WHY SHOULD "I" GO WITH THEM; I DON'T
LIKE THE COLOR BROWN, BLACK, WHITE, GREEN, SO
WHY SHOULD I GO? Yes, and why should *I* go, ever again,
anywhere so what seems others can hear TRUTH VOICED,
OR EVER ANSWER LETTERS, OR GIVE "HELP?"

I am not trying in any way to get you to go, or stay. What
you do is entirely up to you — BUT BEING CANNOT BE
SET ASIDE — LIFE IS TRULY ALL, AND IF YOU CAN
FIND THAT WHICH IS OF MORE IMPORTANCE TO YOU
THAN WHOLENESS, by all means follow same! For myself,
I FIND ONLY TRUTH IS SELF-SATISFACTION, THAT
WHICH NEVER FAILS ME, AND THAT WHICH "BLESS-
ES" MY ENTIRE UNIVERSE OF IDEAS!

I'm positive that your dear relatives will be most happy to
make whatever adjustment is expedient to help out, if you
will be forthright in presenting it to them — for within a

period of 21 days, THEY ARE NOT GOING ANYWHERE,
are they? And do the 21 days, or by having the "celebration"
a couple of days ahead, actually interfere, basically, with
aught? Not really! But, as I pointed out to start with, I'm not
trying to urge you one way or the other in any seeming
movement you make BUT I AM TRYING TO MAKE THIS
WORK CLEAR, THAT FIRST AND ALTOGETHER, SPIR-
IT, LIFE, LOVE, SINGLENESS, IS SINGLE, HENCE
"COMES FIRST," AND IS NOT TO BE SHUNTED TO ONE
SIDE AND ALLOWED SECOND PLACE, TO BE
"SERVED" WITH WHATEVER ENERGY AND ATTEN-
TION AND TIME AND INCLINATION THAT MIGHT
SEEM TO BE LEFT OVER! Such is DEATH ITSELF, FOR
ALL THAT WE INCLUDE WITHIN SUCH REASONING,
BLAMING, ACCUSING, ANNOYANCE AND SO ON!
                    Always fondly,

Dear----------

Don't think I was curt — I wasn't — but you know, and so
do I, that AS CONSCIOUSNESS IS *ALL*, THE SOLE
IDENTITY-BEING, there can be naught beside, and any
seeming "situation" is all from the dream (human mind)!
Why then rehearse all the foibles of this nonsense? That is
going back to metaphysics, assuming Truth is a mere
"healing" agent that can be applied to errors, meanwhile
allowing the would-be-human-mind (dream) to go right on
concocting more junk! In your "work" or "digging," do you
see that TO INFINITE AWARENESS, NOWNESS, FRESH-
NESS, NEWNESS, PRESENCE, there cannot be any "remembrance" or "hangover" of metaphysics, cause-effect
theory, punishment-for-wrongness, prophecy-concerning-the-

attacking-of-evil anywhere? And remember, EVERY PROB-
LEM is thanks to incurring PUNISHMENT for wrongs done
by you or your ancestors! (Please ponder this line!)

I start with REALITY AND THERE'S WHERE I STRIVE
TO CONTINUE ALL MY INTEREST — FOR THIS ALONE
IS THE "PRECLUDER" OF OTHERNESS, PAST-FUTURE,
FEAR AND ALL THE NONSENSE PERTAINING TO A
"BODY!" You simply could not — repeat, C O U L D N O T
voice the errors — going into the aches and pains, your
thinness and how little you eat, etc. You did it again in the
letter that I got yesterday, the same old stuff of detailed
description of "what-is-wrong" with body! This can only
occur because you are still messing about with the human
sense and trying to heal a body — holding to body as
identity. It would be impossible for you to give such detail if
this were not it — and even when you were here, you did
some of it. This is not scolding, or any such — I'm merely
trying to get you to actually deal ONLY WITH INTELLI-
GENCE, AS INTELLIGENCE. Leave "body," as you sense
it, alone! Body, as Mind "thinks-that-thought," has no
appearance, no outline, no stuff, so you simply cannot,
CANNOT, think about "body" at all! MIND DOES NOT
THINK "ABOUT" BODY AT ALL! It "thinks" the thought
and that is it — finish, period!

Now, don't think I am "yelling" at you — not a bit of it. I
am trying to make it clear that ONLY WHAT IS, *is*, and that
is TOTAL CONSCIOUS AWARENESS. This is not "body."
Leave "body" alone. Leave it wholly to Mind where and to
whom it belongs. Stop trying to make a house out of it — a
house where you'd prefer to live, rather than to BE!

You CAN center your attention on SPIRIT if you really

"get down to business." Most of us say we are "down to business," but we actually mean that we are trying the best we know how TO HEAL THE BODY, TO KEEP SPIRIT'S SENSE OF BODY UPPERMOST IN THOUGHT, TO DEMONSTRATE, AND ALL SUCH! We try to heal, help, change "things" visibly and according to feelings! But this is not REALITY.

Every time you find yourself thinking about body, feeling distress, aches, pains, difficulty of any sort, INSTEAD OF VOICING IT, TELLING SOMEONE (EVEN YOURSELF) ABOUT IT, OR GIVING IT ANY SPOT AT ALL IN TIME OR PLACE — if you will "begin" with (AS) Spirit, INFINITELY TOTAL, WHOLE, COMPLETE, HENCE PERFECT IN ACTION, FUNCTION, ALIVENESS, TOTALITY, AWARENESS, FULLNESS, UTTERNESS, NEWNESS, ALONENESS, SINGLENESS — I am positive you will not find yourself still "thinking" of or sensing lack, things, body, trouble, fear, and an ever-increasing-sense-of-difficulty as you write and mention on the phone! There certainly is enough of INFINITY that you are not fully enjoying that can occupy your "thinking" or "digging" for a terribly long "time" if you will! However, most of us are happy to merely re-think, re-peat, re-iterate, the statements we've made over and over, the same old words with nary a new concept of what we are "saying." We let words trip off the tongue instead of BEING INFINITELY NEW, FRESH, WHOLE, ENTIRE-FOR-THE-FIRST-"TIME" — NOW. Rather, we still think in terms of body and feel if "only we-could-see-Reality-then-we'd-heal-body!" This latter is still the old practice of metaphysics.

What, "how much" of NEWNESS, INFINITY, HAVE YOU ENJOYED TODAY — I MEAN, COMPLETELY NEW

INFINITY, TOTALITY, WHOLENESS, SINGLENESS, PURE UNCHALLENGED ALIVENESS TODAY? If "none," then are not the statements made, mere "wine-in-old bottles," hence sour wine, useless faith, a marking-of-time in hopes-that-sometime-one-of-these-statements-will-do-something-to-something? Oh yes, I know that "we believe" with all our heart — that we know "this-is-Truth," but WITH WHAT SO-CALLED MIND ARE WE MAKING THESE STATEMENTS, AND WHAT GOOD DO THEY DO? Saying Truth, and BEING THE SELF THAT *IS* TRUTH is not the same! Like in the Bible, we "say": "Yes, Lord, I believe — help thou my unbelief!"

As I say, I am pointing this out to get you to start with WHAT LOVE KNOWS ITSELF TO BE, FOR THAT IS MIND-IN-ACTION. Herein is no hangover of metaphysics, time, past, or sense-of-body! Why? Because there is NO OTHER MIND. Merely saying there is no other mind is like saying boiling water is not hot! But you'll find that water will scald just the same! Why? Because we are still dealing with water, NOT IN REALITY, NOT DEALING AS TRUTH! For TRUTH HAS NO CONCEPT OF WATER AT ALL — JUST SO, SPIRIT HAS NO CONCEPT OF "BODY"! Yes, I know this will jar you, but it is so! "Body" as we appear to sense it (including all it seems to do and be) is without place in Mind. There is no similarity between "body" as we use that term and a "thought-in-Mind" as I use it in these books! Mind never spends Its time thinking body, or rethinking it, for to have "body" at all in Mind, it would be only now being conceived-perceived, hence is naught that *CAN BE THOUGHT ABOUT!* (Such thinking "about" implies past tense, so PRESENT MIND DOES NOT HAVE ANY "BO-

DY" ANYWHERE TO "THINK about.") And how can you know any "THOUGHT MIND IS NOW THINKING" (CONCEIVING-PERCEIVING) UNLESS YOU *BE* THAT ACTUAL MIND RIGHT NOW — AND IF YOU *ARE* THIS MIND, YOU ARE SO BUSY BEING, THAT YOU DO NOT CONCERN YOURSELF OVER "body" OR ANY OTHER "thought" YOU ARE CONCEIVING, EVEN THOUGH YOU DO CONCEIVE-PERCEIVE BY VIRTUE OF YOUR WHOLENESS! Do you begin to get what I mean here? Think on this. Shall discuss at Seminar.

Fondly,

Dear----------

I find ABSOLUTE HONESTY demands that I not accept, claim, talk for or advocate a separate mind that always insists on lack. If one gives it even a half-chance, it will proclaim he is human, can't "afford" Reality, has no "money," can't meet his daily requirements, etc. The only way to wipe lack completely out of even a seeming existence is this work, for REALITY LEAVES NO SECOND, NO LACK-LADEN MIND WHICH SUFFERS FROM ITS OWN IGNORANCE! To actually stick HONESTLY WITH REALITY, THE SOLE SELF THAT IS I, every form of seeming privation, lack, limitation, fades forever! This AWARENESS is not some "thing" that can be bought, nor can one value it according to pounds sterling! It is of more value than all the gold, precious gems, oil and real estate existent. Only by parting with a false sense of value (money generally) can one actually behold REALITY — that is, so long as one thinks his money is more valuable than THIS UNDIMENSIONAL ALL-INCLUSIVE CONSCIOUS AWARENESS, then he suffers a warped sense of values and will get naught from the work even if he should sit through it. Also, if one assumes that with the payment he can "buy" riches, again he will be fooling himself — but he who honestly digs into what REALITY IS, discovers THAT SELF THAT IS NOW TOTALLY SELF-SATISFIED, INCLUDING ALL "THINGS," whether called money, lands or what — but he includes them as AWARENESS BEING AWARE OF ITS IDEAS, THOUGHTS. He discovers that the LIFE HE IS, IS THE SOLE SUBSTANCE, VALUE, and things are present to "use" in our daily round should it seem sensible to do so, but still, like the alphabet, these items are wholly thoughts IN mind, cannot be earned, inherited, come by in any manner of human endeavor — they are present TO Mind, IN Mind, because of the COMPLETE NATURE OF THE ONE INDIVIDUAL.

Hope this makes sense. We intend to devote much "time" to clearing up the false sense of money, why it seems to be scarce, and all the other nonsense connected therewith. TRUTH WORKS — IS THE SOLE POTENCY EXISTENT RIGHT NOW. One can never work "with" It, but ONE DISCOVERS THAT HE *IS* IT! There is a vast difference. Metaphysics would advocate at-one-ment, whereas REALITY IS THE SOLE ONE *BEING* NOW! Metaphysics is impotent, aside from the faith, which always withers. REALITY IS CHANGELESS WHOLENESS *BEING!* I'll be delighted to have your mother-in-law if she wishes to attend and will arrange as indicated. It is not the "money" involved, Jim, but if I admit that there IS lack, anywhere, then it must be as real for me as for the one for (or of) whom I am admitting it! This is false, so I "operate" wholly on the FACT that all things are now present in Truth. She will "see" this and find she not only "can pay," but actually BEING WHAT IS, CAN'T KEEP FROM "PAYING!"

Let me hear real soon. Thanks.

Love to all,

Dear----------

Now, as to your not attending the work because you have no money — can't pay! If that isn't the BEST POSSIBLE WAY OF HANGING ONTO LACK, I've never known Truth! "HIS SERVANT YE ARE, ONCE YOU OBEY!" Go, as my guest, and end this weeping over the bier of lack, I beg you! You wait on it, and have been ever since I first met you, and has it grown less by jumping every time it calls to you? You couldn't get to the Seminar on time, and had to leave ahead of time because you had to wait on lack, had to be present to hear its tale of woe, look at it to see how ugly it was. Of course, when you are employed wholly dispensing lack, naturally I suppose you must give it your ENTIRE TIME AND ATTENTION — with such a good job to keep you busy all the time, you simply can't afford to turn to THE VERY SELF YOU BE, AND STAY THEREWITH, FOR THEREIN are no holes, no lack, no pressure, no bankruptcy, no demands, no challenges. THERE IS ONLY INFINITE SUBSTANCE BUSY BEING WHOLLY ALIVE, WHOLLY PRESENT, WHOLLY CONSCIOUS, WHOLLY TRUE TO ITSELF ONLY, BECAUSE THERE IS NONE BESIDE AT ALL!

Now, Lucy, I'm not "scolding you," nor "bawling you out." I'm pointing out the nonsense of human sense that would even write that it SHOULD BE RECOGNIZED AS BEING PRESENT, POOR, UNHAPPY, SET UPON, BEING CLOCKED BY YEARS AND SO ON, AND THAT "IT"

WANTS TRUTH! ONLY TRUTH IS TRUE. There is no Lucy-mind, no lack-mind, no pressured-mind, no unhappy or aging-mind, no personal or evil mind! THERE IS ONLY INTELLIGENCE PRESENT BUSY BEING WHOLLY PRESENT, ALIVE, CONSCIOUS, COMPLETE – ONLY CONSCIOUSNESS PRESENT BEING 100% BUSY BEING WHOLLY CONSCIOUS. That is the SOLE BUSINESS existent. Is this the business YOU ARE CONDUCTING, or are you trying to be what-you-can-never-be, namely, a human trying to maintain and sustain some holes, voids, traps, poverty, falsity all over the place?

THE ONLY BUSINESS BEING INTELLIGENCE, BUSY BEING ITSELF, ALL, there can be no closing down of It, no "age" limit, no "worn out" history, no failure!

You wrote: "I know the only way I can have a problem is to deny SELF." Actually, YOU DO NOT HAVE A MIND WITH WHICH TO DENY REALITY! TRUTH CANNOT DENY ITSELF, BETRAY ITSELF, OR BE OTHER THAN WHAT IT IS – ALL! This Mind *being* Itself is I! It is MIND THAT IS BEING I – not a Lucy who can or must or should become I – such is impossible!

I beg of you for your own joy, get out of the sty and start with AWARENESS AND STAY AS AWARENESS. Whenever a past seems to whisper, instantly declare TRUTH AND GO AT IT AS IF IT WERE THE FIRST TIME YOU'VE EVER HEARD THE WORD! And keep at this FOREVER AND EVER! Do NOTHING over, or because of, or with a problem, or a human mind, for "wherein is it to be accounted of?"

Hope this "helps."

Fondly,

P.S. In "Power" ponder letter starting on Page 137, and don't listen to "talk" and sympathy!

Dear----------

You are not the only one who assumes humanity can seem to be about, but WHO OR WHAT MIND SO ASSUMES - AND WHERE IS ANY SUCH ASSUMPTION, SPIRIT BEING THE SOLE LIFE PRESENT? Am I going to quit Reality, my SOLE IDENTITY, just because my "senses" appear to "sense nonsense?" And is there a particle of difference between what I mention above and what you write about "lumps" and anticipating in four months "will then come the harvest?" Does any prophecy deal in NOWNESS? Should I not now send notice to everyone that I'll do no more work in the field hereafter because no doubt in thirty years I may appear to believe that I'm old and can't do so and so?

Joanne, for your own sake, WAKE UP AND GET WITH IT! Over and over one is so prone to anticipate incapacity. Why? Because HE ACCEPTS EVIL AS A GROWING, LIVING, EXPANDING, EVOLVING NOTHINGNESS THAT CAN FINALLY EAT UP REALITY, NOWNESS, SINGLE-NESS, PURITY! No one, and I mean, no one, can STICK WITH SINGLE INDIVIDUAL PURITY, ONENESS, AS THE ONLY, and anticipate inability next month, next week, the next hour! To dwell in what-will-happen-tomorrow is to be 100% within the would-be confines of theology which believes that evil will grow worse, and Spirit will grow weaker, darker, less and less significant, less and less present. Look at the Book of Revelations, if you doubt me — are you

not going along wholly with this, in that you anticipate that a
third of the stars of heaven will be cast onto your earth, your
body, and you will then not be able to do this or that? Yes,
of course you have a great sense of human relief when you
give into the inevitable demise of what humans call life –
when you accept, no longer even questioning that evil is the
victor, so why struggle. Yes, evil causes all flesh to do its
bidding! BUT WHERE IS MIND – WHERE AM I – WHERE
IS ISNESS – WHERE IS OMNIPRESENCE, INTELLI-
GENCE, AWARENESS, NOWNESS? WHO and WHAT AM I?
HAS SPIRIT QUIT, GIVEN UP, THROWN IN THE TOWEL,
IS NOW "RESTING" AND MEANWHILE REMEMBERING
THE SEVENTH DAY OF A LONG REST? Just when do you
intend to take your stand that *ONLY* TRUTH IS TRUE?

This is not meant to be "harsh," but in Actuality WHEN
IS LIFE THE SOLE AWARENESS, SUBSTANCE, STUFF
EXISTENT? WHEN? WHERE? And as this ONE LIFE NOW
PRESENT KNOWS ITS ENTIRETY, *ITS TOTAL SATIS-
FACTION* OF BEING ENTIRE, TOTAL, WHOLE, SINGLE,
WHEREIN NO VOID CAN BE, NO WANT CAN BE, NO
ALIENNESS CAN BE, NO "OTHER-STATE" CAN BE –
AND THIS ONLY IS SATISFACTION – WHERE CAN
THERE BE A CONSTANT YEN TO BE "HEALED" OR TO
"SEE" SOMETHING WHICH WILL SET YOU FREE OF
BONDAGE, OR A DESIRE TO "GET" AWAY FROM
METAPHYSICS, A PHYSICAL SENSE OF BODY, A LUMP
-THAT-IS-OOZING, AND ALL THE REST OF THE PIC-
TURES THAT THRONG THE WOULD-BE HUMAN-MIND-
THAT-IS-A-VOID-AND-NOTHING-BESIDE?

It is not a matter of going to Evansville, or London, or to
heaven, hell, or the cemetery, or whatever – it is wholly a

1atter of putting off the ALLNESS OF ALL, ONE,
INGLENESS, till "it is a more convenient human time to
all for Reality." What I'm trying to say is — stop
anticipating the passage of time — stop trying to outline what
ou are evidently SURE will be the lamentable condition of a
hysical body come next month, two months, next year!
top trying to live June and July instead of BEING NOW
HE ONE YOU "AM." Start being HONEST WITH NOW,
HE PRESENT. Every time you "look ahead to conditions
f months away," you are wholly within the throes of time,
strology, theology! THEOLOGY AND ASTROLOGY ARE
)NE AND THE SAME — IT IS THEOLOGY THAT FIRST
ARGUES "TIME," AND HENCE DIAGNOSIS (HISTORY)
AND PROGNOSIS (PROPHECY). Within this theology is
reation of matter, and all that is the matter with matter, and
vith the hypnotic emphasis that only this matter matters!

It may well be that going here or there is not sensible, but
vhy decide so far ahead, and banking wholly on the certainty
hat YOU WILL *NOT,* REPEAT, *N O T* BE ABLE TO
MAKE IT, FOR TRUTH WILL HAVE STOPPED BEING
'RUE, AND OMNIPRESENCE WILL BE ABSENT "AT-
'HAT-TIME!"

When we "watch" REALITY as closely as we appear to
vatch a picture we call "body," we will find that ONLY
;PIRIT IS, AND IS WHOLE. NOWHERE IS SPIRIT,
NTELLIGENCE, "LEAKING," OR INFIRM, " "DODDER-
NG," OR SUPPORTED ON OR BY A CANE, OR A CAIN!

Will you please look up in BACHELOR GOD: 127:4-2;
l29:24-28 next page; 131:20-19, and, at your leisure, read
arefully the whole chapter on ALIMONY, especially
l33:18-18 next page.

Remember this, Joanne, sooner or later one MUST BE HONEST WITH THE SELF HE IS. IT CANNOT BE PUT OFF, NOR EXCUSED ON THE BASIS OF PRODIGALITY. THERE IS NO SUCH. THE VERY LIFE THAT APPEARED TO BE PERVERTED BY THE PRODIGAL, *IS* ACTUALLY THE SOLE LIFE THAT SPIRIT IS, *PRESENT!* Hence, at no point did so-called prodigality actually rub off on Spirit, Life — at no point did the seeming folly of futility ever succeed in substituting itself for ACTUALITY. It *IS* THE SOLE LIFE NOW, THE SOLE AMNESS THAT IS I, THE PURE ONE BECAUSE THE ONLY ONE, HENCE THE ABSOLUTE PRESENT AUTHORITY, AND THERE IS NO OTHERNESS (CALLED PRODIGALITY, PERSONALITY, HYPNOTISM, ASSUMPTION, SUPERSTITION) THAT CAN TALK TO, WITH, OR ABOUT THE PURE ONE THAT AMNESS IS. THIS AMNESS KNOWS WHOLLY THAT IT IS, AND IS WHOLLY WHAT IT IS NOW. THIS LEAVES NO OTHER-NESS OF ANY SORT TO KNOW, BE, OR NOT BE, AUGHT! Time will not clear away what is NOT! Waiting will not clear away what is NOT! Human effort, resolve, desire, prayer, repetition of words, struggle, alarm, self-pity, or fear will not clear away what is NOT! ONLY REALITY IS REAL, A FACT NOW, HENCE AUGHT THAT IS CON-TRARY TO TOTAL PERFECTION PRESENT, HAS NO PLACE OR HISTORY OR FUTURE OR ADVOCATE. HOW THEN CAN IT BE TREATED, HEALED, FOUGHT OFF, DEALT WITH? It can't, because IT ISN'T!

                              Always fondly,

Dear----------
   I urge you to state FACT *before* you even open your eyes

in the A.M., and then begin to totally devote every moment and all your attention to what you have stated concerning the WHOLENESS OF NOW, ISNESS, FOR THIS WILL PROHIBIT ANY THOUGHT AT ALL ABOUT SICKNESS, JOINTS THAT HURT, BODY THAT IS OLD, OR ANY OF THE MANY OTHER "COMPLAINTS" YOU ARE PROMPTED TO ITERATE. YOU SIMPLY CANNOT KEEP YOUR *ENTIRE* ATTENTION ON FACT, REALITY, ACTUALITY, WHICH MEANS PURE SINGLENESS, PERFECTION, INDIVISIBLE WHOLENESS, AND STILL HAVE TROUBLE. YOU HAVE NO MIND WITH WHICH TO "MIND" TROUBLE OR AUGHT BESIDE.

In THAT WHICH IS, see 113:23-26.

You are constantly trying to heal something, which means that you are starting with lack, evil, that which is NOT, and trying to chase it away. It cannot be done. All such is metaphysics, and it is only the frustration that results that makes you assume "this work" is difficult. TRUTH is so easy, for IT IS ALREADY SO. But if you insist on starting with aches, pains, body, and all manner of troubles, you defy TRUTH, refuse LOVE, repudiate PURE SINGLENESS, and deny SELF, WHOLENESS, SATISFACTION. Is it then any wonder you have "trouble?" Not because there IS evil, lack, man, but because you struggle so to act as if you WERE MAN, LACK, TROUBLE PERSONIFIED! You can't ever bring it off, so quit it now, and begin with WHAT LOVE IS, AND STICK THEREWITH, FOR THIS LEAVES NO OTHER MIND AT ALL.

When you say "no" to IS — that REALITY is *not* ALL — you are in trouble. REALITY is never positive. IT IS ALL. (This may hit you hard, but it is so). There is no negative to oppose a positive. CERTAINTY HAS NOTHING TO DO WITH BEING POSITIVE! We are not operating from a "positive" point of view in this work! "Positive" is human will — human determination — a human choice that you will stick with it on a human basis!

If you can be made to back down (in front of evil-lack-man), it is because it has become so real to you that you are on the run. Only then will you suffer! You may experience fear of the worst sort — TRUTH IS NOT GOING TO TREAT THAT! Just because you are scared, don't let that be a reason for going along with the lie. When you stick with what you are stating, the panic will disappear. If you give in, you are stuck — for the other is just temporary — a nightmare. TRUTH IS NOT MAGIC — NOT AN OPEN SESAME — NOT A WORD YOU SPEAK IN A WHISPER. Don't be panicked. The more you stick with Fact, the less often will these things, suggestions, pains, occur. The more "positive" one is, the more "positive" he is that there is a negative forcing him to be positive, and the more negative he will become. The more positive you are, the more you are being driven by the negative — being backed into a corner. *STATING WHAT TRUTH IS, AND STOPPING THERE, DOES NOT CONSTITUTE THIS WORK.* Don't try to meet the error or handle it, and don't yield to it. The UTTER CERTAINTY OF REALITY IS ALL THERE IS. This is SELF — this is HEAVEN AT HAND, COMPLETENESS HERE NOW — SELF-SATISFACTION.

"Positive" is what you *think* Truth is. TRUTH IS NOT WHAT YOU THINK IT IS, BUT WHAT TRUTH KNOWS ITSELF TO BE — THE SELF YOU BE! THE UTTER CALM ABSOLUTENESS OF TOTALITY IS TRUTH. BEING IS

INFINITY IS, THEREFORE, was-ness and will-be-ness isn't. Intellectualism — outlining — is "positive thinking." The positive is changeable — it can become and is negative. CERTAINTY is LOVE ITSELF - no decision. LOVE IS ACTION, FOR IT IS SINGLENESS BEING ITSELF, I. Positive is always an opinion you have arrived at through rationalization. The positive is always based on man, lack, and is always evil — based on what you will accept and what you will NOT accept! The more you fight the thing, the more you have it. Regardless of the ages of the past or future, nothing has touched SPIRIT, THE LIFE YOU BE, SELF, THAT WHICH IS THE I-THAT-I-AM. Can you "positively" *prove* N O W is NOW? How? Negative conditions are silly, impossible. Don't try to chase trouble or negatives out of the body, the temple, for no such is. Nothing, being *nothing*, why not expose the nothingness of nothing so no one will get tripped by it? Magic (disease, lack, age, pain) comes from darkness — witchcraft, ignorance, Self-denial. Why should we assume we must get rid of that which is altogether magic? Humanity is the entirety of superstition — matter — the argument that you come forth from biology is altogether mysticism — mystery.

Who invented lack? Where does disease come from? You may rationalize it, but who or what is doing the saying? The mystery of unWholeness, where does it originate? Where can you find lack (man) in the midst of TOTAL SINGLE REALITY, OMNIPRESENT EXISTENCE, BEING? If you insist on working in mysticism, with disease, lack, body, personal identity, you are in trouble, when ONLY NOW IS — SO WHY NOT TALK TRUTH ONLY? State 100% what WHOLENESS IS, STICK WITH IT. DEFINE ONENESS,

ENTIRENESS, COMPLETENESS, SPIRIT, FOR THIS IS
THY SELF NOW IN ITS ENTIRETY. KEEP ON DEFINING
WHAT WHOLENESS, INSEPARABLE COMPLETENESS IS.
EVEN IN THE SEEMING "human," the moment the
"victim" being hypnotized starts absolutely concentrating on
any Fact, the spell is broken, and the whole "spell" vanishes!
PERFECTION HAS NO REFERENCE TO BODY, STATE,
OR CONDITION. IT IS THE ABSOLUTENESS OF SINGLE-
NESS. IF YOU ARE OPERATING AS SINGLENESS, IT
MUST BE ABSOLUTE — UNCONDITIONAL COMPLETE-
NESS. THERE IS NOTHING TO IRRITATE WHOLENESS
BECAUSE IT IS SINGLE. There are no laws of relativity. If
you have a problem, it is the argument of a mystery,
darkness, ignorance. SINGLENESS ONLY IS. My best
always.

Sincerely,

Dear----------

Will you please look up and ponder the following in
"Bachelor God": 206:3-15 next page; 202:11-11 n.p.;
130:5-7; 178:2-12; 178:23-27; 165:30-18; 61:2-4; 156:3-28;
155:1-3, 18-29; 57:16-13. Am sure as you ponder these, they
will "clarify" many points.

There are no "senses" to which aught can appear, and no
"man-mind" existent at all, no dream, no humanity, hence
no evil or Satan, tempter, tempted, temptation! THERE IS
SPIRIT ONLY — ONE CONSCIOUS ALIVENESS, AWARE-
NESS. This ALIVENESS IS THE WHOLE SELF, THE
ONLY SELF EXISTENT — THE AMNESS THAT IS I.
Herein the only "things" are those thoughts which MIND IS,
FOR THE FIRST AND *ONLY MOMENT-NOW* CON-

CEIVING. Naught "has" existed in "time." Only NOW, PRESENT TENSE, IS OMNIPRESENCE, LIFE, AWARE-NESS BEING ITS WHOLE NEW SELF. This Mind is not thinking in terms of "was" or of "*thinking-about-thoughts!*" Mind is not even concerned with "things," so drop any nonsense of assuming you DO have a little mind to think "about" body, organs, limbs, aches, pains, limitation, frustrations, and the like.

I waste no time or effort at all over an assumed Alfred-mind and that-which-seems-to-be-its-vessel, its assistant, its toy, its servant or slave, its sponge, its mirror-of-trouble-and-lack! I start WHOLLY WITH ONE WHOLE COMPLETE TOTAL PERFECT PRESENCE, LIFE, SPIRIT, GOODNESS, HONEST TRUTH, and I stick there throughout the day. Not just saying over the words, but no matter how "tempting" the delicious "body" may seem to be with its lovely sauce-of-trouble-poured-all-over-it and its topping-of-misery, garnished with pain, frustration, limitation, disappointment, personal responsibility and such — I STICK WITH WHAT SPIRIT IS BEING, namely, ALL OF LIFE PRESENT, THE TOTALITY OF AWARENESS OF INFINITE PERFECTION WHEREIN NO POSSIBILITY OF OTHER-NESS OF A LACK OF TOTAL *being* could intrude. When the pain screams, I do not deny it, fight it, or even talk back to it — I TALK THAT MUCH MORE "INTELLIGENTLY" OF THE ALLNESS OF ONE COMPLETE AWARENESS WHICH IS OMNIPRESENTLY ALIVE TO ITS OWN UTTER PERFECTION, GOODNESS, BEING — and I keep at this until I am no longer trying to straddle two minds and listen equally to both!

Remember, THERE IS NO DISEASE. THERE IS ONLY

OMNIPRESENT ALL-POTENT INTELLIGENT AWARE-
NESS THAT IS YOUR SELF IN ACTION! This precludes
any little mind to holler about pain, body, food, or what! IT
IS NOT "BODY" that appears to have trouble (your
would-be senses to the contrary!) — it is a would-be second
mind. But if you HONESTLY AND PERSISTENTLY "DIG"
AT WHAT OMNIPRESENT AWARENESS OF LIFE HERE
NOW *IS*, YOU MUST FIND IT IMPOSSIBLE TO ALSO
CLING TO AN ABSENCE OF LIFE VIA ANOTHER MIND!
I urge you, stop trying to heal aught, or overcome aught or
get out of any trouble! Rather, delve into what AWARE-
NESS, ALIVENESS, CONSCIOUSNESS *IS*, FOR THIS IS
HERE AND NOW YOUR COMPLETE IDENTITY. AWARE-
NESS KNOWS THIS, AND THIS AWARENESS IS YOUR
SOLE IDENTITY-I RIGHT NOW. THIS PRECLUDES A
WOULD-BE KAREN MIND TO KNOW AUGHT. Only
metaphysics would have you try to see this via a Karen-mind
WHICH DOES NOT EVEN EXIST!

Only LOVE *can* and *does* consciously "see" or "know"
this Truth, honestly. *No other* so-called *mind COULD BE
HONEST*, because it doesn't exist, not even to declare pain
or trouble!

Fondly,

Dear----------

As you know, I do not "continue" to give treatment — I
work once and then if one still needs further help, am glad to
give same. AS REALITY IS ALREADY ALL, AND THERE
IS NAUGHT BESIDE ANYWHERE, THIS "WORK" IS
IMMEDIATE, TOTAL, COMPLETE, FOR IT IS NOW THE
ONE AND ONLY AWARENESS OMNIPOTENTLY BEING

PRESENT AS THE SOLE SELF AMNESS IS! There can be no wait for ISNESS to "become" IS — IT ALREADY IS WHAT IS, AND THERE IS NAUGHT TO CONTRADICT OR CHALLENGE THE SELF YOU BE, THE AMNESS YOU ARE! To this ONE, no accident can occur, no thought (body) can alter or be Intelligence or ever become the Identity Isness IS!

Please ponder well — that is, STATE OUT LOUD THE FOLLOWING, and then in each case, "dig" at the statement to see if it is so, how totally so, where, when, etc.! I find by using the word, "state," in place of the word, "start," — the meaning of "dig" becomes clearer. I never work to MAKE TRUTH true, but state TRUTH BECAUSE IT IS ALREADY SO — and thus FACT precludes whatever nonsense may appear to be suggested or suggesting!

These citations will keep you really busy, and are certain to prove of great help, for while digging at these FACTS, you will have no "attention" left to bestow upon contraries: UNCHALLENGED SELF 49:8-12; DEITY 17:23-25; SUPPLY 71:2-4; THAT WHICH IS 195:18-22. BACHELOR GOD 147:9-11, 19:18-26, 70:30-12, 90:1-15, 28-27 and 99:10-6; LECTURES 159:1-3, 8-9.

Do not let yourself feel guilt because of the nonsense, for all such is malpractice, an honoring of a lie in lieu of Fact! You have no problem or error to unsee, overcome, clear up, or to clear out — ALL YOU HAVE IS WHAT INFINITE INTELLIGENCE "BE'S," IS, AM, FOR THIS IS THE WHOLE OF YOUR BEING NOW — WHAT YOU WHOLLY BE OR AM RIGHT NOW, AND THERE IS NAUGHT TO DENY THIS, OPPOSE OR CHALLENGE IT! Do not assume the trick of imagination is an authority that can outwit

FACT, CONSCIOUSNESS, BEING! Sticking with what
AWARENESS IS, DIGGING AT THIS INFINITE TOTAL-
ITY, THIS UTTER SINGLENESS, LEAVES NO PLACE
FOR THE void, the lack-man-imagination or substitution!
WHERE ACTUALITY IS THE ONLY (and there is nowhere,
nowhen ACTUALITY IS NOT ALONE THAT WHICH IS
PRESENT, REAL!), there can be no "influence" from any
angle, source, place, cause, effect, etc., for no such "origin"
exists!

Again, do not fall for the nonsense we've been taught in
metaphysics, that when we SEE SO MUCH OF REALITY,
we must pay for it by being the target of evil, Satan, void!
That is so much hogwash! If it were a matter of there being a
man who had a mind that could reach out and take aboard
Truth, then he might have such a reaction, but the FACT
BEING THAT IT IS SPIRIT ONLY THAT IS MIND, AND
NEVER AUGHT BESIDE, THERE IS NO ADVANCE, NO
PROGRESSION, NO LEARNING OR IMPROVING POSSI-
BLE — THERE IS ONLY PERFECTION BEING CHANGE-
LESSLY SO, AND THERE BEING NO OTHER, THEN
WHERE IS THIS ATTACK COMING FROM, WHERE IS
THE JEALOUSY, THE ENVY, THE HATE, THE MAL-
PRACTICE? Silly, eh? No matter how we dig at Truth, we
never unearth aught but that which is ALWAYS ALREADY
NOW SO! FACT BEING ITSELF IS OUR IDENTITY! There
is none beside. It is not a you or me that "discovers" this —
IT IS MIND KNOWING ITSELF THAT IS I, AND THERE
IS NONE ELSE. ALWAYS, IT IS MIND THAT IS LIFE,
SUBSTANCE, IDENTITY, LOVE, SINGLENESS. THERE IS
NAUGHT ELSE, HENCE NAUGHT "BESIDE" TO BE-
COME AUGHT, OR STOP BEING AUGHT, OR TO

CHANGE AUGHT!

> Affectionately,

Dear----------

You ask how we know there is a God, a Truth, etc. Let me put it this way: HOW DO YOU KNOW THERE IS EXISTENCE, THAT YOU EXIST, THAT YOU ARE CONSCIOUS, OR EVEN THAT YOU BE? HOW DO YOU KNOW YOU ARE ALIVE OR THAT THERE IS AUGHT?

You see, don't try to discover "if" there is a god — such cannot be done, for all such seeking is based on theology, a thesis that takes such-and-such as a foundation and works up its case from there — a "lie" proving there is truth to its lie — whereas, in our work, we do NOT HAVE "A GOD" — LIFE IS ALL (and, often, is termed, "God," meaning TOTALITY, WHOLENESS, ALLNESS) — EXISTENCE IS ALL, BEING IS! This very ALIVENESS IS THE SOLE SELF, THE ACTUALITY WE BE, AND IS INCLUSIVE OF ALL ITEMS OF WHICH THIS PRESENT INTELLIGENCE IS CONSCIOUS — but that's all any idea-thing-item is — a mere identification *within* CONSCIOUSNESS, *by* CONSCIOUSNESS, and naught beside! EXISTENCE CANNOT BE "TAKEN FOR GRANTED!" It IS! REALITY BE'S! GENUINENESS EXISTS — or else there is only vacuity, and you are not, so you do not "wonder," nor can you ask a question, for YOU ARE NOT! Naturally, to declare you BE NOT, yet say you can be conscious of NOT BEING, is absurdity!

The "god" that people are trying "to find" is not findable! Why? Because such a creature or creation is IMPOSSIBLE within ACTUALITY, for the entire premise precludes FACT and deals only in assumptions, inclusive of the would-be mind doing the assuming!

If the above seems puzzling, don't worry about it. Just keep on reading, defining what you read aloud, and then digging to see "WHY" these statements can be made, and "WHY" they are FACTUAL RIGHT HERE NOW. When one struggles, it is generally because he is trying to intellectually (hence, from a finite or lack-laden point of observation) investigate INFINITY — place TRUTH under scrutiny, and then pass judgment. It is always based on duality.

IN ACTUALITY, THERE IS NO "SUPREME POWER," for such implies comparison, hence improvement, degrees, etc. MIND IS WHOLE ALREADY, SINGLE, PURE, ALL. THERE IS NAUGHT MORE, NAUGHT LESS, AND THERE IS ONLY THIS INDIVIDUAL ONE, the total and actual IDENTITY THAT IS I. This leaves no little "I-Aiken" to be aught, go anywhere, accomplish or prove aught, for Truth leaves ONLY TRUTH, SINGLENESS, BEING!

See NOW 142:4-21; 95:24-14.

Hope this helps to clear it up for you.

Cordially,

Dear----------

About attending the Forums — I honestly feel that had you put your foot down and insisted on coming in the past, you'd not be faced with some of the pictures that seem so real now. You see, once the nonsense seems to "back you down," it grows, and grows more aggressive each time, and can always seem to shut you off from the GOOD THAT YOU BE! I do wish you'd put an end to all the excuses and COME. It will "help" you far more than anything else.

I know all the "reasons" one does NOT attend — I hear

them on every side. But isn't it odd that EVIL NEVER SEEMS TO TOLERATE ANY EXCUSES – IT ALWAYS HAS A "REASON" WHY YOU SHOULD SERVE IT, AND IT KEEPS YOU AT IT, YEAR IN AND YEAR OUT! And the very trouble that keeps you home IS BECAUSE YOU STAY AT HOME KEEPING THE TROUBLE! Why not let the "trouble" shift for itself, while you turn to the SOLE SELF YOU BE WHICH IS UTTER GOOD RIGHT HERE NOW!

The longer the lie bluffs you, the easier it is for the lie to bluff you – and the more quickly you discover "excuses" or reasons" why you must "stay on the job to watch the evil!" For two and a half hours in the morning and evening for three short days – don't you owe it to your husband to take advantage of the ONE AND ONLY AWARENESS THAT MEANS HAPPINESS, JOY, BLISS TO HIM AND ALL?

You know, dear friend, you remind me of the fellow that was caught in a place where the water was rising fast, and would finally drown him. Well, he was so busy swimming about to keep his head above the water that he had no time to "take-off" to listen to how he could turn off the water and pull the plug so he'd be safe – so, he kept on swimming, swimming, swimming, and the water got higher and higher and higher, and he cried out louder and louder until there was no more space left for him or air – just all water! Well, we start out with trouble and are so busy with the trouble that we won't take the time off to find out how to stop the evil, and pull the plug so it vanishes! Oh yes, we say: "But what else can I do? I've got so much trouble! Someone must stay here and watch over it! I'd like to be free of it, but I'm not going to leave it – no, not even for a moment! But why doesn't it go away? And with what mind am I seeing it, since to Spirit, MY SOLE MIND, no trouble is going on? But I see trouble, so Spirit must be crazy. I'm going to believe my trouble, and to heck with Spirit! After all, trouble makes itself known right here now. Spirit? Well, I don't know much about It, for I don't have any time for Spirit, Goodness. I'm too busy with trouble!"

Oh, please wake up and COME TO THE WORK! Let the would-be trouble shift for itself for a change! You've served it so faithfully for years — why not give TRUTH A CHANCE, for a change? In THAT WHICH IS, ponder 56:11-29; 57:6-29. And then, PUT IT INTO PRACTICE! Don't allow yourself to go back to thinking all the junk. GIVE REALITY A CHANCE! Up to now, you've been most liberal with the lie — you've given IT A CHANCE — THE CHANCE TO KEEP YOU HOME, TO OUT-PICTURE ALL SORTS OF A MESS, TO DRIVE AND HOUND YOUR EVERY STEP, WAKING MOMENT, ATTENTION! Now, do as much, and as faithfully, for SPIRIT, ONE ALL HERE PRESENT!

Appreciatively,

Dear----------

Remember, THERE IS NEVER A CRISIS IN SPIRIT, N O W, ISNESS, OMNIPRESENCE, and there is naught that can be added or taken therefrom! ALL ALONE IS *a l l*, and this leaves naught beside to do aught to aught, nor another mentality that can worry, be sick, perform, or stop aught!

EVERY "THOUGHT-IDEA-BODY" IS JUST THAT THOUGHT IN MIND NOW. "IT" CANNOT CHANGE — AND MIND NEVER CHANGES. THIS IS FACT.

LET US KEEP WITH FACT, and not go about trying to

hange pictures, or in some way try to salvage humanity
vhich is NOT.

Do not deny error, BUT ALWAYS STATE FACT,
'RUTH, SINGLENESS ONLY, for this alone is POWER,
\UTHORITY, and against such there is naught to raise its
oice, for there is naught else! This is the way to "work." All
lenial is affirmation, really, and no good.

NOT A SMITCH OF EVIL, LACK, CAN TOUCH YOU
\ND YOURS, FOR WHAT CAN "CONTEND" WITH
;OODNESS, ITSELF, IN TOTAL WHOLENESS OF SPIRIT.
:TICK WITH THIS, DIG AT WHAT YOU "DECLARE" TO
'IND OUT IF YOU REALLY ARE STICKING WITH
(OUR DEFINITIONS – IF THE WORDS ACTUALLY ARE
:IGHT AND DO THEY MEAN WHAT THEY *DO* MEAN –
\ND ARE YOU STICKING THEREWITH, OR IMMEDI-
\TELY TURNING YOUR BACK ON WHAT THE FACT *IS*.
:emember, you do not need to MAKE Truth THE FACT –
'T IS FACT NOW! This means you have no lack, no man, no
rror, history, condition to meet, contend with, reverse, deal
vith at all, for THERE IS ONLY TRUTH, REALITY, THE
'RESENT *PRESENT!*

Cordially,

)ear----------

Yours of the 11th reached me and I have given you the
ielp you requested. As, no doubt you know, I work only
mce – if additional help is needed, don't hesitate to ask –
ut, you see, TRUTH ALONE BEING TRUE, THE ACTUAL
'ACT, THEN IT IS WHOLLY TRUE, THE FACT, RIGHT
NOW – AND ONLY THE FACT (TRUTH) IS TRUE! No
lelay, no resistance, no opposition, for ONLY THE PRES-

ENT IS PRESENT. NOWHERE WITHIN THE PRESENT
CAN YOU FIND A "WAS," A PAST, HENCE NONE OF
THE SITUATION THAT HAS PURPORTEDLY LED YOU
TO A BRINK OF DISASTER OR TROUBLE — NO PAST IN
WHICH A DIAGNOSIS COULD OCCUR, HENCE A PROG-
NOSIS AWAITING YOU! Only NOW, THE PRESENT, IS,
AM, BE! So let us stick wholly, completely with WHAT THE
ALL PRESENT (OMNIPRESENCE) IS, AM, IS *BEING!* Do
not flit back to the many "was's" — the past, the "has-been."
NOW IS NOT A HAS-BEEN! NOW IS FRESH, WHOLE,
SINGLE, PURE. The would-be past cannot taint or color,
influence or interfere with THE PRESENT, WITH NOW
WHICH IS BEING ALL THAT AM, THE WHOLE CON-
SCIOUSNESS, AWARENESS-I THAT IS!

WHOLENESS is inseparable, indivisible, ONE ONLY. It is
NOW, PRESENT, and has never been wed, hence cannot be
separated or divorced! It is SINGLE, INDIVIDUAL, TOTAL,
WHOLE, ALL. These are not mere words, but actually what
IDENTITY IS RIGHT HERE NOW. This leaves no additional
mind, whether called Alfred's, Linda's, husband's, or what!
There simply is no additional PRESENT, MIND, CON-
SCIOUS AWARENESS, INTELLIGENT IDENTIFICATION
OF NOW *being!* To this ONE TOTAL, WHOLE, *SATIS-
FIED*, COMPLETE, PURE, SINGLE LOVE, ALL-INCLU-
SIVE OF ITS PERFECT CONCEPTIONS-PERCEPTIONS
(THOUGHTS), there is naught more or less — no other mind,
life, identity to blame, accuse, be blamed, be accused!
(Ponder that sentence well, please!)

If, like Esau, you sell your ONENESS, SINGLENESS for
a mere mess of pottage, the price comes high — and what do
you have to show for it save a mess, a gone-to-pot of

vhatever you call home, etc.? But, sticking with WHAT
AWARENESS KNOWS AS ABSOLUTE CONSCIOUS
ALIVENESS, SINGLENESS, ALLNESS RIGHT HERE
PRESENT IN TOTO NOW, precludes another mind called
Linda, or husband, or whatever, where all the nonsense, the
"mess" is cooked up, stewed, brewed, and spit forth! ALL
OF SUCH NONSENSE IS IN THE "WAS," IN THE
"HAS-BEEN," THE PAST! None of it is in the PRESENT,
IN THE NOW, IN INFINITE INTELLIGENCE OR AWARE-
NESS AS ALL NOW, SINGLE, UNDIMENSIONAL COM-
PLETENESS HERE NOW – WITHIN THIS ALIVENESS
THAT IS TOTALLY BUSY BEING 100% ALL THAT IS!

If you "really mean business," you'll drop all thought
pertaining to what "appears to be the situation, how it came
about, who's to blame, the sins of omission, commission,
guilt, evil, morality, criticism, accusations, what your friends
advise, prescribe, and all such." Rather, you will begin with
what INFINITE CONSCIOUS ALIVENESS IS NOW BEING
AS THE SOLE AWARENESS PRESENT IN ITS ENTIRE-
TY, ITS ABSOLUTE SELF-SATISFACTION. This precludes
aught beside, for ACTUALLY, FACTUALLY, NAUGHT
HAS CHANGED NOW, THE PRESENT! STICK WITH THIS
AND BE CONSISTENTLY PERSISTENT, AND PERSIS-
TENTLY CONSISTENT. Do not go back to wallow in
self-pity, fear, worry, hurt feelings, a need to justify yourself
and all such, for all that is a TOTAL DENIAL OF SELF, IS
MURDER, CORRUPTION, AND A SELLING OUT FOR
LESS THAN THE THIRTY PIECES OF SILVER!

Please ponder well in BACHELOR GOD, Pages 95;
99:6-3; 127:8-25; 43:2 through line 6, page 46. Please
ponder this well, AND STAY WITH IT. Do not let yourself

keep coming back to a Linda-mind and the nonsense "it" would utter. It is not a matter of a separation, or dis-ease of any sort — the real difficulty (seemingly) is that we accept another mind wherein all this stuff seems to be brewed and enacted!

Cordially,

Dear----------

Mary, the ONLY CONSIDERATION YOU NEED AT ALL, IS THE ALLNESS OF ONE TOTAL LIGHT, ONE INFINITE MIND, ONE TOTAL CONSCIOUSNESS (which is Substance, Itself), ONE ABSOLUTE AWARENESS, ONE PURE SINGLE LOVE WHEREIN THERE IS NO "OTHER" AT ALL — wherein there is nothing beside — wherein there is naught else! This, and THIS ALONE is your SOLE CON- SIDERATION, YOUR ONLY "WORK," THE ONLY "JOB" YOU EVER-NOW HAVE! It is THIS ALONE THAT IS OUR SOLE "OCCUPATION," if I may use the word. There is naught else "to DO!"

You are to leave bodies, things, items, thoughts (as a definition for "things"), ideas (as a definition for "things- bodies-items"), ENTIRELY ALONE. DO NOT THINK OF THEM, DO NOT THINK ABOUT THEM. DO NOT TRY TO SEE THEM "AS GOD, MIND, SEES THEM!" DO NOT THINK OF THEM AS PERFECT, WHOLE, AND SUCH — DO NOT THINK OF "THINGS-IDEAS-BODIES-IDEAS" AT ALL! Be concerned WITH OMNIPRESENT AWARENESS solely, for this ONE BEING ITSELF is the ONLY SELF EXISTENT — nay, IS EXISTENCE, SUBSTANCE ITSELF.

So long as you strive to "know the Truth concerning body, item, thing," you will be in the bondage of metaphysics, religion, superstition — in the throes of humanity, cause and effect!

I do nothing about, with, for, or concerning "things." MY SOLE "WORK" IS CONCERN (INTEREST) WHOLLY IN CONNECTION WITH MIND, AWARENESS, WHOLENESS, ALLNESS, ONE, PURITY, PRESENCE, ACTION, FUNCTION — all terms for LIGHT ITSELF, CONSCIOUS ALIVENESS ITSELF. Naught beside exists, so why be concerned therewith — and why be concerned with "body" or "thing" when such is ONLY NOW BEING CONCEIVED-PERCEIVED, SO HAS NAUGHT TO OFFER MIND, NO WAY TO AID MIND, NO WAY IN WHICH TO CONTRIBUTE TO (or hinder or thwart) MIND, OR EVEN FOR MIND TO CONSIDER, RECALL, "THINK-ABOUT!"

We repeatedly point out that IDEAS HAVE NO "USE" TO MIND — CONTRIBUTE NAUGHT TO MIND, AND DO NAUGHT FOR OR AGAINST, WITH, OR BECAUSE OF MIND. THEY ARE BUT "THOUGHTS, " SO WHAT? MIND IS ALL, WHOLLY WITHOUT THOUGHTS. IT IS, BECAUSE IT *IS* ALL. IT CAN CONCEIVE, BUT IS NEVER CONCERNED WITH THE CONCEPTION! So why this constant concern with "WHAT" MIND CONCEIVES? That could only be of interest to a separate mind, a second mind, a non-existent mind! Such is only of interest to man, humanity, metaphysics, for all such is theological superstition which "begins always" with lack, evil, void, otherness, impurity, negation, the "want," the "need," the lack-man so-called sense!

I urge you to STATE WHAT SPIRIT IS, WHAT LIFE IS, WHAT PURITY IS, and then see if THIS IS "WHERE" YOU CONCENTRATE ALL YOUR CONCERN!" (Badly put, but it makes it clear!) There is no Mary-mind or body — there is ONLY SPIRIT PRESENT, AND IT KNOWS THIS, AND IS THE WHOLE SELF YOU BE THIS ETERNAL MOMENT! There is no "otherness" at all, so stop trying to "see" it as "perfect" for there is ONLY ONE PERFECTION, NAMELY THE SOLE INDIVIDUAL ONE SELF WHICH IS GOODNESS ITSELF IN OPERATION. THERE IS NAUGHT ELSE AND THIS ONE ALONE IS "CONCERNED" WITH OR "INTERESTED" WHOLLY IN ITSELF — never in Its thoughts! It "conceives," yes, but that is the LAST "TIME" MIND HAS A THOUGHT OF THAT THOUGHT! Mind cannot "recall" an idea-thought — never has "time" to deal with or in, so never RECALLS, REMEMBERS, RECONSIDERS, OR THINKS ABOUT a thought-idea-body-thing! So leave things ALONE, and get busy with ALL, ITSELF, FOR THIS ONLY IS YOUR IDENTITY NOW.

Fondly,

P.S. In POWER, please dig at 101:1-32; 140:27-33 next page; 150:22-6.

Dear----------

I've answered your letter at quite some length in the August, 1968, Monthly Letter.

But briefly — when you ask for "help," just WHAT DO YOU EXPECT? DO YOU LOOK FOR TRUTH? IF SO, IS IT NOT CHANGELESS? OR DO YOU MERELY SAY YOU "WANT TRUTH," BUT ACTUALLY YOU WANT HEALING? CHANGE? AN ALTERING OF THE HUMAN PICTURE? IF SO, THEN YOU ARE TURNING TO THE WRONG ONE FOR HELP! He who wants "healing" should look to metaphysics, medicine, etc. He who wants his human pictures changed, altered, improved, must begin with otherness — and TRUTH WOULD BE DEATH TO ANY SUCH!

If you want TRUTH WHEN YOU CALL HERE, YOU GET TRUTH, AND TRUTH ONLY. WE ARE NOT INTERESTED IN WHAT TRUTH IS *NOT*, WHAT CAUSED TRUTH TO BE *NOT*, WHERE, WHEN, HOW, AND WHY TRUTH IS *NOT*, AND WHO IT IS THAT IS SUFFERING FROM TRUTH *NOT* BEING! BUT IF YOU WANT TRUTH, YOU GET IT, TOTALLY, WHOLLY, HONESTLY, AND IF YOU WILL OPERATE WHOLLY, HONESTLY, ENTIRELY, CONSISTENTLY WITH THE TRUTH YOU HEAR, YOU CANNOT CONTINUE ON WITH TROUBLE. LET ME REPEAT, YOU SIMPLY C A N N O T KEEP ON WITH WHAT TRUTH IS *NOT* — YOU CAN ONLY BEHOLD THAT TRUTH IS, ONLY TRUTH IS, WHOLLY IS, EVERYWHERE IT IS, AND THERE IS NO OTHERNESS POSSIBLE UNDER ANY CIRCUMSTANCE FOR THERE IS NO CIRCUMSTANCE, NO CONDITION, NO RELATIVITY, NO CHANGE HAVING TAKEN PLACE, OR THAT CAN TAKE PLACE, OR EVER DID OR WILL TAKE PLACE, FOR THERE IS ONLY NOW, AND IT IS WHOLLY OMNIPRESENT, PERFECT, ENTIRE, SINGLE, AND THERE IS NAUGHT BESIDE. SO, WHERE IS DISEASE, WHO HAS IT, WHAT SAYS SO, TO WHOM DOES IT SAY IT, WHY, WHEN, HOW, AND DOES IT, REALLY?

But he who is dishonest and "asks" for Truth, yet all the while has his thought centered, concentrated, consistently and only on disease, lack, fear, time, problems, limitation, aches, and misery, humanity, manhood, age, difficulty and so on, will "get" just what he is "looking at," concentrating on,

where, when, and an abundant crop of it. At no point is he
HONESTLY BEGINNING WITH FACT OR INTERESTED
IN FACT, AND IS ONLY, EXCLUSIVELY, INTERESTED
IN, AND INTENDS TO HANG ONTO, HIS MISERY TILL
THE LAST TICK OF TIME, THE LAST BREATH HE CAN
DRAW, TO EXTRACT FROM HIS LITTLE FINITE MEN-
TALITY ALL THE MISERY, SMALLNESS, TROUBLE,
BLAME, CRITICISM, DISAPPOINTMENT AND FRUSTRA-
TION HE CAN MANAGE – THEN ACCUSE TRUTH OF
HAVING LET HIM DOWN! Yet he has not EVEN BEGUN
WITH FACT. IF HE HAD, HE'D FIND TRUTH IS AL-
READY WHOLE, WELL, PERFECT, COMPLETE, ENTIRE,
JOY, ACTION, POWER, PRESENT, AUTHORITY, BEING,
AND NAUGHT BESIDE CAN BE. TRUTH PRECLUDES
PROBLEMS AND THE WOULD-BE MINDS ENTERTAIN-
ING SUCH! One cannot begin with TRUTH and still have
error anywhere, for WHERE TRUTH IS ALL, AND IT IS
ALL EVERYWHERE, THERE CEASES TO BE ANY
PLACE FOR DARKNESS OR NON-TRUTH WHICH YOU
MAY "CALL" DISEASE, PAIN, LACK, RELATIVES,
FRIENDS, BODY, OR WHATEVER! But when you "call,"
and all the time you merely want SPIRIT TO COME BY
AND CLEAN UP YOUR GARBAGE AS A HUMAN, YET
LEAVE YOU OPERATING AS A HAPPY HUMAN, A
WELL AND PROSPEROUS HUMAN, YOU DON'T KNOW
WHEREOF YOU ASK, FOR THERE ARE NO HUMANS
WHERE SPIRIT IS THE ALL, THE ONLY, THE ONE
ALONE! I do hope this answers all your questions! In THAT
WHICH IS, ponder pages 108 and 109.

A merry "NOW" to you – BUT GET BUSY AND BE
HONEST WITH TRUTH – STOP LOOKING TO IT TO

MAKE YOU A HAPPY HUMAN, FOR NO SUCH EXISTS AT ALL!

> Cordially,

Dear----------

Just a note to greet you, and to remind you that just because a nation or a whole planet seems to be in mourning — seems to assume that there is a "grand old man" departed these shores of time — NONE SUCH IS GOING ON IN REALITY! So don't assume it can "also happen to me, Joyce!"

Remember, WHATEVER SEEMS TO BE GOING ON IN THE DREAM — IT IS STILL THE DREAM THAT IS DREAMING IT ALL. THERE IS NOT A BLADE OF GRASS "SEEN" BY ONE IN THAT DREAM, SAVE BOTH THE BLADE OF GRASS AND THE EYE SEEING IT AND THE "SENSE" SENSING OR IDENTIFYING IT, *IS DREAM DREAMING!* NONE OF IT IS GOING ON IN REALITY AT ALL, so one does not try to "change the picture" or the "situation" one seems to be "sensing," nor do aught to the shape, form, dimensional "body" that appears to be the pivotal point wherein and around which the "dis-ease" seems to be centered or operative!

If only I could make this "clear" to our folks! If they'd only actually "think" what they "read" or "say," they would stop being disturbed by pictures (and "feelings" are just as much a "picture" as what the eye or the ear reports)! Leave the picture, the sensing, the feeling, the seeing and hearing out of it altogether — rather, "start" with INFINITE INTELLIGENCE (and there is none other, for to declare there is a finite intelligence is absurd)! One cannot, simply

cannot, assume that PERFECT AWARENESS, CONSCIOUS-
NESS, TOTAL ALIVENESS is only partly aware, partly
conscious, partly alive to being present, active, whole!

You see, disease of any sort, financial, physical, political
or what, only appears to be operative IN THE DEGREE ONE
IS DIRECTING "PART" OF HIS ATTENTION TO WHAT
TRUTH-IS-NOT! He who keeps "digging" at what ALIVE-
NESS, WHOLENESS, TOTAL SPIRIT (SUBSTANCE-
AWARENESS) IS *being*, is so utterly "full" of REALITY
(badly put) that there is no "room" to "entertain" or
"think-on" what-would-be-if-Reality-were-not! Of course,
none of us wishes to deliberately assume Truth is NOT, but it
is the whole fabric of humanity, so when we go in for
assuming we are human, we are also provided (by the dream
who is doing the whole thing of dreaming-up humans, and
what they are "supposed" to be doing) with all the lack
which is the human's foundation! Also, with a seeming
ability to assume that we CAN assume! But none of this is so.
So let's not try to overcome it, feel guilt because of it, or try
to account for it, to it, or give any account of it! Rather,
stick with AWARENESS, and keep at it without cessation —
FOR THIS IS THY BEING! You do not and cannot
"overcome" disease, for there is no such. Nor can you
overcome humanity, or stop being human, BECAUSE YOU
ARE NOT HUMAN, AND THERE IS NO SUCH. Nor can
you harness or quell the human mind, FOR THERE IS NO
OTHER MIND AT ALL, ANIMAL OR WHAT, DISEASED
OR WHAT, HUMAN OR WHAT! There is ONLY SPIRIT
BEING ITSELF AND IT IS PERFECTION BEING, so
where can one even raise the question: "What am I doing
wrong, or what ought I to do in order to overcome, or get the

victory over this condition?" SPIRIT, THE SOLE YOU BE, THE VERY SOUL THAT IS AMNESS, can't be ill. There is no way that the mind-you-are-NOT can be ill! Where, then, Truth-*fully* can you "locate" disease, name it, and then suffer with it? In NOW, ponder well 85:17-18 ("economy" can also be read as "disease" or "body").

Fondly,

Dear----------

Do hope you are actually starting with LIGHT ALONE IS ALL — ALL THE SUBSTANCE, BEING, IDENTITY, CONSCIOUS AWARENESS. There is no other self-I at all.

To start out with body, and keep thinking in terms of the conditions of body, its aches, its limitation, its age, what it eats, how well it sleeps, what is happening to it, and all the rest of it, and then trying to cover it over with Truth, as you would cover a slice of bread with butter, is metaphysics!

To state that ONLY TRUTH IS TRUE, ONLY LIFE IS ALIVE, ONLY EXISTENCE EXISTS, ONLY NOW IS, leaves you with no "body" to think about — it leaves you wholly apart from things to meditate on. Items fade out of focus — so I beg of you, GET BUSY WITH GOODNESS, LIFE, LOVE, SINGLENESS, PURE AWARENESS, LIGHT AS WISDOM, AND KEEP DIGGING THERE, TO THE PRECLUSION OF ANY MATERIAL, PERSONAL, PHYSICAL ORGAN OR BODY-IDENTITY!

So long as body is uppermost in your thought, you simply will not, and cannot actually consider TRUTH. So long as body is uppermost in your consideration, it will be the activity of body that takes every moment of your attention, and you will be trying to change the picture presented to the five-computer-senses. This is to worship body as your god!

GOODNESS IS NOT THAT WHICH THE SENSES "SENSE." BODY IS BUT A THOUGHT IN MIND, BUT LEAVE IT ALONE, FOR MIND DOES NOT SPEND ITS TIME ON THINKING, RETHINKING, RE-RETHINKING THOUGHTS. MIND CONCEIVES, AND THAT IS IT, BUT MIND IS WHO AND WHAT YOU BE — NOT ONE OF THE ITEMS MIND CONCEIVES!

IT IS MIND, IT IS LIGHT, THAT SHOULD BE YOUR ENTIRE CONCERN, and LOVE, SINGLENESS, PURE AWARENESS AS SUBSTANCE, FOR THIS IS YOUR IDENTITY NOW, AND IT IS WHOLE, PERFECT, ABSOLUTELY FREE THIS VERY MOMENT. NO MATTER HOW LONG YOU HAVE BEEN MESSING ABOUT WITH A LIE, YOU CAN BEHOLD TRUTH THIS INSTANT AND THE LIE FADES OUT IMMEDIATELY. YOU ARE NOT BOUND TO KEEP ON MESSING ABOUT WITH ACHES AND PAINS. YOU CAN START WITH FACT THIS INSTANT IF AND WHEN YOU WILL. NAUGHT BINDS YOU. YOU ARE WHOLE, FREE, PERFECT NOW. ALL OF GOODNESS IS YOUR VERY IDENTITY NOW AND INTELLIGENCE KNOWS THIS. THERE IS NO STUPIDITY ANYWHERE, FOR THERE IS NO PLACE FOR IT. THERE IS ONLY LIGHT EVERYWHERE, SO NO DARKNESS, SUPERSTITION, UGLY PICTURES TO APPEAR AS SHADOWS, ANYWHERE. THIS IS FACT. BUT IF YOU TRY TO "SEE' THIS VIA THE SENSES, THE COMPUTER WILL STILL COMPUTE ACCORDING TO THE NONSENSE FED INTO THE THING VIA THE TAPE OF EDUCATION, SO YOU WILL KEEP ON "SENSING" THAT "TRUTH DOES NOT COMPUTE — INSUFFICIENT DATA!"

See THAT WHICH IS 160:5-15.

Fondly,

Dear----------

In the book NOW be sure to carefully go over the chapter on BUSINESS. Read it aloud if you can, and with each sentence, pause and ask yourself if what you have voiced IS THE TRUTH, THE FACT. Then ask yourself if there can possibly be any other mind also present that can refute Fact, contradict Truth, repudiate Action, halt Being, change Identity, silence Intelligence, or minimize UNDIMEN-SIONAL TOTALITY! Once you have answered yourself, then ACT IN ACCORD WITH THE STATEMENT OF FACT YOU HAVE MADE, i.e., stick with what INTELLIGENCE, CONSCIOUSNESS, PURE AWARENESS, declares ITSELF TO *BE*, and do not go back to the depths of what your senses would say was the situation!

The arguments of void, vacuum want, trouble, frustration, may perhaps dog you for awhile, yes, but that is no reason why you need to listen, be irritated, or accept them. With each so-called "attack-of-lack, limitation or humanity," immediately start out with WHAT INTELLIGENCE KNOWS ITSELF TO BE RIGHT HERE NOW, and stick with THIS, for THIS FACT BEING ALONE THE TRUTH, PRECLUDES what the "suggestion" or "human evidence" would have you accept! If you will stay with INFINITE AWARENESS AS THE SOLE INDIVIDUAL ONE PRESENT, of a certainty the suggestion then has no soil on which, or in which, to seemingly operate! It will soon stop even seeming-to-suggest aught.

You see, we do NOT try to drive the money changers (the

problem) out of the temple (body, our daily experience), but rather we DO STICK WITH FACT, FOR TRUTH LEAVES NO PLACE, POWER, IDENTITY, OR EVEN PRETENSE OF EVIL. It is here that we differ radically from all forms of so-called teaching! They would have one wrestle, resist, struggle-to-overcome-or-become, thus making evil a present reality, hence incapable of destruction! Whereas, we stick with FACT, FOR *ONLY* TRUTH IS TRUE, so what remains to fight with or against? With 2 x 2 = 20, you do not fight it, do you? Of course not. You merely stick with WHAT IS FACT and that leaves no problem to deal with, or one that is dealing with you!

The ALLNESS OF ALL, THE PRESENCE OF OMNI-PRESENCE, THE ACTION OF OMNIACTION LEAVES NAUGHT BESIDE, so where and what is the "problem," and who or what says so? On what authority? You see, we do not deal in duality. ONE IS ALL, AND THAT ALL IS THE ONE-BEING-I-AM. I can be no other — not as a human trying to "become," — but it is SPIRIT THAT IS TRULY THE ALONE ONE AND THERE IS NO OTHER ALLNESS "TO BE." We never declare that "man" or the "human" is One, for that is a total fraud! It is SPIRIT, THE MIND THAT IS, LIFE BEING, PURE LOVE PRESENT IN ITS ENTIRE-TY, THAT IS THE SOLE AMNESS THAT IS I, and there is none beside. Always, IT IS SPIRIT, GOD, WHO IS ALL, and Spirit is never idle, never out of a job, never displaced, misplaced, or mismanaged! WITH LOVE, ALL IS PER-FECTION PRESENT, TOTALLY FUNCTIONING IN ITS ALLNESS, ITS ABSOLUTE AWARENESS AS INTELLI-GENCE, THE LIFE THAT IS I. Stick wholly with LIFE, and leave the so-called human sense out of it, and lo, you cannot

fail to discover the glory of BEING IN ITS ENTIRETY!
                     Most cordially,

Dear----------
    Now, Becky, you simply MUST stop the habit of "finding
fault" with others and BEING UPSET AT WHAT THE
FOLKS IN THE HOUSE DO, OR DO NOT DO — WHAT
THEY SAY, THE MANNER IN WHICH THEY SAY IT,
AND WHAT THEY DO NOT SAY! So long as you have
ANOTHER, YOU D E N Y *YOUR*SELF! That means, YOU
GO WITHOUT — PUT YOURSELF OUTSIDE OF YOUR
OWN HEAVEN, SINGLENESS, POWER AND AUTHOR-
ITY! You cut yourself off from ALL GOODNESS, WHICH
IS YOUR SOLE IDENTITY, FUNCTION, ACTION, IDEN-
TITY. I do not care how much human "justification" there
may seem to be, TRUTH BEING ALL, SINGLE, TOTAL,
COMPLETE, WHOLE, there is no justification in refusing
Truth, denying Truth, refuting Fact, opposing Self, fighting
against Health, repudiating Harmony, and insisting on being
but one-among-many, and also insisting on getting pushed
around! ONLY YOU ARE DOING THE PUSHING, THE
OUTLINING, THE DECLARING OF WHAT "OTHERS"
APPEAR TO BE DOING AND SAYING. YOU ALONE ARE
DOING IT ALL, FOR THERE IS ONLY ONE SELF, ONE
LIFE, *ONE LOVE PRESENT AND IT IS I!* So long as you
refuse to be YOUR SELF *ONLY*, you will tolerate (suffer)
falsity, lack, humanhood, conceit, deceit, malice, pain, fear,
death! YOU DO IT TO YOURSELF, BECKY, THEN "SAY"
IT IS ONE OF THE CHARACTERS YOU DREDGE UP
FROM HUMAN IMAGINATION! You alone are writing your
daily diary — you alone concoct the characters, ONLY

BECAUSE YOU REFUSE TO BE SINGLE, ONE, ONLY, WHOLE, TOTAL, COMPLETE!

I urge you to stop this nonsense, and actually START BEING HONEST WITH YOUR SELF, THE ALONE PRESENCE, LOVE, PURITY, SINGLENESS, INFINITE AWARENESS THAT SPIRIT IS. Then, whenever the nonsense of otherness pops up, do not pursue it, deny it, run it down, or sit in the puddle with it and complain how muddy and smelly you are becoming, or how rank and unpalatable the mess appears to be. Rather, START WITH WHAT LOVE, ONENESS IS. YOU CANNOT HOLD TO ERROR WHILE SINGING THE PRAISES OF WHOLENESS, WHOLESOMENESS, COMPLETENESS, ONENESS!

More and more I find it so important to STICK WHOLLY WITH WHAT LOVE IS. DO NOT KEEP CALLING GENE AND POURING OUT IN HIS EAR THE MESSES YOU DREDGE UP WITHIN A BECKY MIND! I would not inflict the putrid junk within a so-called Alfred mind on anyone, not even myself! It is "adding burdens, grievous to be borne, upon the backs of others" who are already bent under their own seeming load! Why add yours to theirs? Especially when you DO HAVE THE INSTANT REMEDY AT HAND? YOU CAN CLEAR OUT THE WHOLE UNIVERSE BY FUMIGATING IT WITH LOVE, SPIRIT, GOODNESS! You CAN, IF YOU WILL, BEGIN WITH SPIRIT AS ALL, AND CAN STICK WITH THIS UNTIL YOU NO LONGER ARE TEMPTED TO ANSWER BECKY'S TELEPHONE CALL TO YOU. REMEMBER, SHE ONLY WANTS TO GOSSIP TO YOU, TO CONVINCE YOU THAT GOD IS A LIAR, TRUTH IS HOLLOW AND UNREAL, FACT IS FICTION, LOVE IS IMPURE, SINGLENESS IS DUAL, OTHERS

"DO" EXIST AND THIS PROVES THAT LIFE IS A LIAR, CORRUPT, STINKING, SELFISH AND SO ON, AND ON, AND ON!

I try to keep so busy with WHAT LOVE IS, that I cannot take "time out" to answer the mental phone call from Aiken, for "he" only wants to insist on what is NOT TRUTH, NOT LOVE, NOT LIFE, NOT COMPLETENESS, NOT HEALTH, NOT UNCHANGING TOTALITY, NOT THE UNCHALLENGED SELF, BUT RATHER THAT THE SELF IS HUMAN AND IS UNDER CONSTANT BARRAGE, ATTACK, FRUSTRATION, STRAIN, AND ALL MANNER OF VICISSITUDES! No, No, Becky, I WANT NOTHING AT ALL TO DO WITH AN AIKEN MIND OR ITS WORLD, FOR IT IS MADE UP WHOLLY, ENTIRELY, ABSOLUTELY OF JUNK, LIES, INSINUATIONS, CONCLUSIONS DRAWN FROM ITS WOULD-BE FIVE SENSES WHICH ARE SENSELESS! If I am to "listen" to aught, IT MUST BE TO TRUTH, FACT, LOVE, AUTHORITY, PURITY, ACTION, FUNCTION, HARMONY, JOY, PEACE, TRANQUILITY, SELF-SATISFACTION, HAPPINESS, THE ABSOLUTE THRILL AND EXCITEMENT OF WHOLENESS WHEREIN NO LACK, NO ERROR, NO IGNORING OF SUCH can even pretend to be! I refuse, SIMPLY *REFUSE*, to spread the infection of verbal poison around over my "friends!" I will not spray them with the ACID OF HATE, MALICE, CRITICISM, GOSSIP, ACCUSATIONS, MALICIOUS REPORTS concerning "others," for IN TRUTH THERE IS ONLY THE ONE I AM, AND I WILL NOT TRY TO CONVINCE MY "FRIENDS" THAT I AM MULTIPLE, IMPURE, GROSS, ANIMAL, HATEFUL, IGNORANT, A DEATH-HEAD WITHIN THEIR EAR OR EYE! I will not do this! Nor will I let "others" do it to me! It is the basest form of cruelty, and you cannot imagine how that "infection" spreads and tries to kill the joy and happiness and freedom of what appears to be "my fellows!" Do not gossip evil to yourself or to another — speak TRUTH or keep still! And do NOT OUTLINE HOW OTHERS SHOULD BEHAVE! Again, you are putting *things* "out there," when in Fact, all items (even what seems to be people) are WITHIN THE ONE SELF YOU BE! When you ACT IN ACCORD WITH WHAT YOU BE, you will NOT be outlining how "others" should act or conduct themselves! But, rather, the whole of your UNIVERSE WITHIN CONSCIOUSNESS IS TRULY HEAVEN! Herein there is naught that CAN "WORK OR MAKE A LIE!" Then, where do YOU stand?

Fondly,

Dear----------

No matter what "may seem to go on out there somewhere," your sole attention should be ON THE ALLNESS OF INFINITE UNDIMENSIONAL LIGHT AS YOUR TOTAL IDENTITY — THE SOLE SUBSTANCE YOU BE. YOU HAVE NOTHING TO DO WITH "BODY" AT ALL, WITH ORGANS, WITH PEOPLE, WITH THINGS. SO LONG AS YOU KEEP DECLARING TRUTH, HOPING IT WILL IN SOME WAY ALTER OR KEEP "THINGS" IN ORDER, YOU ARE PLAYING PRODIGAL — PRACTICING METAPHYSICS.

We are told, even in the Bible, to TAKE NO THOUGHT FOR BODY. Yet, most of the people who turn to Aiken's work insist on constantly "thinking in terms of body," about body, concerning body, and how to keep it well, what it

ants, the help it needs, the services of other bodies to keep
is body happy and properly active and all the rest of it —
nd then they wonder why the road seems so difficult! ALL
UCH "THINKING" IS ONE WITH LACK — NAY, IS
ACK, LIMITATION, CONSTRICTION, RESTRICTION IT-
ELF!

He who states what INFINITE CONSCIOUSNESS IS, and
ctually defines his words, and keeps thinking, digging,
ctually working to find out the deepest possible meaning of
hat he has declared, will have no time or attention to
estow upon what the "senses" would declare about body,
rgans, lack, money and such! One cannot ENTIRELY KEEP
HOUGHT ON THE TOTALITY OF UNDIMENSIONAL
OMPLETENESS, and still harbor all sorts of fear, criticism,
orry, anxiety, organic or glandular difficulties, age, gender,
roperty, and all the rest of the HUMAN NONSENSE — that
onsense that is CAESAR, LACK, MAN, A DENIAL OF
OVE'S SINGLENESS! This is Fact. So, we either actually
top talking and get down to business, or we lie in our teeth
hen we voice Reality, for It is but so much theory to us if
nly chatted, but NOT LIVED IN OUR EVERY MOMENT!

Fondly,

ear----------

I have been "giving thought" to what you wrote in your
st. This letter is not to in any way "dissuade"you from
hat you intend, but it is meant to "help" you see Reality
S THE VERY BEING YOU ARE — so I know you'll take it
 this sense.

Should you be making a mistake in addition, do you
uppose soaking in a tub, in the ocean, or at some spa would

help your addition, correct or improve it in any way, or would you have to start with REALITY, and STAY WITH REALITY WHICH PRECLUDES ANY MISTAKE, and thus put down the correct answer?

Going to an undertaker does NOT give you the correct sense of LIFE, SELF. You must turn to LIFE IN ITS ENTIRETY in order to behold ALIVENESS, YOUR VERY IDENTITY NOW. Putting your confidence in "the physicians" as did Asa, merely means you will continue to "sleep with your fathers."

The ONE PLACE ON THIS PLANET WHERE YOU WILL ACTUALLY "GET HELP," TOTAL FREEDOM, IS AT THE SEMINAR — not by soaking an idea in a spa — any more than soaking the letters of the alphabet will do aught toward writing a book! Soaking body is the same as soaking a nail, a tack, a piece of thread — but it will not make these items happy, well, or wise! There is no mind in any of them, any more than there is mind in your body. You cannot be in the nail or thread, nor can you be in body — all these items are thoughts (ideas, things) of which THE MIND YOU BE IS CONSCIOUS! If you appear to have any trouble with any of those items, it is because you are NOT STARTING WITH THE SOLE SUBSTANCE THAT INCLUDES THEM, but are trying to establish "them" as entities, intelligences or themselves — and the suffering that seems to result is wholly due to trying to work with a mind that is utterly false! But the moment you start "seeing" with the ONLY MIND YOU ALREADY BE, in that instant YOU ARE FREE.

Carol, the "trouble" is not for "years" with your body but because "for years" you have refused to actually get down to business and be HONEST THAT INFINITE OMNI

PRESENCE ACTUALLY IS THE VERY ALIVENESS, EX-ISTENCE, THAT IS YOU for this TOTAL EXISTENCE precludes another mind, an-absentee-mind which can concoct every notion that refutes Truth. Then where is there a mind to testify to error, say "it" knows it and can suffer from or with it? You cannot say that Spirit (your Mind) suffers pain, and as THERE IS NO OTHER MIND AT ALL, NO OTHER I-IDENTITY — WHAT OR WHO IS LEFT TO SUFFER TROUBLE? Carol, you simply MUST deny all that is true of the SELF YOU BE in order to have this other so-called mentality! And the one thing that "it" needs to keep on for years and years to come, is to keep you *away* from hearing TRUTH, FOR LISTENING FOR ONE FULL WEEK TO TRUTH WOULD LEAVE NO PLACE OR MIND TO ENTERTAIN NONSENSE! The ONE SURE "CURE" FOR BODY OF ALL AILMENTS IS REALITY, SINGLENESS, TOTAL UNEQUIVOCAL HONESTY WITH OMNIPRESENT FACT! But if you can be enticed away from WHAT YOU BE — can be enticed to argue for what YOU ARE *NOT*, then error can seem to wax stronger and stronger, even as it did with the prodigal. Why was he not "healed?" Because he was always seeking a healing, thus constantly denying OMNI-PRESENCE *NOW!* He was willing to look for help tomorrow, but was unwilling to admit REALITY TO BE PRESENT NOW IN ITS ENTIRETY! And if you assume you can "soak" Truth through your skin and thus become whole, you have utterly bypassed FACT!

Nothing is wrong with body, an idea in Mind! And there is no human mind existent unless God is a total liar, hence there is NO LIFE AT ALL! If such be the case, where is body? There simply wouldn't be any — and as there is body,

it MUST BE IDEA IN MIND ONLY, AND AS SUCH, MIND
IS BEHOLDING IT AS IT IS, NAMELY, A PERFECT
CHANGELESS IDEA, THOUGHT, "THING." The moment
you begin to lower the bars, willingly ignoring Truth, or
rationalizing for what the error (human mind) would outline,
it begins to snowball! I urge you both to STICK WITH FACT
— NOT JUST "TALK" IT ON FAIR DAYS AND FORGET
IT ON RAINY ONES! I URGE YOU TO RECONSIDER
AND COME TO THE SEMINAR! In FORUMS, please
ponder 98:17-29; 99:21-25, 28-9; 255:3-9; 130:13-24,
198:20-9. I urge you, do not try to "heal" aught, but get
busy with what ALL is here and now. This precludes error,
and leaves naught you need to "know" about it pro or con.

I do hope this is of some "help," and it will be, if you will
not listen to medicine, matter, the suggestion you are a body
conceived biologically and as an outcome of theology! To
listen to such leads but deeper into chaos from which you
must sooner or later emerge by beholding that NO SUCH
EVER WAS — NO HISTORY, TIME, ASTROLOGY, PRO-
PHECY, EVER WAS! Let us stick with WHAT IS, and waste
no more effort trying to soak "what was" out of a
dream-body! Real body is but a thought in Mind, what YOU
INCLUDE WITHIN AWARENESS, and it can't be soaked,
for it is not dimensional — and the "other" is but a figment
of a non-existent dream purportedly dreaming — yet no such
dream or its dreaming can be found in OMNIPRESENCE,
YOUR SOLE PRESENT IDENTITY!

Do let me hear from you — and sure hope you come to
the Seminar — and you WILL if you genuinely wish to
behold FACT and drop fiction!

Love,

Dear----------

Please ponder well the letter that begins on page 137 of Power. Do not depart from the ONENESS, THE ENTIRETY, THE TOTALITY THAT SPIRIT (I AM) *NOW IS*.

You see, Velma, the moment we try to "change the picture," we are working from the "seeing of the eye and the hearing of the ear." But "starting with" or admitting the OMNIPRESENCE OF TRUTH, INSTANTLY IT IS EVIDENT THAT THERE IS *ONLY* REALITY (EXISTENCE) PRESENT, HENCE IT ALONE IS ALL THAT IS ACTING *(BEING)* AND THERE CAN BE NAUGHT BESIDE!

Too often we merely "say" the "words" while our conviction (our "faith") is in evil, lack, the pictures that seem to surround us — we accept that we DO have a little mind that is filled with all manner of frustrations, limitations, "reasons" for this or that! It will even tell you that you have a husband that is limited, needs care, and requires much time and attention, hence that you are bound, limited, imprisoned. It will tell the next fellow that it is his organs, his heart, his eyes, his liver, his "old" body, and so on. Another it will tell that it is the Iron Curtain, politics, gender, lack of money, or something else! To argue for humanity is to take ALL THAT FLESH IS HEIR TO! You cannot have a little bit of humanity! You either have it *all* (meanwhile excluding Truth), or SPIRIT IS ALL AND THUS PRECLUDES A HUMAN MIND WITH ALL THE JUNK IT CLAIMS ABOUT ITSELF AND ITS WOULD-BE WORLD!

You either BE WHAT TRUTH IS, OR ELSE YOU DO NOT EXIST! And in this ONE MIND THAT I AM, there is naught that can "work or make a lie." In the ONE MIND,

OMNIPRESENT, *OMNIACTIVE ALIVENESS*, there is no human mind at all, hence none to paint pictures, try to heal or overcome pictures, put up barriers, demand of Love, "What doest Thou?" No, LOVE (THE ONE I AM) IS NOT CHALLENGED, BECAUSE THERE IS NO OTHER EXISTENT, HENCE NONE TO DO THE CHALLENGING!

Stick with what MIND IS KNOWING ITSELF TO BE, for this is your ACTUAL I-IDENTITY *NOW*. Within this ONE PERFECT FULLY ACTING MIND, THERE IS NAUGHT CONTRARY. ONLY OMNIACTION IS GOING ON EVERY-WHERE. You cannot place the point of a needle anywhere that LOVE, SINGLENESS, PURITY, ONE ALONE, IS NOT BEING THE PRESENT PERFECT ONE! Within THIS ONE MIND, EVERY IDEA (body, thing) IS A PERFECT THOUGHT. The thought (idea) cannot change, for IT IS *NOW* PERCEIVED AS THE IDEA THAT IT IS! This leaves no personal (human or man) mind to claim things to be objective, persons, etc. ONLY AS MIND PERCEIVES *ITS* IDEAS DO THEY EXIST. There is no other mind at all. And no idea (body) that MIND "THINKS" (perceives) can change, alter itself, become diseased, have a separate mind or experience! Each THOUGHT (idea, body, thing, item) OF MIND IS UNDIMENSIONAL! Each thought must be EVERYWHERE MIND IS! No thought has a specific "location" or geographical spot! It would have to be physical or material to have this occur! No idea can lose his mind, because NO IDEA HAS EVER HAD A MIND TO LOSE! EVERY IDEA IS *IN* MIND, BUT HAS NEVER HAD A MIND! Hence none can have an impaired mind, disordered mind, partial or undeveloped mind!

We do not have to "treat" these seeming "conditions" —

we merely have to be alert that we do not argue for a human mind, humanhood, manhood which claims to be this disordered disorderliness! We NEVER have to do aught to the "problem" for that is not the culprit — but we must be alert lest we accept the suggestion that there IS another mind, a human one wherein all that is human can go on. And remember, that which is human is DEAD ALREADY. It is not subject to Truth for there is NO TRUTH IN IT — IT IS A LIAR AND THE FATHER OF THE LIE — but IT HAS NO PLACE IN OMNIPRESENCE (WHICH IS HEAVEN HERE AND NOW). If not in OMNIPRESENCE, IT IS NOT IN EXISTENCE, SO HOW CAN IT "BE ACCOUNTED OF"? AND WHO OR WHAT WOULD "CLAIM" IT CAN DO THIS ACCOUNTING? Stay with the ALLNESS OF PERFECT SPIRIT RIGHT NOW, FOR THIS PRECLUDES ANY OTHERNESS, WHETHER IT APPEARS AS YOU OR ANOTHER.

Where there is no human mind, there is no humanity, hence none of the things "flesh is heir to." Where there is ONLY SPIRIT, ONLY WHAT SPIRIT IS, IS IN ACTION, FUNCTION, *BEING!* It is this simple! And, regardless of the suggestions of another mind, I am sure a Seminar will "clear away" any sense of another mind, the sole and only lie, devil, Satan, hell, death! (I'm not giving you a commercial, but do feel it would be completely "out of this world" for you)! Anyway, do give it thought, and don't let the "time of year" interfere, for ONLY *OMNIPRESENCE, NOW, IS!* The would-be human depends on time, loves time, measures by time, classifies by time, lives in and because of time, and never has time! NOWNESS, EXISTENCE, PRESENCE, IS-NESS, I AMNESS *precludes* time, hence any history, past, need to gain or regain, need to grow, develop, "understand!" NOW PERFECTION, I AM, *is*. This is Fact and precludes fable, cause, reason, or appearance of such!

Cordially,

Dear----------

As for the pictures that salute your senses, DO NOTHING WITH THEM, OR TO THEM! Turn wholly to what LOVE IS KNOWING ITSELF TO BE, namely, ALL THE SUBSTANCE, PRESENCE, LIFE, INTELLIGENCE, IDENTITY-I, AMNESS. Within this ONE MIND there are no human pictures, no argument of birth, death, imperfection of any sort, anywhere, for any reason.

There simply is no "other way" to be free of human pictures save by starting out with REALITY and STAYING WITH REALITY, for within TRUTH (CONSCIOUS AWARENESS) THERE IS ONLY PERFECTION. Nowhere within Reality can one find aught human, mortal, coming-and-going, superior or inferior. Nowhere in Mind can one find degrees of INTELLIGENCE! INTELLIGENCE IS NOT DIVISIBLE, NOT FRACTURED, NOT SCATTERED ABOUT, a little here and a little more there! INTELLIGENCE IS ONE WHOLE BEING, THE SOLE IDENTITY YOU BE! There is no otherness at all. And within the INTELLIGENCE YOU *BE*, every "body" (item-thing) is but a PERFECT THOUGHT, IDEA, CONCEPTION. Nothing more, nothing less.

In other words, whenever you think of the boy, stop seeing him as your eyes, your education, your sentiment and emotions are conditioned to "see" him, but rather beginning with ONE INFINITE AWARENESS (your ENTIRE BEING

being the ONLY INDIVIDUAL, the ALONE AMNESS-THAT-IS-I), you will see that every item (whether called body, alphabet, planet or what) is but a thought, an idea, something of which Mind is aware, which Mind includes within Its CONSCIOUSNESS. But not one of these items is aware, not one has stuff to it — it is within Mind, conceived by Mind, known only to Mind, and perfectly perceived by Mind. Every idea (body) is undimensional, everywhere within Mind, hence cannot have the shape it appears to have to a limited finite sense!

Keep your own counsel — don't discuss "conditions," for to do so is to start with what the senses assume to be the state of this or that. Then you will do the "sensible" thing relative to your daily affairs. It is not a matter of being afraid to "talk," but rather that TRUTH BEING ALL, there is no reason to "come down to the plain of Ono!" If it seems required to talk with the teachers, don't be afraid to, any more than you'd be afraid to talk about a misspelled word — but don't argue for Truth — It needs no argument in Its behalf, FOR IT IS NOW ALL, AND THERE IS NO OTHERNESS. Stick with this. Don't try to "heal" or "change" aught, for TRUTH ALONE BEING PRESENT, OMNIPRESENT, THERE IS NAUGHT BESIDE AT ALL, ·NO OTHER MIND, STATE, CONDITION, ACTION, BEING OR AWARENESS — AND ALL, BEING ALL, IS PERFECT NOW. This *precludes* another mind, one that is not perfect, whole, entire! But trouble continues only so long as one is prodigal, insisting on another mind, hence on lack! No such exists TO THE ONE ALONE WHEREIN THERE IS NO OTHER. Ponder in NOW, 83:18-28, and in DEITY, 51:13-24; 49:18-6.

Cordially,

Dear----------

Yours just came and I shall try to get an answer off that makes it clear that AS ONLY EXISTENCE EXISTS, ONLY ALL IS ALL, ONLY NOW *IS*, there can be no little mind anywhere (call it by any name you wish, yours, another's or what) beside. Therefore, there is no little mind to conjure up nightmares, frustration, raise its voice to say to the SOLE PURE SINGLENESS THAT AWARENESS-SELF *IS*: "WHAT DOEST THOU?"

Only because you would ask "why" for error, do you claim there IS ERROR — to wonder is to wander, and to assume another mind, time, place, stuff, personality, or awareness of lack — of darkness, the pit, the grave! If you assume you CAN GIVE INFORMATION TO ANOTHER, OR HAVE DONE SO, THEN YOU MUST ASSUME MORE THAN ONE MIND. CONSCIOUSNESS DOES *NOT* "COMMUNICATE" WITH ANOTHER, FOR THERE IS NO OTHER AT ALL — THERE IS NO OTHER MIND, CALL IT NATALIE, CALL IT FRANCES, OR WHAT, THAT *CAN* COMMUNICATE ITS FEARS, TROUBLES, DOUBTS, MYSTIFICATION, CONFUSION, AND ALL THE REST OF IT TO YOU, OR TO ANOTHER — CANNOT COMMUNICATE OTHERNESS TO THE SINGLE ONE THAT TRUTH IS!

THERE CAN BE NO MAL-PRACTICE — THE COMMUNICATION OF ELECTRICAL ENERGY, DOUBT, FEAR, HATE, MALICE, RESENTMENT, JEALOUSY, OR DOWNRIGHT RESENTMENT THROUGH ANY MANNER AT ALL. INTELLIGENCE IS WHO AND WHAT YOU BE.

YOU ARE NOT A "RECEIVING STATION" FOR NON-
SENSE, NOR CAN YOU BROADCAST NONSENSE, FOR
THE SAME REASON! ONLY INTELLIGENT AWARE-
NESS, EXISTENCE ITSELF, IS PRESENT, AND IS THE
WHOLE OF YOU. THIS MIND KNOWS WHAT IT IS, FOR
IT IS BUSY BEING ITSELF ONLY, AND KNOWS IT, FOR
IT IS THIS "KNOWLEDGE," THIS AWARENESS ITSELF,
THIS EXISTENCE, THIS LIVING-ONE BEING ALIVE! To
THIS ONE, there is no question concerning what IT IS. And
where would It go to find another mind that would question,
deny, refute or attempt to destroy this FACT, THIS
EXISTENCE? Nowhere! Why? Because there is no other
mind at all, no question at all, no time at all, no past at all,
no future at all, no progression or retrogression at all — there
is only TOTAL PURE SINGLENESS WHOLLY ALIVE TO
ITS ENTIRETY, JOY, BLISS, LIFE, AND THIS IS THE
ABSOLUTE SOLE ONE THAT IS YOUR VERY AND
ONLY IDENTITY. THERE IS NO CHOICE, NO DECISION,
NO DEMONSTRATION POSSIBLE, NO HAVING TO
STRUGGLE TO "MAKE" THIS SO, NOR ANY STRUGGLE
TO "PREVENT TRUTH FROM BEING SO," NOR ANY
OTHER MIND THAT IS CLAIMING "IT" CAN DIRECT
NASTY, FALSE, OR DEADLY "THOUGHTS" AT YOU,
LIKE SO MANY MENTAL BULLETS, AND KNOCK MIND
OUT OF ITS TOTALITY, SELF, OMNIPRESENCE, NOW-
NESS!

You cannot, and let me repeat, you canNOT reverse
SELF, FOR IT IS LOVE BEING ITSELF, AND TO THIS
ONE THERE CAN BE NO MORE, NO LESS, AND THIS IS
THE FACT RIGHT NOW. THERE IS NO OTHERNESS AT
ALL TO WHOM AUGHT CAN BE PROVEN, OR DIS-

PROVEN — THERE IS ONLY FACT ITSELF, AND THIS IS YOUR IDENTITY NOW — NOT BECAUSE A LITTLE "YOU" SEES IT, BUT BECAUSE THE SOLE OMNI-PRESENT INFINITE INTELLIGENCE THAT IS OMNI-PRESENCE ITSELF, THE ABSOLUTE POWER OF AWARENESS PRESENT HERE NOW AS AMNESS-I, IS *BEING* IT! This is your Identity NOW!

Cut off any notion of another mind, coming or going, yours or another's — and that "time" is enabling these minds-which-are-NOT to attack aught! STATE FACT, THEN DEFINE THE FACT STATED, AND KEEP AT IT TILL THE SUGGESTION OF DIFFICULTY, LABOR, AND ALL THE REST OF IT CEASES TO EVEN KNOCK AT YOUR DOOR — FOR THAT IS ALL IT CAN "EVEN APPEAR" TO BE — A SUGGESTION PURPORTEDLY STEMMING FROM ANOTHER, WHETHER YOU CALL IT YOURSELF (Natalie), OR OTHERS ON THE OUTSIDE. Sticking with INTELLIGENCE ONLY, there is no outside, no inside, there is ONLY WHOLENESS, and this is your IDENTITY NOW. Naught can deliberately swamp you, attack you, or make you assume that it is "difficult" to BE! For, who or what is *BEING?* IT IS SPIRIT THAT IS DOING IT ALL — SO WHAT OR WHO "ELSE" CAN BE TIRED OUT BY IT? NO ONE, FOR THERE IS NONE BESIDE — TRUTH IS NOT TIRED FROM BEING — NOW IS NOT FATIGUED BY BEING NOW. AND NOW IS WHEN YOU *BE!* But it is TRUTH THAT IS BEING THE SELF, not a Natalie or Frances who is "trying" to "become" the Self!

NAUGHT IS WRONG — THERE IS NO "BACKSLID-ING" IN NOW. THERE IS NO SIN, NO FALL, NO PRODIGALITY WHERE TRUTH ALONE IS THE SOLE

OMNIPRESENT CHANGELESS, UNCHALLENGED TO-
TALITY THAT IS I, and this leaves naught beside. Know
YOU ARE FREE NOW, FOR THERE IS NO CONFUSION
IN MIND, AND THERE IS *ONLY* MIND. I shall try to send
you a tape shortly.

Love,

Dear----------

In the book FORUMS – relative to what may "appear" as
"extra sensory perception" – I would urge you to read
carefully what it says: 222:4-12. You will notice I say,
"appear" – why? BECAUSE WHERE ALL IS ALREADY
ALL, there is no waiting for tomorrow to DISCOVER WHAT
OMNISCIENCE ALREADY KNOWS AS PRESENT FACT!
Here is a poor illustration of what I mean: As a playwright,
do you not NOW KNOW THE END OF THE PLAY? Yet to
the one in the audience it may seem that the play is only
starting and he wonders "how" it will "work out." Would
you call the end of the play, to the playwright, a prophecy?
Or is it the "inevitable" outcome of what has been set as a
pattern? So, STATING FACT AS IT IS, ALL AS NOW
CONSCIOUSLY WHOLE AND COMPLETE, all GOOD IS
PRESENT IN TOTO HERE NOW. To THIS AWARENESS,
there is no prophecy, no "waiting for It to COME ABOUT,"
for IT IS FACT NOW. Yet, to what may seem a man-bound-
sense, "time" appears to be important, and such an one
would "hope and trust that eventually" a good end would
come about! We, while still "seeming to browse within a
human pattern or framework," actually cut through all this
junk and BEHOLD FACT AS ALREADY PRESENT, ALL
GOOD OPERATIVE HERE NOW – we "experience" THIS

GOODNESS AS PRESENT. Yet, to what may appear as our fellows, "they" may assume that WE HAVE IMPROVED, BEEN HEALED, ARE CHANGED, etc. – yet to the SENSE OF AWARENESS, SPIRIT, NAUGHT HAS CHANGED, FOR ALL IS ALL WITHOUT INTERRUPTION, AND IT IS ALL HERE NOW – no prophecy, no actual prescience at all – just NORMAL AWARENESS, INFINITE INTELLIGENCE, CONSCIOUS ALIVENESS IN OPERATION AS THE SELF IT IS! In other words, regardless of what the "senses" may "seem" to say, ALL GOOD IS SEEN AS FACT, CHANGELESSLY PRESENT. Sticking with this clears away the pretense – and to the "others" it may seem as if we have "foretold" an event – but to MIND, IT IS ALREADY THE FACT, having naught to do with past or future! LOVE DOES NOT WORK WITH OR IN "TIME!" Pre-cognition and prophecy both are the same – both deal with time, a future, both denying NOW AS ALL! When you start with ALL, it is easy to "see" what is inevitable from the viewpoint of error – it MUST FAIL, PROVE FUTILE – APPEAR AS THE NONSENSE IT IS, HENCE "COME" TO NAUGHT!"

In your reference to Page 62 in THAT WHICH IS, it seems to me very clear that man is a myth. It points out that "ADAM, MAN, THE MORTAL, COULD *NOT* ABIDE IN LIFE'S PRESENCE. Line 18 says, "THIS THEOLOGICAL MYTH OF FLEETING LIFE, VULNERABLE IDENTITY – THIS SEPARATE PERSONAL EXISTENCE THAT IS *SUPPOSEDLY* CAPABLE OF CHOOSING BETWEEN GOD AND EVIL – COULD ONLY *PRETEND* TO THRIVE *OUTSIDE* TRUTH'S BOUNDARY!"

We point out that WHERE ALL ALONE IS THE ONLY,

THERE CAN BE NO "CHOICE," NO DECISION TO MAKE — AND THAT WHERE SPIRIT IS, HEAVEN IS, HENCE THERE CAN BE NO CONFUSION, NO MAN, NO ADAM, NO CREATION — THERE IS ONLY SPIRIT!

Starting with line 23, to quote in part, it says: THAT WHICH DENIES TRUTH (the ALONENESS OF LOVE, THE INSEPARABLE TOTALITY OF SINGLENESS, PURITY, HEAVEN AT HAND) — IS ANTI-TRUTH (IS *NOT* TRUTH, HENCE NOT TRUE!), ANTI-INTELLIGENCE (is ignorance, humanity-which-is-NOT), etc. — BECAUSE IT HAS NEVER EXISTED IN TRUTH.

He who starts out with murder, is starting by TOTAL DENIAL OF LOVE, GOD, LIFE, ALLNESS — IS BEGINNING WITH A CHALLENGED ONE, HENCE IS STARTING WITH A DEVIL WHICH DENIES GOD AS THE ALONE ONE! He who starts with a mistake will continue with a mistake wherein NO TRUTH CAN BE! But, he who starts with TRUTH, CLEAVES TO TRUTH AND TRUTH ALONE, WILL END WITH TRUTH WHEREIN NO CONFUSION CAN BE!

He who starts with a murdered President, is JUDGING WHOLLY BY HIS SEEING, HEARING, etc. — AND YET WE ARE TOLD NOT TO SO JUDGE, FOR "ALL SUCH JUDGMENT IS UNRIGHTEOUS JUDGMENT!" If you begin with ONE SINGLE TOTAL LIFE PRESENT WHEREIN THERE IS NO OTHERNESS, CAN YOU ALSO TELL ME THAT LIFE, GOD, DIED, WAS MURDERED? IF LIFE WAS *NOT* MURDERED, THEN WHY TALK OF IT — AND IF LIFE *WAS* MURDERED, THEN YOU ARE DEAD, AND ALL THOSE "WHO TALK ABOUT THE PRESIDENT" ARE EQUALLY DEAD, FOR LIFE IS NO MORE! But if

LIFE IS STILL ALIVE, PRESENT, then why pick something with the eye and pass judgment on CHANGELESS LOVE, claiming something "did" happen to IT? You cannot satisfy any of the senses, so long as you work with them, for all of them lie, and they testify only to lies! They see what they believe, and then believe they "see" or "experience" that lie!

We do not "work" in any such fashion. We start ALWAYS with the ALLNESS OF CHANGELESS LIFE, FOR THIS ALONE IS WHO AND WHAT WE BE! May I suggest you ponder well in POWER, 102:3-8, 33-20, next page. Page 103:33-3; 101:29-32; 150:22-6, next page.

I do trust this long explanation on these two points you raise will clear up any confusion you might have had. We have discussed death so often in the Monthly Letters that I hesitate to answer your letter in it. LIFE IS ALL THERE IS, AND LIFE DOES NOT DIE. There is NO DEATH ANY-WHERE IN THE WHOLE OF OMNIPRESENCE. LIFE ALONE IS TOTALLY PRESENT NOW, THE SOLE POWER, THE ONLY INTELLIGENCE, THE ABSOLUTE SUBSTANCE, THE ONLY IDENTITY. For anyone to keep messing about with the theological nonsense of evil, death, otherness, duality, hell, the pit, is IGNORING OMNIPRES-ENT TRUTH, DENYING SOUL, REFUSING INTELLI-GENCE, AND "APPEARS" TO MAKE HIS DWELLING IN HELL, IGNORANCE, FEAR, SUPERSTITION! This is being prodigal. BUT AS SPIRIT IS THE SOLE, THE ONLY ONE PRESENT, NONE BESIDE CAN BE, HENCE NO "OTHER" EXISTS TO BE PRODIGAL, IN ERROR, IN BODY, IN EVIL, IN HELL OR THE CEMETERY, EVER! Which "side" are you going to "think on?" TRUTH IS ALL — this leaves no evil to think of, none to think it, none to be it, or to be nfluenced thereby!

Cordially,

)ear----------

Do ponder well in NOW 173:4-11 on the next page. Go
ver this with real care, ponder exactly what each sentence
neans, and AS IT IS TRUTH, HENCE TRUE RIGHT NOW,
vhy wait, and with what "mind" do you wait, and what for?
Meanwhile, while you "wait," you keep denying your Self,
ence keep on going without! This is duality, this is
Self-betrayal, this is "murder" for all and sundry that is
vithin your present sense of awareness, for you are putting it
ll "out there," hence outside of OMNIPRESENT LIFE,
OUR TOTAL IDENTITY NOW!

As for allowing emotions to upset you, or cause you to go
lying off to far spots in the state, isn't that foolish? Do you
"need" to "run away," and do you assume "distance" will
elp? THERE IS NAUGHT BUT WHAT IS WITHIN THE
AWARENESS YOU BE — NO SPACE, NO TIME, NO
"OTHERS" AT ALL, SO WHY KEEP TURNING TO SUCH,
BLAMING SUCH (AND BLAMING YOURSELF IS PART
)F THE SAME NONSENSE) — NONE OF THIS IS
BEGINNING OR STAYING WITH ONE SINGLE WHOLE
)NE! Begin to be HONEST WITH YOUR SELF — BEGIN
)EMANDING OF YOURSELF THAT WHAT IS YOUR
DENTITY IS NOW YOUR IDENTITY, AND ALL THAT IS
NCLUDED WITHIN THIS IDENTITY IS NOW INCLUDED
THEREIN — DEMAND THAT YOU STICK WITH WHAT
OU BE AND NOT KEEP GOING OFF ON THESE SILLY
MOTIONAL EXCURSIONS INTO DARKENSS, CON-
"USION, FRUSTRATION, PAIN, AND ALL THE REST OF

THE GRAVEYARD GAMBITS! DEMAND THAT YOU
STICK WITH WHAT YOU BE, WITH WHAT LIFE IS, WITH
NOW, WITH ISNESS. KEEP DEMANDING OF YOURSELF
THAT YOU DO THIS, AND *SEE* THAT YOU *DO* STICK
You can, and why not start NOW? So silly to go through all
this nonsense. Just declaring or seeing it is a lie DOES NOT
HELP – THE ONLY "HELP" IS WHEN YOU START WITH
FACT, AND DEMAND OF YOURSELF THAT YOU STICK
WITH THE FACT OF WHAT YOU BE, NAMELY WHOLE
TOTAL, ALL-INCLUSIVE! You have nothing "out there,"
so stop heaping your "feelings" on such! Whatever you see as
wrong in one "person," you'll find is equally "wrong" in
another, for you are working within make-believe when you
allow two or more minds to compete with each other! So
seeing your husband "out of work," now you see your friend
"out of work," and then you'll see a lot of others "out of
work," and on and on and on – but WHERE IS REALITY
SINGLENESS? All these "others" are but your refusal to
DEMAND THAT YOU STICK WITH TRUTH, FACT
ONENESS, WHOLENESS! Naught "out there" can possibly
fill the hole, but IN REALITY THERE IS ONLY REALITY
HENCE NO HOLE TO FILL, AND NAUGHT TO ASSUME
SUCH, OR TO PRETEND "IT" CAN FILL AUGHT!

Fondly,

Dear----------
    SPIRIT, THE SOLE SELF, DOES NOT USE A CANE
NOR KNOW OF A CAIN – IT IS NOT LIMPING ABOUT
NOR IS IT UNBALANCED. IT IS *CHANGELESS* WHOLE
NESS *NOW*. IT KNOWS THIS – IT KNOWS ALL THAT IT
IS, AND IS BUSY BEING WHAT IT KNOWS ITSELF TO

BE. THERE SIMPLY IS NO OTHER MIND AT ALL, HENCE NONE OTHER TO "KNOW" OR "NOT KNOW, NOT AGREE WITH TRUTH, NOT ACKNOWLEDGE TRUTH!"

There simply is no Alfred mind to agree with what REALITY IS. On the same basis, there is no Alfred mind to disagree, or to claim it staggers about, loses balance, ever was balanced, has now become unbalanced! There is no Alfred mind to go crazy, insane, un-balanced, or unsteady in balance, for there is no Alfred mind at all — none balancing, judging, *weighing* itself! There is no Alfred mind to assume it is a self, and a balanced one at that, a weighty one, an important one, and suddenly now find it is not so important, not so weighty, not so "big" in any sense of the word, so is now staggered, thrown off balance, unsteady, insecure, misplaced, or any such metaphysical or mentalized state or condition! ALL THERE IS, IS OMNIPRESENCE BEING WHOLLY WHOLE TO ITSELF ONLY, IMPORTANT TO ITSELF ONLY, WITHIN ITSELF ONLY, NEVER MOVED, NEVER INFLUENCED, NEVER MEANING AUGHT TO OTHERS OR ANOTHER, NEVER EXPECTING, NEVER JUDGING, NEVER FRUSTRATED OR BLINDED BY CONDITIONS, CIRCUMSTANCES, INSECURE, SHAKY, DODDERING, SLIPPING, EMOTIONAL, OR AUGHT ELSE MORTAL OR HUMAN, FOR REALITY IS CHANGELESS SINGLENESS, THE SOLE AUTHORITY BECAUSE IT DEALS ONLY WITH ITSELF, WITHIN ITSELF, IS COMPLETE TO ITSELF, AND IS DOING ALL THE KNOWING AND BEING THAT IS ITSELF, AND THERE IS NAUGHT BESIDE. THIS IS FACT. THIS IS SO NOW. THIS ETERNALLY IS SO. THERE IS NO WAIT. THERE IS NAUGHT

TO "SEE." THERE IS NAUGHT TO "OVERCOME," OR
TO "BEHOLD." THERE IS NAUGHT TO "STUDY,"
"PERCEIVE," TO "STOP," OR TO "START." THERE IS
NO "SENSE" OF BODY" AT ALL, FOR "BODY" TO
MIND IS MERELY A THOUGHT WITHIN THIS CON-
SCIOUSNESS I AM. IT IS NOT AN OBJECT, AN ITEM
"OUT THERE." IT IS NEVER PHYSICAL, ORGANIC,
NOR CONTROLLED BY NERVES, ORGANS, LIMBS, OR
TIME. THERE IS NO SUCH BODY ANYWHERE, NOR
ANY MIND TO ASSUME SUCH A SUPERSTITION.
THERE ARE NO WITCHES, NO HUMAN MINDS OR
HUMAN BODIES OR HUMAN THINGS OR TIMES OR
CONDITIONS! THERE IS ONLY PRESENT ISNESS, AM-
NESS, CONSCIOUSNESS ALIVE TO ITS FULL AWARE-
NESS. THIS AMNESS IS NOT "THINKING" IN TERMS OF
"THOUGHTS," BUT IS BUSY BEING ALL THE WHOLE-
NESS IT IS, ALIVE TO ALL THE JOY IT IS, THE TOTAL
SUBSTANCE IT IS, THE SINGLE-ALLNESS IT IS. THIS IS
AMNESS THAT IS I, and IT IS ALL PRESENT, IS-ING,
BE-ING, RIGHT HERE AND IT (MIND) KNOWS IT. There
is no otherness to know or not know, believe or not believe,
be metaphysical (meaning, *mentally* PHYSICAL), or not.
This is Fact. There are no idiots to reverse or deny or even
trying to "see"this! THERE IS ONLY FACT HERE! The
human mind, so-called, is an idiot because a total malicious
murderous liar concerning itself!

MIND NEVER "TALKS" ABOUT "BODY" — FOR ALL
SUCH "TALK IS MENTAL PHYSICS!" MIND ACTS IT-
SELF BY BEING BUSY ACTING IN ACCORD WITH ITS
ALLNESS. The "metaphysician" — the mental physicality —
sits and waits for a healing, meanwhile declaring, declaring,

declaring till the air is blue, but NEVER ACTS THE FACT BEING DECLARED. They call this: "Waiting for the spirit of God to move upon the face of the waters — wait here till I come again — and after two months (or more) the spirit descends upon the waiting ones so they speak in unknown tongues!" How true, how true, for who knows the jabber coming forth? NOT INTELLIGENCE WHO KNOWS NO WAIT, no return, no recovery! How can Spirit be "adopted" or "visited?" Not even by disease, trouble, fear! In Love, Purity, there are *no* visitors!

The "metaphysician — the mental physician" always waits for DEMONSTRATION — always waits for a RETURN OF HEALTH, A RECOVERY OF SOME SORT! Recovery of what "has-been" lost!

Have you EVER had someone call on you for help in metaphysics that was not waiting for a RECOVERY? Were they not waiting to GET BACK WHAT PURPORTEDLY WAS LOST IN THE PAST, IN A "WAS," IN TIME, IN THAT WHICH SUPERSTITION SAID WAS GONE BEFORE? Is there any ISNESS in this? Is this "starting" with OMNIPRESENCE, FULLNESS, WHOLENESS *NOW?* He who "looks for help, a healing, a recovery," I maintain is working still in metaphysics, mental physics, a mental physicality, or a physical sense of mind! If he did not assume his IDENTITY was a mental physicality, he'd not keep messing about the body-physical, worrying over it, making statements of Truth over it like a priest trying to exorcize an evil spirit, or saying as Jesus did over the lad: "Come out of him and enter no more into him!"

REALITY DOES NOT WORK THIS WAY. IT STARTS WITH WHAT SPIRIT IS. It is not concerned in any possible way with what "body" is, how it is, where it is, when it is, or how it came about, when, where, or if! REALITY IS SOLELY CONCERNED WITH THE FULLNESS OF HERE NOW. WITH THE TOTAL OF WHOLENESS NOW. WITH THE ABSOLUTENESS OF NOW, THE COMPLETE PRESENCE OF THE PRESENT, THE ISNESS OF IS, THE JOY AND COMPLETENESS OF AWARENESS, CONSCIOUSNESS BEING WHEREIN NAUGHT ELSE CAN BE! It never, simply NEVER DECLARES AUGHT ABOUT OR CONCERNING, OR CONCERNS ITSELF WITH "BODY" IN ANY manner whatever! Only in metaphysics, MATTER-MINDEDNESS, PHYSICAL-MINDEDNESS, DOES "BODY" SEEM SO IMPORTANT AND PLAY AN ALMIGHTY ROLE. AND FOR PHYSICALITY THERE IS NO HOPE, NO HELP, NO PLACE, NO REALITY, NO EXISTENCE. It can only be "found" where SPIRIT-IS-NOT-ALL-PRESENT! So-o, he who keeps trying to "heal, or help "body" will never get anywhere beyond his faith in superstition, witchcraft, malpractice, mattering-mind and minding matter! And not really there, for such is NOT!

Yes, I'd say, LET US ACT AS *BEING*, rather than have our "being" a mere act! And remember, the size of a lie, or how old it appears to be, its reason, etc., it is still a lie, and Fact leaves it nowhere.

Fondly,

Dear----------

As to going "into bankruptcy" — SPIRIT IS THE SOLE AND ONLY SUBSTANCE, SUPPLY, "STUFF," ACTION... AND CANNOT GO "OUT OF BUSINESS," BE BANKRUPT, POOR, PRESSURED OR WHAT. This is FACT!

Whatever would appear to deny it must come from "another mind," and takes place only with that "other mind," and deals only with what concerns that "other mind," hence is entirely fallacious.

One will never, repeat, N E V E R meet financial or business problems so long as he treats with a human mind, deals with a human mind, delves into a human mind, tries to defend and protect the human mind, or keeps clinging to the demands of cause and effect, the trappings of a human mind! We tried so hard to make this clear at the Hollywood Seminar in October, but wonder how many saw what we were saying. Yes, they repeat the words, but all the while trying to memorize them so as to apply them to the human mind and its difficulties! NOT ONE, REPEAT, NOT ONE EVER TRIES TO "APPLY" TRUTH TO SPIRIT, THE SOLE SELF, BECAUSE SPIRIT, THE SOLE ALIVE AWARE-NESS-CALLED-I NEVER IS DISEASED, WORRIED, BE-SET BY OTHERS, NOR IS STRUGGLING TO "KEEP THINGS GOING."

He who declares that CONSCIOUSNESS ALONE IS ALL, and sees what he is saying, then acts in accord therewith *BY BEING THAT CONSCIOUSNESS ONLY,* finds this precludes a human mind with all that mind claims to experience, worry over, deal with or know! Every time any suggestion of humanhood (lack, privation, business, others, and such) confronts you, if you will INSTANTLY DECLARE TRUTH, THE ALLNESS OF THE ONE UNCHALLENGED UNOP-POSED UNDIMENSIONAL ALIVENESS, AWARENESS, this cuts off messing about with "what" the "other mind" claims to know or worry over or about — cuts off its vain boast that it can do you dirt "if" you don't listen to it and do its bidding!

I simply cut right through all the nonsense by DECLAR-ING TRUTH, AND THEN GETTING BUSY WITH THAT TRUTH I'VE DECLARED, TILL THERE IS NOT A MOMENT LEFT OVER FOR ME TO MESS ABOUT WITH THE OTHER MIND, HENCE WITH THE STINK IT IS RAISING! This applies whether it is money, ill health, criticism, political mess, weather, or what! INTELLIGENCE IS NOT MESSED UP, AND INTELLIGENCE IS THE SOLE SUBSTANCE, THE ONLY STUFF, THE WHOLE AWARE-NESS THAT IS I, AND THIS LEAVES NO OTHERNESS. THIS IS TRUTH. WHY THEN "LOVE AN ENEMY" CALLED A HUMAN MIND THAT IS FILLED WITH ALL SORTS OF DEATH (LACK, VOIDS, TROUBLE, POISON, HATE, FEAR, ANXIETY)?

Generally then the "irritation" or "problem" vanishes for want of another mind to recognize, classify, experience and mess with it by INCLUDING IT AS ITS EXPERIENCE — but sometimes I have to keep steadily and without stoppage of any sort, at TRUTH ONLY, because I seem so attracted to the "other mind" and what it claims to know and experience — I seem drawn to it as if by a magnet, and I hold to it like a halo surrounding the Truth I'm declaring — I seem to still see and hear and know of it beyond and above the Truth I declare. Why? Because I'm not really, NOT ACTUALLY, 100% DOWN TO BUSINESS, BUT AM DOING SOME "SHARING" — am still interested in that "other" state! This is playing prodigal. Finally, when this has gone on long enough, I generally get "wise to MYSELF" and then we immediately have a settlement, and I am free. But so many times we are apt to assume that the Truth will clear away the error! But what is that save STILL CLINGING TO THE ERROR, AND OUTLINING, OUT-PICTURING "HOW" AND "WHEN" AND "WHY" WE WANT IT TO CLEAR UP – STILL CLINGING TO THE ARGUMENT THAT TRUTH WILL SAVE US, RESURRECT US, LIFT US UP – STILL CLAIMING A SAVIOR, MESSIAH, A PROMISE THAT WE DEMAND TRUTH OR GOD TO KEEP! Right back to religion! And in business we do this more than in any other walk!

UNTIL YOU DECLARE ABSOLUTE TRUTH, THEN ACT THEREWITH BY *BEING*, (HOLDING TO THIS FACT AS THE ONLY, THE PRESENT REALITY WHEREIN THERE IS NONE BESIDE, HENCE NO OTHER STATE, OUTLOOK, CONDITION AT ALL) yes, BY *BEING* FACT, YOU WILL NOT KNOW YOUR SELF AS YOU BE, but will still be acting as a prodigal!

No matter how far the prodigal went afield, he never had help. So with us, we will know NO PEACE, SUPPLY, SELF, so long as we insist on having a human mind, and the troubles it is heir to! No such mind exists, hence no such problem exists – so how can one say that he DOES HAVE THE PROBLEM, IS BANKRUPT, OUT OF BUSINESS AND SUCH, yet keep declaring there is no man-mind! The mere presenting of the "problem" is evidence he is OPERATING AS THAT HUMAN MIND, FOR ONLY THEREIN IS THE "PROBLEM!" You will find no lack anywhere save in the human mind, so if you HAVE LACK, you are operating as a human mind, and suffer only from your own SELF DE-NIAL! You consider human business as more pressing, of greater importance, as requiring your every thought, than you do DECLARING TRUTH, STAYING WITH TRUTH,

BEING OR ACTING THAT TRUTH YOU DECLARE,
BECAUSE IT ALONE IS OUR SELF AND ITS ONLY
DEMAND IS THAT YOU STAY WHOLLY WITH IT AND
NOT KEEP DASHING BACK TO THE PLAIN OF ONO!

One cannot save a human mind and its experience. One
cannot heal a human mind and its ills. WHY? BECAUSE
THERE IS ONLY TRUTH, HENCE NO HUMAN MIND,
HENCE NO EXPERIENCES OF HUMANITY, NO LACKS,
NO VOIDS TO FILL!

Hope this helps. Please ponder well the letter that starts
on 137 of POWER. Give "NO THOUGHT TO BUSINESS"
but stick with SELF, TRUTH, AWARENESS ONLY, FOR
IT IS *ALL*.

Fondly,

Dear----------

As to your questions relative to "ideas" — yes, I do state
that Mind "uses" Its ideas to the full. But, by that I do not
mean that Mind actually "employs" Its ideas to do something
for Mind. I was merely trying to overcome the difficulty of
semantics and show that every idea Mind conceives, It
conceives perfectly RIGHT NOW, and hence Mind perceives
the UTTER PERFECTION OF IDEA RIGHT NOW IN ITS
TOTALITY — NOTHING IS LEFT OUT, NOTHING YET TO
COME. MIND USES ITS ABSOLUTE "POTENTIAL" IN
CONCEIVING EVERY IDEA, hence that idea is "being"
completely what it is, namely PERFECT. Under no sense did
I mean to imply that the idea had a mind, a life, a destiny of
its own and that it in some way could "help" Mind. I was
striving to make it clear that there are not "lesser ideas" and
"greater ideas" as is stated in metaphysics! To quote Mrs.

Eddy: "The greater help the lesser in one grand brotherhood," or words to that effect. NO! Every idea of Mind is complete, whole, changelessly the idea Mind conceives-perceives it to be, and that idea is nowhere else, and exists to no One else!

Again, I point out over and over that ideas are not important to Mind, but as Mind has the capacity, the potential, the ability to CONCEIVE, IT HAS TO CONCEIVE, OTHERWISE MIND WOULD BE FUNCTIONING AS LESS THAN THE UTTER WHOLE ONE IT IS! I do hope I make this clear. It is so hard to find words that even partly convey the meaning we intend.

In the new tape I just mailed, it tells how to "ponder." I mean by the word, not just to "say" words, but to "think through thoroughly" what the words mean that you do say concerning Spirit! If what you declare IS TRUTH, then IT IS FACT RIGHT NOW, HENCE WHATEVER WOULD PRETEND TO CONTRADICT IT, INCLUDING THE WOULD-BE MIND DOING THE CONTRADICTING, *MUST* BE A LIAR, HENCE UNTRUE. WHEN? NOW! So you are WHOLE RIGHT NOW. From now on ACT WHAT YOU'VE SAID, and do not go back to acting and reacting to the lies that imply or declare an absence of GOOD!

Too often one declares Fact, then goes right on with error, and hopes that someday what he has "said" will clear away the mess that he is ACTING! If what you say is SO, why not enjoy that Fact RIGHT NOW? Do you have one mind that is in error and another One that is SO? Are you doubleminded? If so, you are wholly unstable even in the most simple act you perform daily! While Mind includes the alphabet, there is no Mind IN THE ALPHABET, NOR IN ANY "BODY."

IDEA IS *IN* MIND, not the other way about. Mind only is "I Am." The items you include in Awareness are only thoughts, items, "things" of which you ARE AWARE. Under no circumstance could you be one of those items, but "body" is just that and no more.

Trust this is clear. It is stated over and over in the books, so read and "ponder" what you read.

Cordially,

Dear----------

Yours just came and I have given you the "help" you requested. I will help you DAILY, until I hear from you. I do not ordinarily do this, but as you asked, I will "make an exception." But, YOU MUST KEEP ME POSTED! If I do NOT hear, I shall shortly quit "working."

TRUTH IS SO THIS VERY INSTANT. THERE IS NO WAIT, NO DELAY, NO WANDERING ABOUT "UNTIL" IT GETS "READY" TO *BE* ALL *IT IS!* ALL OF TRUTH IS ALREADY PRESENT, THE WHOLE AWARENESS, THE WHOLE INTELLIGENCE *NOW.* AS OMNIPRESENCE IS ALL, THERE CAN BE NO "REMEMBERING," NO "FORGETTING," FOR MIND IS *NOW IN ACTION!* What is GOING ON NOW, doesn't have to be "stored away" somewhere, and then "recalled!" WHAT IS GOING ON NOW, MIND NOW IS SURE OF, AS AWARENESS!

AWARENESS BEING ITSELF IS YOUR WHOLE IDENTITY. YOU ARE NOT IN A "BODY," NOR DEPENDENT ON ITS HEAD OR BRAIN TO "REMEMBER, RECALL, DIG UP, OR REVIEW" AUGHT! Mind KNOWS NOW, and NOW IS ALL THERE IS.

All "remembering" depends on time — on a "past." and

the "remembering" is always done in a future-to-NOW! Just stick with N O W only. Leave events, the past, time, body, wholly out of your "work." Stick totally with ALLNESS, OMNIPRESENCE, OMNIACTION NOW BEING!

In POWER, ponder well, over and over, page 101 — whole page. Read it aloud, then see if you define the words, know what they say, and are they FACT? If so, WHEN, WHERE, HOW, WHY? Then can aught also "exist" to contradict the Fact, your Self? How many "SELFS" HAVE YOU? Are there two of you — one, OMNIPRESENT AWARENESS *being*, and the other an injured physical body?

As for the suit — I do not like to even comment about that — but I do think that if there has been negligence on the part of the city, or department, and certain damages appear, it is only right that they are forced to attend to their responsibilities! If it were reversed, they'd surely make YOU do so, eh? But, should you have your attorneys so move, do not get your SELF involved by paying attention to the five senses — to emotions and such. Do it wholly as you would if you were writing a play — see the characters carry out what should be, but DO NOT ASSUME YOU ARE ALSO A CHARACTER, AND ARE "SUFFERING THIS OR THAT!" INTELLIGENCE IS WHAT YOU BE, and It cannot "suffer" (put up with, tolerate, cling to, accept, or feel it is subject to) evil, lack, manhood, otherness, duality!

Roy, NO ACCIDENT HAS OCCURRED TO INFINITE AWARENESS — AND ONLY LOVE IS YOUR IDENTITY — LIFE BEING ITSELF IS THE SOLE AMNESS THAT IS I. There is none beside. Naught has happened to SPIRIT, and SPIRIT BEING ALL IS WHO AND WHAT I AM. NONE OTHER. Here is Fact. Stick with this, and act wholly here.

IT IS TRUTH, FACT, THE SOLE ACTUALITY PRESENT. Aught that may "appear" to contradict FACT, is false, an illusion, a fraud, superstition! Is theological mumbo-jumbo. Naturally, if you BEGIN WITH A LIE, THE "CONDITIONS" OF THE LIE WILL SEEM TO BE ALL THAT IS REAL! But he who STATES FACT, AND STICKS THEREWITH, BEHOLDS THE LIE TO BE JUST THAT — a lie, without place, authority, power, *history or existence!* Don't try to "heal" aught. Spirit is ALL, and does not need "healing." Spirit is thy SOLE SELF NOW!

Cordially,

Dear----------

I beg of you to keep your SOLE ATTENTION on the ALLNESS OF LIGHT AS THE SOLE SUBSTANCE, THE ONLY "STUFF" YOU BE, and do not give a single thought to body, to how it feels, what it says, how it acts or does not act, how it functions, or refuses to function, FOR BODY CANNOT TALK TO YOU, FUNCTION, DO OR NOT DO ANYTHING MORE OR LESS THAN A TABLE FORK CAN, AND HAS NOTHING MORE TO DO WITH YOUR IDENTITY, YOUR SELF.

You do not keep talking about the organs of a fork, how a fork feels, how it "falls down" or it "cannot see well," or it "has a family, a daughter who insists on that fork doing so and so," or how little money that fork has "coming in," and how hard that fork "tries to declare the Truth, and to know the Truth, and practice the Truth!"

YOU KNOW THE FORK DOES NAUGHT BUT STAYS WHAT IT IS, NAMELY, A FORK ONLY! And if it were not for INTELLIGENCE YOU WOULD NOT KNOW A FORK

FROM A KNIFE, OR A BODY FROM A PILLOWSLIP.
LEAVE THE FORK OUT OF YOUR THOUGHT, STOP
DECLARING IT IS YOU, AND TELLING ME HOW THAT
FORK "FEELS, HOW IT SUFFERS, WHAT PAIN IT IS
IN," AND ALL THE OTHER NONSENSE ABOUT A
FORK! Or a body! For one is no more "I" than the other.
YOU ARE NOT A FORK, NEVER GAVE BIRTH TO A
FAMILY, NEVER HAD A FAMILY, NEVER WERE GIVEN
BIRTH TO, AND YOU, TRUTH, HAS NO BODY AT ALL —
NONE AT ALL, SO STOP TALKING ABOUT WHAT YOU
(TRUTH) DOES NOT, REPEAT, *DOES NOT* EVEN HAVE!
MIND IS GOODNESS ITSELF, PERFECTION, SINGLE,
AND THIS IS WHO AND WHAT YOU BE — SINGLE
INDIVIDUAL PURE ALONENESS, AND THERE IS NONE
BESIDE AT ALL! There is no little belief-mind to malprac-
tice, believe, claim, or kick up at all, be human, material, the
offspring of a "fling-in-the-hay" or aught else! Stop insulting
and degrading your SELF by telling, re-lating, re-peating such
corruption, adultery, lies!

YOU, BEING CONSCIOUS, CAN STATE FACT AS
LOVE, SINGLENESS KNOWS FACT TO BE, NAMELY,
ALL LIGHT FUNCTIONING UNDIMENSIONALLY, AND
WHEREIN NO POSSIBLE DARKNESS OR DIMNESS CAN
BE. YOU CAN STATE THIS, AND CAN THINK IT
THROUGH. YOU, THEN, CAN, REPEAT, *CAN* ACT WHAT
YOU CONSCIOUSLY STATE, FOR WHAT YOU STATE IS
ALL THE FACT THERE IS, AND THAT FACT YOU
STATE IS THE FACT RIGHT NOW. "Body" or "fork" has
nothing to do with YOUR STATEMENT OF FACT, OF
SELF, OF IDENTITY. And you need not then spend all your
effort messing over a fork, talking about, watching it, trying

to change it into a dinner plate, or something else! YOUR
SOLE ATTENTION SHOULD BE ON WHAT INTELLI-
GENT LIGHT KNOWS ITSELF TO BE, FOR THIS IS
YOUR VERY MIND DECLARING WHAT YOU, LIGHT,
BE! It takes no more effort or air to state FACT, than it does
to re-late, and re-late and re-late lies concerning a fork! So,
get busy and BE HONEST AND TALK TRUTH ONLY, AND
ACT WHAT YOU CANNOT AVOID BEING, NAMELY,
PERFECTION, ALL POWER, HERE NOW!

Look up in THAT WHICH IS 52:24-7 on 54;
59:26- page 61; 174:5-26 on next page; 177:20-26;
174:23-26,27-1; 175:23-4; 176:15-22, 25-8. These will help
you greatly. PERFECTION ALIVE TO ITSELF IS YOUR
WHOLE IDENTITY INTACT NOW. IT HAS NO AGE, NO
MATTER, NO BELIEFS, NO LIMITS, NO TROUBLES, NO
CHALLENGE, NO OPPOSITIONS AT ALL. THIS IS NOW
FACT. IT CAN NEVER BE MORE FACT THAN NOW, SO
WHO OR WHAT CAN "PUT IT OFF FOR A MORE
CONVENIENT SEASON?"

HOPE YOU ATTEND THE SEMINAR IN HOLLYWOOD
IN NOVEMBER. YOU CAN, FOR OMNIPOTENT PERFEC-
TION, OMNIPRESENT SINGLENESS IS WHO AND WHAT
YOU BE. THERE IS NAUGHT ELSE, HENCE NAUGHT TO
SAY YOU "NAY."

Fondly,

Dear----------

Please, in FORUMS, ponder well and then A C T what it
says on page 24:17-27. Do not feel depressed — that is the
stock in trade of human sense that comes from nowhere, has
no place, and is going nowhere — that's enough to depress

anything, eh? Well, as ONLY CONSCIOUSNESS IS, AND
THAT ONE IS JOY ITSELF *being*, there is no other mind to
feel aught!

You KNOW that SPIRIT IS NOT DEPRESSED — THAT
JOY IS NOT DEPRESSED. Well, JOY and SELF is ONE
AND THE SAME ONE! So what is left to be depressed? You
see, it is ALWAYS a so-called "other" mind that is "feeling"
this or that, but NEVER INTELLIGENCE, JOY, BLISS! The
ONE YOU BE is CHANGELESS, so how can YOUR
IDENTITY ebb and flow, re-act to this or that, such as bad
news, a disease, a diagnosis and its attendant prognosis,
history, or that-which-lies-ahead?

All depression, fear, anxiety is RE-ACTION, but never
ACTION, never BEING! Where OMNIACTION IS, there can
be no re-action, because there is naught to react — ONLY
ISNESS IS, AND IT IS TOTAL BEING FUNCTIONING TO
THE FULL AS THE SOLE TOTAL JOY IT IS. To have a
reaction one would have to share SINGLENESS with
otherness, hence he would have to destroy SINGLENESS in
order to allow for duality! And if there were duality, there
would be no Singleness, hence there would be naught! Not
even reaction!

Where LIFE (GOD) *IS*, HEAVEN IS. There is nowhere
LIFE (GOD) IS NOT, so nowhere Heaven is not — so where
can trouble be, and as LIFE IS WHAT YOU ARE *BEING*,
you are *not* being depressed! As ONLY SUBSTANCE,
LOVE, *is*, what is left to depress, and what or who would do
it or experience it?

No, there simply cannot be more than the ONE SINGLE
INFINITE CHANGELESS MIND. This leaves no "other"
mind at all, hence naught such a so-called mind would

pretend — no "other" mind to whom "it" could pretend! So it all boils down to this — let us be HONEST WITH THE ONE SOLE MIND PRESENT, stick with this, be determined to "stick" with Fact, and be equally determined that you will not "go-along-with-the-many" in claiming that there is also-another-mind which is full of trouble or anxiety and things! This requires constant awareness on your part, or you will slip right back into the "old habits."

OUR ONLY "SEEMING" TROUBLE IS THE ACCEP-TANCE THAT WE DO HAVE ANOTHER MIND, FOR IT IS THAT "STINKER" THAT IS DOING ALL THE "PROJECT-ING" OF THE UGLY PICTURES, PRODUCING THE "SENSES" THAT THEN "SEEM" TO SENSE THEM, KNOW THEM OR SUFFER FROM THEM! The whole of it is that other or dream mind — so, let us stick to the ONLY MIND, and be determined not to go off and swallow all the nonsense of "another mind!" Where there is no "dream" (other mind), there can be no junk dreamed (dredged) up!

                                      Cordially,

Dear Friend:

In our work we may seem to get a call for help. What do we do? Do we go into the "reasons" for the condition — that someone has been "thinking evil, negative, or false thoughts" — not "standing porter at the door of thought?" NO! There is neither cause nor effect in REALITY. We do not have any mind to go wrong, do wrong, experience wrong, or be wrong, for THE SOLE MIND PRESENT IS SINGLE, TOTAL, WHOLE, AND OMNIPRESENT ACTION, including Its universe of NOW-THOUGHTS-IDEAS-THINGS! In other words, we "begin" at once with the ALLNESS OF REAL-

ITY, SUBSTANCE, CONSCIOUSNESS, SPIRIT. THIS PRE-
CLUDES ANY OTHERNESS OF ANY SORT, HENCE
NAUGHT THAT CAN "CAUSE" OR APPEAR AS A
"RESULT-EFFECT" — we are NOT interested in the whys
and so on of humanity or human thinking, for there is none
such at all! We do not credit alienness at all, but stick
INTELLIGENTLY, CONSISTENTLY WITH WHAT-IS,
which precludes disease (is-notness!) entirely, for there is no
presence to entertain such, the ONLY PRESENCE BEING
CONSCIOUSNESS IN ITS ENTIRETY HERE AND NOW,
ETERNALLY.

Hope this makes sense to you. With each request for
"help," the above is a short statement as to what I do. It is
the same as if you "feel" pain, "see" an inflamed swelling on
your body or another's, "hear" a prognosis for what seems to
be one body or another, taste, or smell aught contrary to Fact
— in every "case" do you not BEGIN WITH THE WHOLE-
NESS OF ALL which precludes any death, disaster, otherness, either as what calls itself Roger's mind, or that of
another? THERE IS BUT ONE OMNIPRESENCE BEING
OMNIPRESENT IN ITS TOTALITY, AND THIS PRE-
CLUDES ANY OTHER MIND, WHETHER PERSONAL,
RACIAL, HISTORICAL, *HYSTERICAL,* EMOTIONAL, AN-
IMAL, PHYSICAL, MATERIAL, PAST, FUTURE OR IN
BETWEEN, MALE OR FEMALE OR NEUTER GEN-
DERED! You see, REALITY leaves naught to harp or
manifest disease, no disease to be manifested, hence none to
heal or fail to heal! This means financial, the same as
domestic, political, astrological, theological or what! The
ALLNESS OF ALL, THE ONENESS OF ONE, THE
WHOLENESS OF SINGLE WHOLENESS precludes any

mind or minds, hence the stuff purportedly therein, or the would-be capacity to entertain, experience, fear, or "handle" such negative, Reality-deny-ers, or denials! (Badly put, but you see the intent.) You cannot fail in your "work" nor can you fail to have such "work" to do, for everywhere within what seems the human, we are confronted with humanity or lack, but now we know WHAT TO "DO," and "HOW" TO "DO" IT with positive guaranteed certainty RIGHT NOW!

Cordially,

Dear----------

Now, as you know from reading the books, I work only once — then, should one appear to "need" further help, he must request same. I do not "take up work and keep working," as most metaphysicians do. This work is NOT metaphysics, but IS FACT RIGHT HERE, RIGHT NOW. THERE IS NO DELAY, NO WAIT, NO GUILT TO OVER-COME, NO "UNDERSTANDING" TO OBTAIN. ALL THAT IS ASKED IS THAT ONE BE TOTALLY HONEST WITH THE SOLE SELF, SPIRIT, AWARENESS, LIFE, PURITY! You say that the doctors have told you that life is almost over for you! This is the chatter of a monkey, a flea, a speck of dust — mere nonsense. Why? BECAUSE LIFE IS SPIRIT ONLY. ONLY LIFE (GOODNESS) IS ALIVE, AND IS CHANGELESS HERE NOW — IS ALL RIGHT HERE NOW — IS TOTALLY PRESENT IN ITS UNCHALLENGED PERFECTION, ITS SINGLE ABSOLUTENESS, ITS ABSO-LUTE TOTALITY, COMPLETENESS, ACTION, AWARE-NESS!

If Life can end, and LIFE AND EXISTENCE IS THE SELFSAME ONE, then did the doctors know what they were

talking about when they said that EXISTENCE was going to
end shortly? And on top of that, said that LIFE, SPIRIT,
MIND, AWARENESS, CONSCIOUSNESS (GOD) HAS A
CANCER THAT IS EATING UP TRUTH, HENCE CHANG-
ING IT, DESTROYING IT, WIPING IT OUT?

What manner of LOVE IS SPIRIT, PURITY, WHOLE-
NESS wherein there is no void, no lack, no otherness
possible, hence no impurity, no adultery, no idolatry? Where
in the WHOLE OF OMNIPRESENCE, ALL-PRESENT, CAN
YOU FIND A HOLE, AN ABSENCE OF TOTALITY, AN
IMPURITY, A CONTRADICTION OF COMPLETENESS?
Only when you turn your back on FACT, and go along with
so-called "senses" which have never seen Truth, felt It, tasted
It, or come in contact with It. Which are you going to turn to
NOW — will it be a judgment after the hearing of the ear, the
seeing of an eye, or will it be CHANGELESS PURITY
PRESENT IN ITS TOTALITY, WHOLENESS, HONEST
AWARENESS, CONSCIOUS ACTION? Will you admit that
THERE IS BUT ONE ALL PRESENT, hence it is THIS ONE
ONLY WHO IS DOING ALL THE KNOWING, BEING,
ACTING — AND IT IS THIS MIND THAT IS MY IDEN-
TITY NOW — HENCE THERE IS NAUGHT BESIDE, SO
NO WOULD-BE "OTHER" CAN CLAIM OR PRETEND OR
GIVE FALSE EVIDENCE THAT "IT" ALSO EXISTS? IT
HAS NO PLACE IN WHICH TO EXIST, NO SUBSTANCE
TO OPERATE IN!

I have given you the "help" you requested. Do NOT
LOOK FOR A HEALING, but rather, GET BUSY WITH
WHAT REALITY *IS*, WHAT TRUTH *IS*, WHAT LIFE *IS*,
AND YOU'LL STOP BEING AFRAID, STOP ASSUMING
THERE IS A VOID IN LOVE! Please ponder well in THAT

WHICH IS page 57:6-17; 65:9-29; 93:8-14; 107:13-27; 102:6-10, 19-6. Am sure as you really "dig" to see what these statements TRUTH-FULLY MEAN, you'll have no desire to fiddle around with the nonsense of what your would-be "senses" sense!

Cordially,

P. S. And remember, no "loss" can occur in Mind!

Dear----------

Yours of the 7th at hand and I have given you the "help" you asked.

Now, as to typing out the lecture tape I sent you, am wondering why you do not LISTEN, instead of always depending on that sense of SIGHT? There is nothing NEW in the tape — it is merely THE WAY, THE TONE, THE EMPHASIS IN WHICH IT IS PUT, that is of value to you IF YOU LISTEN. If you see it still on the page, it is of no greater "use" to you than the books, the Monthly Letters, or whatever else you READ OF REALITY! By putting it on paper, you bypass the SOLE REASON I SENT IT ON TO YOU!

Remember, ANY ONE OF THE SENSES ARE HUMAN. And if you do not state WHAT INTELLIGENCE IS, and DEPEND WHOLLY THEREON AS THAT VERY MIND ITSELF BEHOLDING ITS OWN ENTIRETY, you are still trying to "see" as a human. See what? "See" INFINITY — and it cannot be done!

ONLY CONSCIOUSNESS IS CONSCIOUS, AND THAT IS SPIRIT ITSELF *being*. There simply IS NAUGHT ELSE AT ALL. Then why keep looking at a body, through a body, via a body, and being concerned with a body? "Body" has no RELATIONSHIP TO YOU AT ALL! NONE AT ALL!

You still seem to assume there IS A DREAM, A MATTER MAN, A HUMAN BEING! And that is why you continue to ask concerning a "process," as per question 4. You may as well ask concerning the process whereby the flat earth becomes round, and yesterday stops being today! All such is a false assumption — failure in thesis, hence, no answer you get will satisfy, for THERE IS NO FOUNDATION IN ERROR TO "BEGIN" WITH, OR TO "EXPLAIN," BE-CAUSE THERE IS ONLY ACTUALITY, FACT, *present!*

I urge you to stop "trying to accomplish, get, acquire, lay-hold-on REALITY!" IT IS ITSELF NOW. GOD IS HIMSELF NOW. LOVE IS ITSELF ALL THERE IS NOW. And this is already your ENTIRETY, YOUR SOLE IDEN-TITY, THE WHOLE SUBSTANCE YOU BE THIS IN-STANT. NO MORE IS TO COME, NAUGHT IS TO DEPART, NO FOG EXISTS TO INTELLIGENCE TO BE CLEARED AWAY, NO LOSS IS TO BE RECOVERED, NO "HEALING" CAN TAKE PLACE IN THE PERFECTION AND WHOLENESS OF PRESENT NOWNESS, AMNESS, ISNESS!

Apparently you still go via Christian Science and assume error, matter, birth-death, physical identity, body, sin, personal mind, general mind, mass consciousness, devil, Satan, hell, pit, ignorance and all that pertains to that (or those) word (s)! But, if so, then you still start out by robbing Intelligence, denying Consciousness, refusing Nowness, de-clining Isness, and refuting I-AM-BEING! You must still be "was-ing," and hoping to "will-be-ing".

In the tape I sent you I tried to point out that these

assumptions are all the devil there is, and so, so long as you entertain them, YOU BECOME THE INVENTOR, CONCEIVER, PERCEIVER, EXPERIENCER OF ALL THE "IMPS" OF NONSENSE, NOT-TRUTH, NOT-FACT YOU CAN DRUM UP! But YOU ALONE, thanks to this falsity of IDENTIFICATION, are doing it all to your own falsification! None of it hits Reality, your Sole Identity — all of it is a pseudo-movement within a pseudo-place known by a pseudo-mind, and suffered by a pseudo-sense! And this same silly nonsense "assumes" a whole world on which to vent its nonsense, BUT FOREVER AVOIDS ANY AND EVERY FACT, TRUTH, ACTUALITY! So why keep at it? Why not STATE FACT, STICK WITH FACT, AND CONTINUE DEFINING THE WORDS AND SENTENCES YOU STATE, TO BE SURE YOU KNOW THEM TO *BE* FACT — WHY, WHERE, WHEN, AND HOW! Leave pseudo "things" alone! You CAN and "ultimately" MUST STATE FACT, AND OPERATE IN ACCORD WITH FACT, FOR IT ALONE IS PRESENT, REAL, ACTION! There is no Louis-mind, personality, identity at all, neither past nor future! *ALL* IS ALL THERE IS. ONE SINGLE MIND — ONE SINGLE IDENTITY, LIFE, AWARENESS, *SUBSTANCE!*

This is the total definition of question 1. I am referring ONLY TO THE SINGLENESS, WHOLENESS, ONENESS, hence the PURITY OF LOVE PRESENT, WHOLE CONSCIOUSNESS ENTIRELY ALIVE TO ITS ABSOLUTE ACTION, JOY, SUBSTANCE OF BEING!

Will answer more fully all these questions in a M.L., but probably July, for the June letter is already written. Have to do them ahead of time so they can be mailed out while I am away. I do hope this helps you. Please turn to 141:6-22 in

NOW. Ponder it well. And I urge you to LISTEN TO THE TAPE — LISTEN, DON'T JUST KEEP "READING." LISTEN TO THE EMPHASIS, LISTEN TO THE WORDS, AND DISCOVER WHAT THEY SAY, WHAT THEY MEAN, AS USED! Am sure you will "get" much more from same. You seem to have the notion you must READ Truth in order to behold Reality — not so! READING DOES NOT MAKE IT MORE REAL, ANY MORE THAN "LISTENING" AND VICE VERSA BUT IT IS ALREADY SO, SO "LISTEN" AND THEN ACT IN ACCORD THEREWITH! Don't think It has to be "studied" or steadied! IT IS FACT, WHAT YOU ALREADY BE, AND NO SO-CALLED "HUMAN" *MANIPULATION* IS REQUIRED — no more trying to "fit it into a slot" is ever required! TRUTH IS, IT IS THE WHOLE OF YOUR IDENTITY NOW — AND IS THE SINGLE ONE — THERE IS NO OTHER AT ALL! You are THE ONLY!

Cordially,

Dear----------

Please, I urge you, see what the meaning of the words you use really is, i.e., don't quote words, assuming that the repetition of them will help, nor that an "intellectual comprehension" of them will do aught to aught. Rather, what I am trying to make clear is — the SOLE ALIVENESS PRESENT is the entirety that is your PRESENT TOTAL IDENTITY. This very AWARENESS PRESENT IS THE ONLY AWARENESS YOU BE — AND IT IS THIS AWARENESS (CONSCIOUSNESS, if you prefer, or ALIVENESS, SANITY, BEING) that is being aware, being conscious, being alive, being present. Is this not so? Then why expect THIS AWARENESS THAT IS BEING AWARE, to in some way effect or affect another mind, a state-of-would-be-thought that pretends to know pain, suffering, lack, fear, ignorance, limitation, dimension, time, frailty and so on?

Can you HONESTLY AND ABSOLUTELY SAY THAT THIS PRESENT CONSCIOUS AWARENESS (which is the ONLY SUBSTANCE THERE IS — the ONLY ACTION, FUNCTION, ALIVENESS, THERE IS) is actually *aware* of lack, is conscious of a large amount-of-unconsciousness-or-void (trouble, dis-ease, un-ease, un-Completeness, un-Wholeness)?

Is not THIS CONSCIOUS AWARENESS PRESENT, CAPABLE OF CONCEIVING (THINKING UP, IF YOU PREFER) ANY ITEM (thing, body, idea) — and isn't every one of these thoughts (ideas) WHOLLY THOUGHT *ONLY?* Is not each of them WITHIN THIS AWARENESS, WHOLLY BELONGING TO THIS AWARENESS ONLY, AND UTTERLY PERFECT, WHOLE, COMPLETE, LACKING NAUGHT, DEPENDING ON NAUGHT, CONNECTED WITH NAUGHT — BUT TOTALLY WITHIN AWARENESS ONLY, RIGHT NOW? Is one of them "made" of matter, atom-stuff, dependent on biology, physiology, and so on? DOESN'T MIND "THINK" THEM INSTANTLY, AND ARE THEY NOT THEN "THOUGHT" RIGHT HERE NOW, AND UTTERLY SATISFACTORILY?

Why, then, revert to a mystical theological assumption, and "try to heal" what does not, and cannot exist in connection with one of Mind's PERFECT THOUGHTS? You admit ONLY AWARENESS IS "THINKING" THE THOUGHT, yet you assume that "thought" was composed by biological activity way back many years ago! What manner of rationalization is this? And again, you then try to "heal" or "change" that atom-thing from dis-ease to ease! Yet you admit ONLY AWARENESS CAN "THINK" THOUGHTS (CONCEIVE IDEAS) AND THAT EVERY ONE OF THESE THOUGHTS BELONGS TO MIND ONLY, AND NOT TO THE THOUGHTS THEMSELVES! As this is so, how can any dis-ease strike any thought-idea? It cannot, and this is obvious when we actually start out "thinking" with MIND ONLY. But most of us start with the body, the growth, the pain, the lump, the ache, the lameness, the difficulty, or whatever! And we keep harping on these "conditions" and crying out for Mind to aid them! Yet MIND KNOWS NAUGHT OF VOID, LACK, TIME, MAT-TER OR DISEASE! MIND IS WHOLLY AWARE RIGHT HERE OF BEING RIGHT HERE, WHOLLY ALIVE TO ITS OWN UTTER TOTALITY, SINGLENESS, ONLY-NESS, FULLNESS, ACTION, POWER, ABILITY, AND SELF-SATISFACTION, SELF-GLORY AND INTELLIGENT ALIVENESS! It never can be ignorant of WHAT IT IS AS THIS PRESENT AWARENESS, AND THIS AWARENESS THAT IS PRESENT, NOW, WHOLLY INCLUSIVE OF THE ENTIRE UNIVERSE OF ITS CONCEPTIONS-PERCEP-TIONS. At no moment does It try to reverse Its WHOLE-NESS and try to be un-Whole, un-Truth, un-Intelligent, or try to become one of the thoughts (ideas-bodies) It conceives!

If you will 100% get busy with what THIS PRESENT AWARENESS IS, you cannot give further attention, heed, or service to lack!

In POWER, please ponder well 125:7-31; 126:26-31; 128:28-33 (use the word, "SELF," or "AWARENESS," in place of "God."); 129:28-2; 124:20-4; 119:5-23. And in THE UNCHALLENGED SELF, 46:1-20.

Pound on this. See if you are CONSCIOUSLY THIS ONE AWARENESS BEING AWARE, or do you still prodigally claim you are a human that Mind knows something of, and is willing to aid or assist! If this is so, then you are but a "thing" and are without *(outside of)* Mind — you have seemingly "cut your SELF off from being the SELF THAT IS, THE PRESENCE THAT IS, THE LIFE THAT IS, THE IDENTITY-I THAT IS! If but a "thing" then you are like one of the letters of the alphabet, merely an "item" known BY Intelligence, but that INTELLIGENCE IS NOT THE I-AM to you! Then you are helpless, and do not have or include a world, nor are you ever AWARENESS, ACTION, BEING *being!*

So glad you are to be at the Seminar. It will be grand — and do come with questions. Am looking forward eagerly to seeing you again, and am bringing a load of mighty grand "thoughts!"

Cordially,

Dear----------

As to making a decision — can you honestly say that you are STICKING WITH THE FACT THAT *ONLY* TRUTH IS TRUE, AND THAT ONLY *NOW* IS? Any decision deals with time, history, and outlining, doesn't it?

You see ONLY INTELLIGENCE IS. IT KNOWS ALL, FOR IT *IS* ALL. THIS LEAVES NO OTHER MIND AT ALL, SO WHAT HAS TO "DECIDE" AND CONCERNING WHAT? WHERE? WHY? WHO OR WHAT SAYS SO? Are you still arguing that you ARE human, and must take care of all these many things that so cluttered up the thought of Martha?

If, as I pointed out in the work in San Francisco, you'd start with ALL, and stay with ALL, RIGHT NOW ONLY, and not allow your thought to wander off onto human identity, human problems, desires, frustration, annoyances — but stay wholly, honestly, consistently with NOW, AND NOW ONLY — WITH OMNIPRESENCE *ONLY*, and just keep at it no matter how difficult this may seem to be, you'll find all the would-be problems vanish, for they will no longer have a mind (a Clara-mind) to water and tend them! They cannot exist by themselves, so if you withdraw all your attention therefrom, there is no way for them to seem to continue or even exist at all. Truly then, to paraphrase it, these "former (long drawn-out notions) things (problems of lack and disappointment) shall NOT COME INTO MIND, nor can they even pretend to be re-membered (given power, locomotion, place, authority and so on) any more!"

You can give up your job and plan on reading, reciting, memorizing every page of these books, yet you'll find they will not help you, and you'll find the same intrusions, the same sort of demands made upon you ! Why? Because they are NOT "OUT THERE!" They are but the outcome of listening to and serving attentively a Clara-mind — another mind, rather than giving ALL YOUR ATTENTION, AWARE-NESS, ALIVENESS TO *BEING* ALIVE IN TOTO, RIGHT HERE NOW! I find I have to do this. And I'm sure I have as many "seeming demands" made upon me as you do! Yet by sticking with WHAT ALONE IS TRUTH, TRUE, FACT, REAL, I cannot be "tempted" to go off and spend hours over lack, limitation, worry, failures, privations, pity, and all the rest of the vacuity — that seeming sense where no SPIRIT IS! It was this serving of the void, giving attention to it, and trying to find ways of meeting it or overcoming it or of getting around it, or filling it up, that floored the god of the Bible! And it will do the same to you.

Never do anything because of a REASON, PURPOSE, MOTIVE, for all such is seeking GOOD via things, or via manipulation, change, improvement! And all such is based on using the human or prodigal so-called mind!

We can get so messed up, and get to feeling so abused, misunderstood, set-upon, that the whole world looks black indeed, but only to a mind-that-is-NOT! To LIGHT, YOUR VERY SELF *NOW*, ALL IS BRIGHTNESS ITSELF! So let us start with FACT instead of what the senses would proclaim!

Just stop and consider — right now TOTAL PERFEC-TION BEING ALIVE TO ITS ABSOLUTE ALLNESS, BLISS, SELF-SATISFACTION IS WHO AND WHAT YOU ARE — YOUR FOREVER-NOW IDENTITY IN FULL ACTION! Can you then be discouraged? Why? With what, and over what? IMPOSSIBLE! Be the JOY YOU BE, NOW!

Cordially,